DUFFY

EXPANDED EDITION

DUFFY

STARDOM *to* SENATE *to* SCANDAL

DAN LEGER

NIMBUS
PUBLISHING LTD

Nimbus Publishing Limited
3731 Mackintosh St, Halifax, NS B3K 5A5
(902) 455-4286 nimbus.ca

Printed and bound in Canada

NB1216

Cover photo: Chris Wattie / Corbis Images
Interior and cover design: Jenn Embree

Library and Archives Canada Cataloguing in Publication

Leger, Dan, 1954-, author
Duffy : stardom to Senate to scandal / Dan Leger. —Paperback edition.

ISBN 978-1-77108-339-3 (paperback)
ISBN 978-1-77108-146-7 (bound).—ISBN 978-1-77108-147-4 (pdf).
—ISBN 978-1-77108-148-1 (mobi).—ISBN 978-1-77108-149-8 (html)

1. Duffy, Mike, 1946-. 2. Television journalists—Canada—Biography.
3. Canada. Parliament. Senate—Biography. 4. Legislators—Canada—
Biography. 5. Political corruption—Canada. I. Title.

FC641.D84L444 2016   971.07'3092   C2016-903778-9

Nimbus Publishing acknowledges the financial support for its publishing activities from the Government of Canada through the Canada Book Fund (CBF) and the Canada Council for the Arts, and from the Province of Nova Scotia. We are pleased to work in partnership with the Province of Nova Scotia to develop and promote our creative industries for the benefit of all Nova Scotians.

For my family

CONTENTS

FOREWORD

WHEN I WORKED ON PARLIAMENT HILL IN THE LATE 1970S AND EARLY '80s, I covered some great stories through the Trudeau, Clark, and Mulroney years. But I'll admit that during those half-dozen years I'd be surprised if I walked down the shiny halls to the Senate more than a few times. Aside from the pomp and ceremony of Throne Speeches, nothing much seemed to happen in the Red Chamber. And every time some new bagman, party hack, or sacked cabinet minister was appointed to the Senate, we'd all snicker and say something like "we'll never hear from them again."

Over the years since, the Senate has popped into the public eye a few times, but not many, and hardly any that changed the image most Canadians had of the place. Television is allowed in the chamber only on Throne Speech days, and few will forget the time the cameras caught a shot of Senator Frank Mahovlich apparently napping during one of the Chrétien-era session launches. It was not a good moment for the "Big M" or for the institution, and only underlined the somewhat unfair notion many Canadians have that nothing happens in the Senate except the waste of their money.

Which brings us to 2013, when reporters, cameras, and public attention were all focused on the Senate in a way they never had been before—the worst scandal to hit the Harper government since it was first elected in 2006. And at the centre of the storm has been one of the country's most recognizable unelected faces, Mike Duffy. Best known for his decades in private and public radio and television, Duffy was one of the hardest-working journalists on Parliament Hill when I worked alongside him during my Ottawa days. We even jokingly called him "the Senator" for the way he played the Ottawa game. He loved the nickname, especially when it got picked up and used by everyone from cabinet ministers to prime ministers. But it was all just a joke, or at least we thought it was until the day Stephen Harper turned it from fantasy to reality.

One thing all reporters and all politicians know is that the issue that can galvanize voters' attention, no matter whether they are Conservative, New Democrat, or Liberal, is abuse of the public purse. The low opinion most Canadians have of politicians often centres around how their money is spent, especially when it is misspent. And that's where this story meets its perfect storm: the Senate, Duffy, and money.

My old friend and colleague Dan Leger knows Parliament Hill, he knows the country, and he knows Mike Duffy. I can't think of anyone else who could tie all this together in a way that brings new light to a tale of money, backroom backstabbing, and political intrigue at the highest levels.

Read it. You may weep, you may laugh. You won't be bored.

Peter Mansbridge
Toronto
November 2013

PREFACE

BY EVEN THE MOST JADED STANDARD, 2013 REPRESENTED A LOW-WATER mark in Canadian politics. It wasn't something new; conditions had been deteriorating for a decade.

The federal sponsorship scandal incinerated thirteen years of Liberal government, scandals in the legislatures of Nova Scotia and Newfoundland and Labrador had exposed elected politicians stealing from the public, and parliamentary debate had morphed into talking points and attack ads. Even with all of that, 2013 seemed particularly sordid. An inquiry was uncovering new outrages in the Quebec corruption case, tainting twenty-seven mayors. Toronto City Council, the country's largest, was a laughingstock over the bizarre antics of its mayor, Rob Ford. On Parliament Hill, a raging scandal involving senators, expenses, and a high-level cover-up posed a tangible threat to the Conservative government of Prime Minister Stephen Harper. It would result in the condemnation and suspension of three of his senators: Mike Duffy, Pamela Wallin, and Patrick Brazeau, and the hurried resignation of Liberal Mac Harb.

This book was written as the rot was ripening. It started out as a column I had written in May for the *Halifax Chronicle Herald* about the troubles of Senator Mike Duffy. I had known Duffy since 1981, when I was a junior wire-service reporter and he was already a television star. Even back then, Duffy was a "personality" whose self-created identity was "the Old Duff"—Parliament Hill's man in the know.

Duffy lived in Ottawa but made forays back to the Maritimes for election campaign stops, conferences, or prime ministerial visits. Wherever he went, people wanted to shake his hand, get a free opinion on politics, and trade a joke. Duffy had the patter down: "a little bird" had passed on some gossip or he had chatted up a certain person close to someone high up. It was all part of the shtick, but I had no reason to doubt his sources back then, and mostly I still don't. Duffy knew people, and people love to talk.

It would be that way for decades. Duffy went from radio to television and then to individual stardom, all the while cultivating his image as an insider and political character. "The Old Duff" became the stage persona of the ambitious Mike Duffy, a Prince Edward Island boy who had done well for himself. Duffy let people think he knew where the bodies are buried, but he wouldn't tell all, as if revealing more would devalue his insider currency. Some colleagues thought that if he wasn't reporting everything, maybe he wasn't such a great journalist after all; reporters are paid to reveal secrets, not keep them. It was only after going into politics, and with his back to the wall, that Duffy started to tell everything he knew, with devastating results.

In 1984, I was posted to the Canadian Press bureau in Ottawa, where I was thrilled to run with the famed Hill media pack, work in Parliament's historic buildings, and cover great events in national politics. I thought of it as an honour, but it was also fun. I got to write about the Hill's cast of vivid characters: a larger-than-life prime minister in Brian Mulroney, parliamentarians of every stripe, and the supporting cast of fixers, bag men, hangers-on, and hacks. And journalistic heavy hitters like Mike Duffy.

I got to know the star reporter a lot better when I was assigned to CP's broom-closet sub-bureau off the Centre Block "Hot Room," traditional seat of the Parliamentary Press Gallery. Duffy was with the CBC, which operated out of the National Press Building across Wellington Street, but he preferred the Hot Room, where he could do his own thing out of sight of his minders at the CBC. The Centre Block was also great for picking up gossip; you couldn't walk down the hall without bumping into a politician.

Duffy and I weren't intimate pals, but we were both Maritimers and enjoyed the occasional pint—often many more than one. The Maritime mafia still had influence on the Hill, and Duffy generously introduced me to "people you should know," often over "libations." We covered many of the same stories: Mulroney's turbulent government, the free trade fight, the Meech Lake Accord and its fallout, and the Liberal pratfalls of the Turner years. We were competitive but always friendly. Later, I learned that not everyone on the Hill had the same kind of experience with Duffy. Bridges got burned and many of Duffy's former colleagues were no longer fans.

After six years in Ottawa, I moved back to Halifax and went to work first for the CBC and eventually for the *Chronicle Herald*. I didn't see much of Duffy any more; he was a network bigwig on CTV and a fixture on the Ottawa scene. Instead of having to pursue the powerful and influential, they came to him. And fame had its rewards: Duffy became one of the highest-paid journalists in the country.

Then, in late 2008, with the Harper government fighting for survival in a minority Parliament, Duffy—along with Wallin, Brazeau, and fifteen others, all Conservatives—was appointed to the Senate. I was surprised, but not shocked. I too had heard about Duffy's passionate designs on a Senate seat. For years, reporters in Halifax and later in Ottawa had jokingly called each other "Doctor" and "Senator." Perhaps Duffy had taken it more seriously than had the rest of us and been seduced by the allure of membership in Canada's most exclusive political club.

Duffy had been leaning toward the Conservatives anyway, which became apparent on his TV show, *Mike Duffy Live*. And the hard-eyed, humourless party of Stephen Harper would benefit from having a yarn-spinning showman to entertain fundraising crowds.

It did seem odd, however, that Duffy filled a vacancy from Prince Edward Island. Why not Ottawa, where he had lived since the early 1970s? Still, I rationalized that the Senate is a funny place, with its antique customs and inscrutable rules, and shrugged it off. Duffy popped up occasionally in the news, usually for some unnecessarily controversial comment, but he generally stayed off the radar until late 2012, when questions arose about the expense claims of some of the Senate's most famous members. As the story evolved, Duffy became the poster boy for everything the public disliked about the "chamber of sober second thought." Because he was so famous, a household name, he came to personify everything that was wrong in the upper house.

In May 2013, CTV's Robert Fife, a long-time friend of both Duffy's and mine, reported sensational information connecting Duffy's expenses repayment to the Prime Minister's Office (PMO). It looked bad for the senator, who had been booted out of the Conservative caucus. In a column I wrote at the time, I suggested that Duffy had fallen into the trap of believing his own bull, a common celebrity delusion. The character of the Old Duff, man-about-Parliament and political insider, had subsumed the real Mike Duffy, and not for the better. A few weeks after the column appeared, I was approached to write this book. Since then, I have interviewed dozens of people who knew Duffy at different stages of his life and many others connected with the scandal that did so much to damage the Conservative government.

I also spoke to Duffy, on a perfect Prince Edward Island day in late August of that same year. I arrived unannounced at his place in touristy Cavendish, across the road from the purported "homestead home of Lucy Maud Montgomery." Duffy's modest cottage at 10 Friendly Lane occupies a tidy lot with flowers and pretty shrubs, a rose bush clinging to a wooden stepladder leaning on a wall. Somebody was home: a clothesline festooned with capacious shirts flapped in the afternoon sea breeze. I knocked on the door and Heather Duffy appeared, none too pleased to see an uninvited face. I asked politely for Senator Mike, and Duffy appeared, raising his arms as if to wave me off. "I'm not talking to you," he said. "I saw that column you wrote."

Through the screen, I told Duffy I was writing a book about the expense scandal, whether he cooperated or not. He hesitated for a moment; then, over Heather's protests, he grabbed a ball cap and stepped out onto the low deck in a blue golf shirt and baggy shorts. We sat on wrought-iron chairs in the sun and had a long talk. Duffy didn't want to be quoted on the record, but he did lay out the scenario he would make so startlingly in the Senate two months later: about being thrown to the wolves by a party and prime minister interested only in covering up a political liability. He knew he was in deep trouble, and felt betrayed by the mighty powers in the PMO. He had evidence to back up his claims, and at some point it would all come out. If that was in court, fine. Eventually, Heather herded her husband back inside. As I started to walk away, Duffy noticed a tourist taking pictures and scowled: "Is that guy shooting for you?" Over the following months, the senator and I exchanged more than eighty emails, which Duffy did not want made public. But they did help me understand the series of events that had rocked the Harper government.

Duffy's story and his part in the Senate scandal laid bare some dark truths about hardball politics and the lengths to which parties will go to protect their interests. It's a story about overreaching ambition and corrosive entitlement, about an insider who became a problem for the Harper government, and when he did, suddenly reverted to being an outsider, and a despised one at that.

Mike Duffy became a media icon for what he claimed to know about the blood sport contested on Parliament Hill. It made him famous and, by Canadian standards, quite well off. But Duffy wanted more than just the insider image—he wanted into the club. When he actually became "an active player on the field," he would learn that the real practice of politics is darker, more ruthless, and far more dangerous than he had imagined.

Acknowledgements

This book would not have happened without the proposal from Patrick Murphy at Nimbus, who saw more in my column than even I did. Peter Mansbridge found time to contribute the foreword, which was very kind of him. Gary MacDougall and Teresa Wright at the *Charlottetown Guardian*, as well as Alan Holman and Tracy Lightfoot, helped me navigate Prince Edward Island. From the Ottawa Press Gallery, I was able to consult Michael Bate, Bruce Cheadle, Susan Delacourt, Robert Fife, Stephen Maher, and Craig Oliver. I made good use of Claire Hoy's book *Nice Work: the Continuing Scandal of Canada's Senate*, Tom Flanagan's *Harper's Team*, and Lawrence Martin's *Harperland*. Senators who were willing to go on the record are named, but several others would speak only off the record. That also goes for several other political sources interviewed on background. I am particularly thankful for Rob Walsh's informal telephone and email course on parliamentary privilege. Terry MacDonald searched property records for me in Charlottetown, and a talented young photographer, Devaan Ingraham, took the cover portrait. My wife, Bonnie Woodworth, read over the completed draft and assured me it made sense. Barry Norris edited the book and made many improvements, for which I am grateful.

Special thanks go to my dear friend Doug Long, who put me up and put up with me when I visited Ottawa. To my family and friends: thank you for your patience, support, and encouragement. It means everything.

Dan Leger
Halifax
January 6, 2014

THE YOUNG DUFF, 1946–71

Mike was respected. He built a solid reputation.

— SENATOR JIM MUNSON, 2013

ELEVEN VILLA AVENUE IS A FINE OLD WOOD-FRAME HOUSE IN BRIGHTON, the most prestigious neighbourhood in Charlottetown, Prince Edward Island's laid-back capital. The two-storey Victorian-era home with its sidelight entryway and Maple Leaf flag over the door stands on the corner of Villa and North River Road, which runs toward downtown, and is just a few blocks from the red sands of Charlottetown Harbour. The house is surrounded by tall trees and adorned with ornamental bushes. A tidy walkway of interconnected bricks runs to low steps up to the screened front door.

Visiting narrow, quiet Villa Avenue today, with its stately homes shaded by tall old trees, it's easy to imagine what it would have looked like in the late 1940s, when Mike Duffy was born and Charlottetown had a population of about fifteen thousand, a quarter of its size today. Much has changed in the city since then. Nowadays, Charlottetown has bustling malls, suburban sprawl, and a downtown arts centre where endless variations of the *Anne of Green Gables* story are told and retold. Charlottetown's waterfront, once bordered by fishing piers and storage sheds from the days when schooners took away the potatoes and fish and brought back everything else, is now full of condominiums and tourist traps thronged in summer with visitors. But not much has changed in Brighton. It is still a tidy, comfortable neighbourhood in a safe, conservative Maritime city where the descendants of Scots, English, and Irish still dominate the population, the economy, and politics.

Charlottetown, established in 1768, was named for Queen Charlotte, royal consort of King George III. It retains a palpable sense of history and civic pride in its role in Confederation and the founding of Canada. At the centre of the low-rise downtown district stands Province House, a neoclassical gem built from Nova Scotia freestone where the Fathers of Confederation met in 1864 to start the process that would become a democratic, fair, and humane country. Charlottetown's motto is *Cunabula Foederis*— Birthplace of Confederation—and in the summer of 2014 the city marked the 150th anniversary of the Charlottetown Conference with dozens of public events. In some sense, the city has marked time since the occasion of its most famous historical event. As the rest of Canada grew and became more diverse, Charlottetown stayed small and peripheral to the lunging aspirations of the growing country. Like Islanders themselves, Charlottetown minds its own business and doesn't brag. It's that way now and it certainly was in the 1940s, when the well-kept house on Villa Avenue was the boyhood home of Senator Michael Dennis Duffy.

Mike Duffy was born in Charlottetown on May 27, 1946, to Wilfrid F. Duffy, a lieutenant-commander in the Royal Canadian Navy during the Second World War who returned to become a provincial civil servant, and Lillian Bernadette Duffy, who would remain an important part of Mike's life until her death in 2010 at age ninety-three. She had been thirty-eight years widowed after Wilfrid, sixty-five, died in 1972 from the second of two heart attacks.

Mike and his four siblings grew up in the days when Island society was divided along well-defined religious lines. The Duffys were Roman Catholics, which prescribed where Mike would go to school, who most of his friends would be, and where he would hang out with his peers. It would even dictate where he was born: not at the provincially run Prince Edward Island Hospital where the Protestant babies first saw life, but at the Catholic-run Charlottetown Hospital, established by the local diocese in 1879 and operated by the Church until its replacement in 1982 by the Queen Elizabeth Hospital.

The old Catholic hospital exemplified the unwritten rules of religious separation that persisted on the Island well into the 1960s. "In those days, this town was divided right down the middle by religion," recalls journalist Alan Holman, an Islander and Duffy contemporary when, as teenagers, they both worked briefly for the *Guardian*, the local daily, then later at the CBC in Ottawa. "Even the doctors' offices worked that way," says Holman. "Catholic doctors took care of Catholics and the Protestant doctors took care of Protestants." It was that way right across Island society, including in its politics. In those days, provincial electoral districts had two representatives each, so it was often possible to elect a Protestant and a Catholic in each riding. The peace was always kept. No one even talked about it much; it was just the way things were.

Growing up, Mike attended classes with the other Catholic kids at Queen Square School in the old part of town and hung out at the Basilica Recreation Centre, while the Protestants played and socialized at the YMCA. As a teenager, he attended St. Dunstan's, in those days both a Catholic high school and a degree-granting post-secondary institution, the Island's first. St. Dunstan's and the mostly Protestant Prince of Wales College were amalgamated into the new University of Prince Edward Island during the province's modernization period in the 1960s. Until then, the two communities mostly kept apart. "The only place where the Catholic kids and the Protestants got together was at the old Rollaway Dance Hall," recalls Holman. "Of course, there were fights."

Duffy came from a family in which politics was part of daily conversation. The *Guardian*—its motto is *"Covers Prince Edward Island like the Dew"*—was delivered to the front door every day. His grandfather, Charles Gavan Duffy, was a Liberal member of the provincial Legislative Assembly and served as its speaker in the early 1920s. Mike would recall his grandfather's deep connection to the Liberal Party, which extended to naming his son after Wilfrid Laurier and to keeping a boxed set of RCA Victor 78 rpm recordings of William Lyon Mackenzie King's speeches. "One realizes how committed my grandfather was to the Liberal federation to have actually paid money for such a collection," Duffy would tell the Senate in his maiden speech in 2009. "When it came to oratory, Mackenzie King was not Winston Churchill." Charles Duffy also benefited from the age-old practice of patronage, which still lurks in the backrooms of Island politics. "Like many good Liberal lawyers, he was eventually elevated to the bench," his grandson recalled. Duffy's mother, in contrast, came from solid Tory stock. His maternal grandfather, a railroad conductor named Peter McCarron, had been a committed Conservative, and Mike would recall that the political divide "led to some great discussions between my two grandfathers."

Mike was no scholar, and admits he had a rather "spotty academic career" at St. Dunstan's. He never quite made it all the way to graduating from high school, but journalists didn't need to be well educated when Duffy got into the business. And he was developing other interests anyway. While still in grade school, he made his first radio broadcast, in a spelling bee with other ten- and eleven-year-olds. In an interview with Catherine Clark of the Cable Public Affairs Channel in 2012, Duffy recalled his wonder at standing in the same studio from which legendary fiddler Don Messer broadcast his immensely popular Down East music show. "I go in and I say, you hear this on the radio at home...and this is where it comes from, in this room with the boom mike hanging down, the guy behind the glass, the control panel and everything. This is magic, this is magic." The radio spelling bee would spark Duffy's lifelong passion for broadcasting. After the show, he went to the school library and got out all the books he could find on broadcasting and radio. "I read everything I could about it," he told Clark.

In 1962, fifteen-year-old Duffy got a chance to become involved in the industry that would define him and take him, many years later, into the Canadian Broadcasting Hall of Fame. He was already writing a column in the *Guardian* called "Platter Chatter," about pop music, and was serving as president of the St. Dunstan's student council when he got a call from a producer at local television station CFCY. The station wanted to start a show featuring local high schoolers. Did Mike know anyone who might want to try it out? For Duffy, the call was a dream come true. He jumped at the chance and volunteered at once. Even though Duffy and the other kids were rank amateurs, the station managers let them do pretty much what they wanted with their airtime. "They were wonderful," Duffy told Clark. The producer acted as "the mother hen," but mostly let Mike and his friends devise the show, which they called *Club 62*, and produce it on their own. Its opening sequence featured Duffy and his teenaged colleagues "dancing around" to the music of Billy Vaughn's 1962 hit "A Swingin' Safari." "And so, then I had something to do other than school. I was full time. I still went to school, but I was working on items for the show. I've been in television ever since."

Well, not exactly. There would be some twists and turns along the way. *Club 62* ran for two years, ending around the time Mike dropped out of school and became what Islanders call a "Christmas graduate." He needed a job. Television was still in its infancy in the Maritimes, so radio was his best option, even for the tenor-voiced Duffy in an era of baritone domination. The Charlottetown station wouldn't hire him, so he left for Halifax and CJCH, a pioneering pop music station, where Bob McCleave, later a Tory MP, took him on.

McCleave gave Duffy two shifts a week, Saturday and Sunday nights, for fifteen dollars a shift, which barely covered his rent at the local YMCA on South Park Street. Duffy lasted only three months before station management decided he didn't have the right sound and let him go. Although everything seemed dark at the time, his brief stint at CJCH would prove fruitful—if only for Duffy's network of connections. McCleave later became part of the political scene in Ottawa, and the aspiring young broadcaster also met Max Keeping, who would loom large in his life many years later. Keeping was a bit older and more experienced than Duffy, and he too was passing through the radio business in Halifax on his way to Ottawa. In 1988, he would play a role in Duffy's transformation from a network television reporter to star host of his own show. But nobody could have seen that coming in those early, disappointing days. Without a job, Duffy had to leave Halifax. A colleague at CJCH, Harris Sullivan, drove him to a good hitchhiking spot heading west on the Bicentennial Highway, handed him five dollars, and wished him good luck.

Discouraged but not defeated, Duffy soon heard about an opening at a radio station in Amherst, Nova Scotia, a couple of kilometres from the New Brunswick border. After a brief visit with his parents in Charlottetown, during which his father suggested he drop his broadcasting dreams and take an electrician's course, Duffy took the bus to Amherst. There, he landed a job at CKDH for the princely sum of seventy-five dollars a week. More important to the young would-be broadcaster, the job included "all the airtime you wanted," writing and presenting the news from around northern Nova Scotia. And that included politics.

Being the newsroom rookie exposed Duffy to issues both significant and mundane and to some of the leading political figures of the day, men who would have a profound impact on the future star reporter. The most prominent Maritime politician of his time, Nova Scotia premier Robert L. Stanfield, would soon depart for Ottawa and the national leadership of the Progressive Conservative Party. The greatest, and oddest, of all the mid-century Tories, John G. Diefenbaker, came through town in 1965. Through the good offices of local Tory MP Robert Coates, a future cabinet minister under Brian Mulroney, Duffy landed an interview with "the Chief" aboard his campaign train. The two men, fifty-two years apart in age, would form a relationship that lasted until Diefenbaker's death in 1979.

But it was Stanfield's successful run for the Tory leadership that really set the political hook for Duffy. In 1967, Mike cobbled together a few bucks and made it to Toronto for the convention that chose Stanfield as the party's leader. It was the event that cemented Duffy's goal of covering national politics. The convention, held in legendary Maple Leaf Gardens in early September, made a lasting impression on the young reporter, one he would never shake. It had all the ingredients of a great political story: colourful characters, gripping drama, and backroom knife play. In 1958, Diefenbaker had led the party to one of the greatest election victories in Canadian political history, but infighting in the ranks had since crippled the Tories. They were reduced to a minority in 1963 under the Liberals' new leader, Nobel Prize–winning former diplomat Lester B. Pearson. Diefenbaker's fiery oratory and old-fashioned populism no longer resonated with a Canadian population that was becoming more urban, modern, and diverse. Dief was a man out of step with his times, and a cabal of Maritimers backing Stanfield, with allies from other parts of the country, were determined to get him out. They forced a leadership review and then a full convention, at which Diefenbaker was also a potential candidate. The convention, in that wildly optimistic Centennial Year, was the first in Canada to be covered by television as it took place.

After five ballots, Stanfield, who was photographed by newspaper photographers calmly eating a banana while he awaited the results, won out over nine other candidates, including luminaries such as former Manitoba premier Duff Roblin, former cabinet members Davie Fulton, Donald Fleming, Alvin Hamilton, and George Hees, and Diefenbaker himself, who threw his hat in the ring at the last minute; Mary Walker-Sawka, the first woman to contest the leadership of a national political party in Canada, got two votes. The dumping of Diefenbaker and Stanfield's successful coalition building with other candidates made the story even more engaging for Duffy and the other reporters on the convention floor. When it was over, a Maritimer had been elected national Tory leader, and Duffy found himself with connections that would be handy for decades to come.

It wouldn't be a straight line from the Maritimes to the capital for the young Duff, but by 1969 he had developed an itch for the national scene that had to be scratched, and he worked the phones relentlessly searching for a reporting job in Ottawa. Coming up empty, he signed on at CFCF-TV in Montreal, not as a reporter but as a lineup and assignment editor, chasing news tips, sending reporters and cameramen into the field, and helping to arrange their stories for the supper-hour telecast. He would toil in the trenches for four years, not getting what he wanted, which was his face on TV, but learning the nuts and bolts of television production.

In those days, television was a laborious craft quite unlike what it has become in the digital age. There was no videotape—everything was shot on film, and film was expensive, even for a big-city station like CFCF. Cameramen were trained to shoot in brief sequences, and only what would be needed for the finished item. Film reels had to be rushed to a developing lab to be processed before they could be edited and made ready for air. Duffy and other back-shop producers added simple production information and wrote introductory and show continuity material. But once it went to air, there was no denying the impact of television news. Audiences fell in love with TV's compelling images and sound and the punchy, straightforward writing. By the late 1960s, television was rocketing past newspapers and radio as the primary source of news for people all over North America.

Duffy revelled in his role at one of Canada's most successful local stations, but his goal was always to get to Parliament Hill: Holman recalls his talking about it as far back as his teenage days at the *Guardian*. After two years at CFCF, Duffy was ready to move on, even if it meant a pay cut. And so, in 1971, at age twenty-five, he moved to Ottawa and took a job at CFRA, part of the CHUM Group of radio stations in Ontario, the Maritimes, and Manitoba. There, he covered the usual routine stories but specialized in coverage of Ottawa's City Hall, where he would go up against Jim Munson, another young Maritimer who would cross paths and swords with

Duffy many times over the years. The New Brunswick–born Munson—later Jean Chrétien's press aide and a Liberal senator and who, like Duffy, would become one of Canada's top television journalists—recalls Duffy as an able competitor in those days. "Duff was aggressive and he had some contacts. I didn't know anybody and he seemed to know everyone. He'd be walking down the halls at City Hall saying 'hi' to this person and that. I didn't know all those people. He was beating me constantly, trouncing me, you might say."

Ever restless and driven, Duffy was soon assigned to Parliament Hill, reporting for CFRA and for Contemporary News, which provided daily syndicated reports for the network of CHUM stations, one of the forerunner companies of CTV. Like Munson, Duffy became a Parliament Hill regular, one of the "corridor commandos" who worked the halls of the Centre Block in the days when journalists were allowed to roam pretty much anywhere they wanted. "Mike was respected," Munson says. "He built a solid reputation." Duffy rented a cheap apartment and set up shop in the city that would define his reputation and make him an unmistakable part of the national political scene.

A STAR EMERGES: THE CBC YEARS

I have a little notepad here of one-liners.

— MIKE DUFFY TO PETER GZOWSKI ON *MORNINGSIDE*, 1985

IN THE EARLY 1970S, CHUM WAS BUILDING ITS AUDIENCE AND DIDN'T mind spending money to promote its products, Duffy among them. In return, Duffy worked hard to build his network, not least by socializing with other journalists, lobbyists, and political prey— anyone who had an answer to his habitual question, "what's going on?" It was all about getting to know people. MPs arriving from every part of Canada would encounter Duffy, an amiable figure on the Hill and already master of its arcane ways. He was well established, but always looking for something better, a little higher up the journalistic ladder, preferably with a bigger paycheque. He took a big step up that ladder when he joined CBC Radio's parliamentary bureau in 1974. Along with covering the Hill, the CBC's foreign reach enabled Duffy to make the occasional foray into the United States. In 1975, he even made it to Saigon shortly before it fell to the North Vietnamese.

Duffy meantime was working hard to build his reputation and foster his image as an Ottawa insider. He told friends that Prime Minister Pierre Trudeau paid close attention to his reporting, despite Trudeau's well-known disdain for the journalistic rabble. Duffy would claim that Trudeau even had an affectionate nickname for him, "Duffy Kravitz," after Mordecai Richler's hustling protagonist in the novel *The Apprenticeship of Duddy Kravitz*. Trudeau reputedly speculated on the identities of Duffy's presumed high-level sources in his government, finally deciding the most likely suspect was the voluble Bryce Mackasey, who won six straight elections in the Montreal riding of Verdun. After serving in five different cabinet posts and long service to the Liberal party, in 1984 Mackasey was appointed Canadian ambassador in the hardship post of Lisbon. Mackasey's reward provoked Brian Mulroney's memorable observation that, in politics, "there's no whore like an old whore." As prime minister, Mulroney cancelled the appointment.

The parliamentary bureau put Duffy at the scene of everything going on around the Hill, and there was a lot going on. The Trudeaumania of 1968 was well past, but the Trudeau government had been re-elected with a majority in 1974. The Liberals didn't have long to savour it. Within two years, the threat of separatism arose mightily in Quebec with the election of the Parti Québécois under the charismatic René Lévesque, who might have been the only other politician in the country with the kind of voter connection that Trudeau enjoyed at his peak. Lévesque was also provocative, and the PQ was soon proposing what would later be known as Bill 101, which reasserted and codified the dominance of the French language in the province and provoked an angry backlash from anglophone Quebecers and many other Canadians. It also generated a Liberal obsession with national unity, one that would have far-reaching effects.

In the 1970s, Ottawa was a far more relaxed and collegial place than it is now, and therefore perfect for a reporter like Duffy, the kind with the personal touch. In Trudeau-era Ottawa, it was still possible for reporters to develop frank relationships with cabinet ministers and senior bureaucrats, and Duffy worked his contacts assiduously. Later, he revealed that Mackasey and Prince Edward Island's Daniel J. MacDonald were his prime sources of inside information about the top Liberal circles. Mackasey might have been through the wars politically, but MacDonald had seen a real war, having fought in the Canadian Army's campaign in Italy and been gravely wounded at the Battle of Senio River, losing his left arm and leg. Trudeau appointed him minister of veterans affairs; the department's building in Charlottetown is named for him. Duffy admired the war hero Islander and kept in touch.

Professionally, Duffy prospered in radio, but, like everyone else, he could see that the medium didn't have the audience impact of television. In the United States, the daily supper-hour newscasts were among the most popular and profitable offerings on the network schedules. Television also had glamour and, in those days, respectability. It was becoming the most trusted source of news for Canadians, a status it would hold well into the Internet age, and Duffy wanted in. Plus, it paid better than radio, a fact not lost on the ambitious future star.

Duffy's switch to television and CBC's *The National* in 1977 made him famous. *The National* was the showpiece of Canadian television news, with a storied history stretching back to its black-and-white launch as a nightly news bulletin in 1954. Its 10 P.M. time slot gave it plenty of space to summarize any story's daily developments. Millions of Canadians ended their day with *The National* in what TV executives call "appointment viewing," because it was reliably there, every night at the same time, with a trusted product. And the early 1970s marked a heyday in public respect for the CBC, which was seen as a high-quality broadcaster. More than that, it reflected the country's growing wealth and cultural sophistication. It had become a central element of Canadian identity.

Granted, there were also fewer alternatives to the CBC or other conventional television networks in that pre-Internet age.

Broadcasting in Canada is a regulated industry with steep barriers to entry, especially at the network level. The Internet would change that, but the digital revolution was still far in the future. As Duffy was in transition from radio to TV, so television was in transition from film to videotape, a technology that would make it faster and cheaper to shoot, report, and edit the news. As the tools of the TV trade evolved from analogue and film to electronic news gathering to digital, so did the networks, although Duffy didn't go along easily. He adapted to the changes, but relied on methods he had learned in the past: making connections, working the phones, and exploiting the gossip mill.

These were still comparatively early days in television. The year Duffy joined *The National*, the miniseries *Roots* was the biggest thing on TV and cable was just starting to reach a significant number of Canadian homes. Three years later, Ted Turner would launch CNN, which would change everything about the TV news business. But at the time *The National* was the Holy Grail of domestic news for a would-be celebrity reporter in Canada. It guaranteed audiences and a decent paycheque for Duffy and other top-notch journalists who honed their craft on the show. For Duffy, however, the transition to TV meant something as equally important as audience and money: it meant access. Ottawa influence makers wanted to reach wide audiences, and Duffy could help them do that.

Politics and journalism have always travelled on the same street, and they have more in common than many people realize. Especially in the early days of Duffy's career, politicians needed journalists to get their message out. Now, governments have become adept at using the media to send messages directly to their supporters and the public. Yet then, as now, journalists needed politicians to supply the raw material for their craft. Politicians and journalists both yearn for broad popular acceptance—politicians to get elected, journalists to get their stories out. When you get right down to it, there isn't much difference between a TV ratings book and a political poll: both measure public interest and name recognition.

Duffy worked hard to develop a web of contacts, as well as his on-air persona and audience, and became one of the best-known faces on CBC's top journalistic program—a different kind of reporter, for sure, but more recognizable than even top correspondents such as David Halton, Don Newman, or Brian Stewart. Duffy was a name, and that gave him access to the highest reaches of politics and the federal public service. Understanding Duffy's popularity with audiences isn't hard. He was folksy, with a way of explaining difficult stories simply and free of jargon, a skill many reporters talk about but few possess. On air, Duffy appeared to be genuinely excited to be where news was happening, a trait shared by all good journalists. He also looked like your next-door neighbour or the guy at the hardware store; his portly frame and thinning hair didn't work against him, they were part of his charm. He was the jolly storyteller, not one of the cookie-cutter correspondents of the American networks, with their immaculate suits, perfect hair, and pearly whites. Duffy was the kind of guy you could invite into your living room to bring you the day's political news in a way that was non-threatening and friendly. He was a Maritimer, after all, a good old boy from Prince Edward Island who seemed, in those days, to lack any pretension. Canadians liked that.

Yet, for all of his obvious ambition, Duffy didn't see himself as a news anchor but as a reporter, and the late 1970s was a star-making period in Canadian political journalism. The popularity of mass media had made household names of journalists such as Charles Lynch, Richard Gwyn, Alan Fotheringham, Hugh Winsor, Jeffrey Simpson, Pamela Wallin, and Peter C. Newman. On the political side, Trudeau ruled in Ottawa with a coterie of hard-eyed ministers. One of them, Cape Bretoner Allan J. MacEachen, was a Trudeau intimate, winner of ten elections dating back to 1953, and the de facto Maritime chieftain of the party. In fact, it's doubtful any Maritimer since, with the possible exception of Peter MacKay in the early years under Harper, has wielded so much federal clout. As Liberal patronage king in the East and a future senator, MacEachen was not shy about appointing Maritimers to his office or installing them among the aides to other Liberal ministers and MPs. He had a powerful Maritime ally in Roméo LeBlanc from New Brunswick, a former journalist who had served both Pearson and Trudeau as a press aide and who was destined for both the Senate and Rideau Hall as Governor General in the Chrétien era. His son, Dominic, would later become a senior cabinet minister in a new Liberal government under a different Trudeau: Justin. LeBlanc had turned to active politics in 1972 and become a key figure in the federal power and patronage structure. Partly because of the influence wielded by MacEachen and LeBlanc through most of the 1970s and early 1980s, Maritimers prospered in federal Ottawa. The down-east network of politicians and mandarins socialized and gossiped. All those talkative Maritimers presented an ideal hunting ground for Duffy, the best-known Maritime journalist of them all, and they often provided grist for his frequent "Duffy's Notebook" items on *The National*.

Duffy was careful to nurture the insider image even in his news gathering. He covered Trudeau's heyday years through the 1970s, including his one and only defeat at the hands of Joe Clark and the Tories in the 1979 election. Duffy was there for Trudeau's resurrection and election victory in 1980. He was there to cover Trudeau's reaction to the Quebec referendum on sovereignty-association in May that same year. The "No" side won with about 60 percent of the vote, but it was still a disturbing moment for federalists and the national unity warriors of the PMO. Duffy gave the story a human touch, portraying the prime minister as deeply concerned, even a bit rattled.

Duffy was also there when Trudeau tried to put an end to constitutional debates by getting a deal with the provinces on patriating the Constitution. On November 5, 1981, Trudeau announced the political deal that six months later brought the Queen to Ottawa to sign the new Constitution Act. It was a big day in Canadian history, and Duffy showed viewers what it meant to be plugged in to the political process, as he was. Leaning against a cookstove in a utility kitchen on the fifth floor of the Government Conference Centre in Ottawa, Duffy narrated the stirring story of Jean Chrétien's "Kitchen Accord," which outlined the constitutional agreement among the federal government and nine of the ten provinces. All except Quebec had signed on, a fact that would have profound significance for the country. But on that day, all was sunny optimism and a sense of historical moment. Duffy reported that the deal had been created in that kitchen by three emerging political stars—Chrétien, Ontario's attorney general, Roy McMurtry, and Saskatchewan's justice minister and future premier, Roy Romanow—and scribbled down on scrap paper. Duffy took the viewer inside the fateful talks and included several long clips of the three amigos basking in their sense of accomplishment, even finishing each other's sentences. And with that story, seemingly from the inside of an historic event, he helped foster one of the great legends of modern politics. The Kitchen Accord became part of Canadian political lore.

There was one small problem, however, and it has persisted for more than thirty years. Newfoundland and Labrador's mercurial premier Brian Peckford was at the constitutional table, and that wasn't how he saw it at all. Peckford, a brash former outport schoolteacher, had become a thorn in Trudeau's side, making demands and issuing manifestos on his province's claims to hydro profits from Churchill Falls and ownership of the Grand Banks oil fields. The atmosphere was much like it would be twenty-five years later, during Danny Williams's crusades against Stephen Harper over offshore royalties. Peckford became a noisy member of the "Gang of Eight" premiers who were pressuring Ottawa for concessions on provincial rights. According to Peckford, other provinces had rallied to a formula he had proposed, not to any so-called Kitchen Accord. Yet Peckford barely was mentioned in Duffy's version of the three pals in their kitchen.

The day after the story appeared, Peckford told the *Globe and Mail* that the authentic deal—the one ratified by all the premiers except Lévesque—had been put together by the delegations from Newfoundland and Labrador, Saskatchewan, Prince Edward Island,

and Nova Scotia. Scoffing at the very idea of a Kitchen Accord, Peckford denied that Chrétien had even been in the room. Still, the Duffy version, which other journalists also reported, became the defining narrative in the patriation drama, and the story persists today. As late as 2012, I corresponded on the subject with Peckford, who now lives in British Columbia. He had written a memoir which he said would set the record straight about who did what at the Conference Centre over those momentous days. He acknowledged that the kitchen yarn "has been the accepted version for thirty years," but it was a "misrepresentation" of what really happened: "an incorrect version of events on how the agreement came together."

But, like any journalist, Duffy had to concentrate more on the history of the day than on history in the long run. The constitutional agreement might fall into the latter category, but the former was how reporters made their mortgage payments, and that was busy as the end of the Trudeau era neared and a period of transition began—grist for a reporter on the make. And it was then that Duffy's knack for self-promotion came to the fore. As political events heated up, Duffy did everything he could to portray himself as the master purveyor of inside dope from Ottawa.

In June 1983, Brian Mulroney's long campaign to undermine and oust Joe Clark bore fruit when he became leader of the Progressive Conservative party. Characteristically, Clark played into his hands, just as he had for the scheming Liberals and New Democrats who had brought down his minority government on a budget vote in 1979. After Clark's subsequent loss to the Trudeau Mark II Edition in 1980, the party's constitution demanded a leadership review at its national convention in 1981. Clark won 66.5 percent support and held on. In a similar vote at the national Tory gathering in Winnipeg two years later, Clark again won similar support, but he surprised everyone, including Duffy, by immediately calling for a leadership convention even though, under the party's constitution, he had every right to keep his job. Clark demanded a clear mandate from the party, and vowed to defend his leadership against all comers. Duffy was there for the announcement, and in his coverage the Duff persona emerges from the news and into centre frame.

Clark delivered an emotional speech to a packed, shocked room, calling for a leadership convention at which he would be a candidate. When he finished, the former prime minister waved and marched down a few steps off the stage and into the teeming crowd. Duffy was standing nearby and, according to his rather breathless account, Clark strode right up to him and shook his hand. Duffy reported the handshake as if it were part of the story, divining from it that Clark was nervous about his prospects at the coming leadership convention. As Duffy tried to ask a question, though, Clark was hoisted on the shoulders of his supporters and carried bodily off through the crowd.

It wasn't all domestic politics that kept Duffy busy and helped to build his reputation. Early in the morning on March 12, 1985, Armenian separatists stormed the Turkish embassy in Ottawa, killing a Canadian guard who tried to stop them. The Turkish ambassador, hearing the gunfire, jumped out an upper-storey window and was seriously injured. Heavily armed police surrounded the compound and a standoff ensued as every news agency in Ottawa rushed reporters and cameras to the scene. Duffy was there, reporting on the siege and the eventual surrender of the hostage takers, with the CBC breaking into regular programming for updates. Duffy's concise reporting won him an ACTRA award that year, the only major journalistic award he was to win during his career.

It was also in this period that his marriage fell apart as the pressures of his rising fame became too much. His wife, Nancy, left with the couple's two children for the BC interior, leaving Mike to continue burnishing his image on his own. Visiting Washington, DC, during the Canada-US free trade talks in 1987, Duffy secured a clip featuring famous Democratic senator Daniel Patrick Moynihan of New York. In the piece shown that night on *The National*, Duffy included "cutaways" which showed him palling around with Moynihan, who playfully patted Duffy on the shoulder.

Duffy's milieu was the Parliamentary Press Gallery. The venerable institution is part professional association and part social organization. It exists both as a body politic and as a lobby group. It has standards of professional behaviour—a jacket and tie is mandatory for the men when they go up to the Hill—and members are expected to respect parliamentary traditions and to conduct their business ethically and professionally. The Gallery is also a mindset: members consider themselves an elite, and if it seems at times more like a pack of feral dogs, that's because the Gallery is that, too. For all its tradition and decorum, the Gallery is populated by ambitious and competitive individuals who want to break news first and get ahead in a demanding profession.

The Gallery also exists in bricks and mortar. Back in the Centennial Year of 1967, with the country bursting with optimism and its economy firing on all cylinders, Parliament took over a building at 180 Wellington Street, across from the West Block, for the Gallery's use. A small theatre was built on the ground floor, to be administered by the Gallery but staffed with public employees who, over the years, would witness some pretty strange events. The National Press Theatre has become the scene of hundreds of news conferences over the years by MPs, cabinet ministers, political dignitaries, lobby groups, and even prime ministers. It was in that theatre that *Toronto Sun* columnist Claire Hoy infamously asked Brian Mulroney, "How does it feel when people call you Lyin' Brian?" The prime minister didn't show up in the theatre again for several years.

The Gallery's sentimental heart isn't on Wellington Street but in Room 350-N, a cluttered, high-ceilinged space on the third floor of the Centre Block in which Duffy was a near-constant presence. The Hot Room, as it is called, is a warren of cubicles and dusty desks where the inner core of the Gallery operates and which, with the indulgence of the speaker of the House of Commons, is the official corporate headquarters of the Parliamentary Press Gallery of Canada. From its north-facing windows, it has a view of the Ottawa River and across to the Gatineau Hills in Quebec. On its walls hang collections of photographs of the Gallery's storied members—class pictures of the generations of political journalists who have worked there. They were a small class back in the days when only a few major publications could afford a parliamentary correspondent. The photos also reveal how fashion changed over time, with fedoras popular in the 1940s and long hair and improbable whiskers in the 1960s and 1970s. The membership has changed, too, with more and more women joining since the 1970s. The Hot Room is a place of ritual, gossip, and cramped complaint. The fireplace in an adjoining lounge sits unused, but engraved on its mantelpiece is a quote from Lord Byron: "But words are things, and a small drop of ink, falling, like dew upon a thought, produces that which makes thousands, perhaps millions, think."

From the Hot Room, it's a quick dash down the hall and a flight of stairs to the foyer of the House of Commons, where daily "scrums"—the name comes from the refined violence of rugby scrums—have been a feature of parliamentary reporting for three generations. Since the advent of TV coverage of the House in the 1970s, most Gallery members have been able to watch the routine proceedings from their offices or from the Hot Room, ending any requirement to endure an hour on the hard wooden chairs in the Visitors' Gallery. The scrums are still popular, and many reporters wander up to the Hill after the *opéra bouffe* of the daily Question Period to pursue their prey—and the prey show up to be pursued. The scrums are a great Canadian parliamentary tradition of close-up interchanges between the journalistic hounds and the political rabbits, even if the roles of hunter and prey are often subtly reversed. After Question Period, MPs come out to the foyer to find out if they are going to make the headlines that day or remain in obscurity. It's where the day's news can be hashed over and analyzed among the reporters and the media spinners from the political parties.

Although the contact is useful, it does encourage a kind of blended thinking on the news of the day, as media critics have pointed out with some justification. Still, MPs and ministers can show up and get a hearing from the Gallery, and the Gallery gets to ask just about any question that comes to mind. For Opposition MPs, it's a godsend: one-stop media shopping for exposure to their feigned indignation. When the House is sitting, it is the centre of the Ottawa spin zone, although not the wrestling match it once was. As prime minister, Brian Mulroney would often pause at the bottom of the steps leading up to his office a floor above the Commons and field questions hollered from the pack. Jean Chrétien did, too, bantering back and forth with the reporters and often providing spicy quotes for the evening news.

The scrums are also a distinctly Canadian institution, a daily free-for-all not seen in many countries, even robust democracies. Visiting American journalists are often amazed that the prime minister would subject himself to questions yelled from the edge of a jostling mob. Americans like their politicians to look dignified and remote, not subject to proximate interrogation. One visitor, a little the worse for wear after getting knocked around in an elbows-up session in the foyer, described the experience, with simple elegance, as "a Mongolian pig fuck," a term Gallery members relished, especially as it came from the Americans.

With the Gallery and the political set jammed together in old buildings full of ghosts and tradition, situations arise when press and politics get too close. Ministers, MPs, and staff sometimes get into their cups with reporters, leading to some odd situations and to many yarns that have lived far beyond anyone's hangover. In Duffy's early years, there were few consequences from such convivial mixing because of an unwritten rule that kept the private life of political Ottawa mostly separate from the public. Gallery members usually knew which MPs had drinking problems and which had troubled marriages. They knew who was gay in the days before BC New Democrat Svend Robinson first declared it openly.

Few journalists saw sexual orientation or marital unrest as news-worthy, so it was rarely covered. And who were they to talk anyway? The Gallery has had more than its share of intemperate characters, and you could hardly report on an MP's peccadilloes if you had a few of your own.

Like so much else about a place thought to be historical and hidebound, however, the bibulous, friendly atmosphere between the media and politicians has changed over time and the Hill has become much more adversarial. Successive governments have limited Gallery members' freedom of movement, usually pretending to be worried about security. If it makes it harder to cover the news, so be it. Stephen Harper refused to expose himself to the scrums and took the back stairs into the Commons, bypassing journalists. His cabinet took its cues from the boss, and ministers rarely made themselves available.

The Gallery is a self-regulating and self-policing institution. It decides who can join, and it imposes its own protocols for pool coverage, news conferences, and the like. There has always been a sense of journalistic solidarity, even among rivals and otherwise dissimilar news organizations. When Duffy was rising in the ranks, the Gallery accepted members from the Soviet Union's TASS news agency, as well as from *Pravda* ("truth" in Russian), the official Communist Party organ, and *Izvestia* ("news"), the Soviet news-paper of record. The Russians had a saying: "In the Truth there is no news and in the News there is no truth"; by 2008, when Mike Duffy was going from Gallery to Senate, that's pretty much how the Harper government saw most of the Canadian media.

Duffy was a leading member of the Parliamentary Press Gallery for many years, but he was never what one would call an investigative journalist. He wasn't the kind to spend hours poring over documents or researching facts. Rather, he was a purveyor of insider talk, about who was saying what to whom, and his scoops were often incremental pieces of information that moved the story along but didn't result in the resignation of ministers or the fall of governments. The Gallery was so well set up and the symbiotic relationship with parliamentarians so solidified that Duffy's daily production didn't have to break new ground. The CBC wanted the day's top stories covered fairly and promptly, and Duffy delivered. That he brought his own style and brand to reporting was all to the good, too, because it helped the national broadcaster differentiate itself from the competition. The CBC didn't need its correspondents to look like matinee idols, beauty queens, or—God forbid—Americans. It knew its audience expected fair coverage, and for the most part that's what it got. If Duffy was able to build his own image and embroider his own myth during those years, that was fine, too. The CBC wanted authentic Canadian voices, and the portly reporter was one of them.

Like the rest of the Gallery, Duffy reported on the daily news of budgets and bills, intrigue and party politics. He seemed to cover it all pretty fairly, without any obvious bias toward one party or another. And even if Duffy had personal political leanings, *The National*'s robust script-vetting system picked it up and edited it out. In those days, no one complained about Duffy's biases. Political journalism was far less polarized than it is now, in any case, and complaints from the parties about bias were rare and formulaic. Major newspapers endorsed parties or leaders during election campaigns—for instance, the *Toronto Star* generally favoured the Liberals while the *Globe and Mail* plumped for the Tories—but their news pages mostly maintained a good balance. Later, after Duffy was accused of harbouring romantic feelings for the Tories, people would wonder where it all started. It's natural to assume that, if Duffy is a Conservative now, he must have been back then. But that is to misunderstand the way news coverage is put together, and it is also to misunderstand Duffy, who was a partisan for no cause other than that of Mike Duffy. He liked being close to power, and in Canada powerful people prefer friendly faces. Duffy cultivated contacts among Liberals and Conservatives, less so among New Democrats. His ability to go on air with stories from his vaunted but mysterious sources was part of his appeal as an insider in the parliamentary corridors. By the 1980s, his second decade on the Hill, Duffy saw himself as more than just another reporter, as he demonstrated in an interview on national radio in 1985.

Duffy was a frequent contributor to *Morningside*, CBC Radio's daily public affairs show. Peter Gzowski was its iconic host, fiercely nationalist, grumpy and wise. He had made the program mandatory listening for many Canadians, especially the political classes. His weekly panel of three veteran insiders—Gerry Caplan, Eric Kierans, and Dalton Camp—were old campaigners who gathered for crusty but amiable argument. Duffy would also appear, in one-on-one interviews with Gzowski from the Hill, for exactly the same reason: he was an insider. Seen as a rising national media figure, he brought his trademark gossip and political personality chat to the show. He also revealed, perhaps unintentionally, a growing interest in the Senate.

On February 22, 1985, Gzowski asked Duffy about the political fallout in Ottawa from the behaviour of unruly Liberal senators who had been controversially appointed by Prime Minister John Turner on Pierre Trudeau's orders and who were obstructing the Mulroney Tories. "Peter, the Senate used to be called the taskless thanks," Duffy said, repeating a well-worn description of the Upper Chamber that, somehow, the wordwise Gzowski had never heard. As the host broke into smoky laughter, Duffy remarked, "I have a little notepad here of one-liners," before going on to say that, if the wayward senators didn't behave, they would "run the risk of getting the place abolished before I'm old and gray enough even to get considered for an appointment." There was a pause, seemingly as Gzowski wondered whether Duffy was being serious. "That's a joke," Duffy quickly added, but this time, Gzowski didn't laugh. After an awkward silence, Duffy laid out the standard Ottawa view of how the Senate should behave: "This is a place where you're supposed to sip Scotch quietly and make sure that you don't cause too much of a ruckus." The words would come back to haunt him.

Duffy was also a prodigious consumer of food and alcohol, and it told on his waistline. He had been gaining weight since his late teens, but by the mid-1980s, it was getting worse. He would routinely go for after-work libations and order bottles of cold white wine, "one for the table and one for the well," meaning a second bottle cooling in an ice bucket for subsequent imbibing once the first one had given up the ghost. He was a faithful patron of Mama Teresa's, a downtown Italian restaurant where the political and journalistic set mixed, and the menu wasn't bogged down with low-calorie options. And Duffy was becoming all too aware of his growing fame, telling dinner mates on more than one occasion, "I'll sit facing the wall so we won't be bothered all night" by his admirers. Inevitably, a few minutes later, Duffy would be twisted around to chat with diners at other tables. Then he would be on the move, shaking hands and chatting up the impromptu audience of fans.

Duffy was also one of those drinkers whose mood and behaviour could change as his alcohol intake increased. When Duffy was drinking, and that was often in those days, he could go from charmer to troll, by times funny and insulting. And he was not shy about approaching women when he was in his cups, working what one former friend called the law of averages: "Mike just kept hitting on women. I guess he figured eventually one of them would say yes." One young woman from Winnipeg, Natalie Pollock, thought he was interesting and found his fame appealing. Pursued by Duffy, she let down her guard, and they saw each other on and off for awhile. At the time, Pollock was on the Liberal Party fringe; she says Duffy told her in 1984 that he was personally close to Prime Minister John Turner. In fact, Duffy claimed that Turner was urging him to take up the red and run for a seat in Parliament, which is the first time his aspirations beyond broadcasting became apparent. Pollock says she found Duffy to be fun to hang around with, but unreliable and far too fond of drink.

For all his quirks, Duffy was one of the most resourceful reporters in town, as he demonstrated on a historic evening in 1987.

Prime Minister Mulroney had summoned the premiers for talks aimed at reconciling Quebec with the constitutional changes Trudeau had wrought with patriation in 1982. They met at Willson House, a boxy government conference facility with big windows enclosing a ground-floor foyer overlooking Meech Lake, north of Ottawa in Gatineau National Park. It was a cold evening in April as the first ministers gathered, delegations in tow. After they had all arrived, journalists were allowed in for a photo opportunity of the premiers gathered around the table with Mulroney. Duffy didn't bother with the photo op, instead lingering back in the foyer where little clumps of tables and chairs were clustered here and there, each with a telephone. As the rest of the media took pictures and bantered with the politicians, Duffy wrote down the numbers on the telephones. Pretty soon the media mob was ushered out, retreating downhill to a warm press room set up in another building.

Two Canadian Press reporters—Robert Fife, later of CTV fame, and I—lingered on at Willson House for the "death watch," just in case something happened. We were armed with a state-of-the-art cellular telephone, which in 1987 meant a four-pound electronic brick with a shoulder strap, handset, and a big, rubberized antenna. As we shivered with the security team outside on the driveway, we could see the delegations gathered around in the foyer. They looked warm. After a few minutes, Duffy came huffing up the hill from the media holding room. "That thing work out here?" he asked, pointing at the mobile phone. We assured him it did. "Let me have it." Duffy pulled out a piece of paper with phone numbers scrawled on it and started dialing. Peering inside the foyer, the three could see one of the provincial officials suddenly look down at the phone on the table next to him. He hesitated for a second, then picked it up. "Dougie, old boy. It's the Duff." The man looked around the room, confused. Duffy waved from outside, and the quarry noticed him. "What's going on in there? What are you hearing?" Sure enough, there was news: Ontario's David Peterson was pushing the other premiers hard to get a deal. Quebec's Robert Bourassa had many demands, but there was progress. They hung up, and Duffy briefed Fife and me, who quickly called in the news on the newfangled phone. Before too long, a gaggle of Gallery members came charging up the hill, demanding to know what was going on. How did CP find out what was happening inside Willson House? Duffy just smiled.

CELEBRITY AND CONTROVERSY: THE CTV YEARS

*I would like to have the Order of Canada
before my mother dies.*

— MIKE DUFFY, 1995

NINETEEN-EIGHTY-EIGHT WOULD PROVE TO BE A BIG YEAR IN CANADIAN politics and for the career of Mike Duffy. A bitter election campaign would take place late in the year in which the Progressive Conservative majority government under Brian Mulroney would be tested on its centrepiece policy, Canada-US free trade. During that year, Quebec and the rest of Canada would diverge again on constitutional questions. The Reform Party under Preston Manning would make its first appearance in a federal campaign, with twenty-nine-year-old Stephen Harper, a recent defector from the federal Tories, writing policy. Reform fielded seventy-two candidates, but won only 2.1 percent of the popular vote and no seats. And Duffy would stun the Press Gallery, the CBC, and his viewers by jumping ship to start his own show on a new network. It was his chance to parlay all that hard work and years of image-building into a personal brand, one that would go beyond what he could ever achieve as a reporter, even as one of the stars of *The National*.

In 1988, the Mulroney government was four years into its mandate and a year into the defence of its far-reaching trade agreement with the United States. The political deal had been reached in 1987, but signed by the two countries' leaders on the second day of 1988. It seems straightforward now, in the wake of many other similar trade deals around the world, but it wasn't then. Well-organized interest groups on both sides of the border sought exemptions or other special treatment: the Canadian dairy industry fought to exempt milk quotas while US lumber interests complained about advantageous stumpage fees in Canada. The very idea of liberalized trade, of more "sleeping with an elephant," as Pierre Trudeau once put it, ignited a deep discussion about Canadian values and identity, what it meant for the country politically, and how it would affect national economic sovereignty. Typically, Canadians agonized and fought over it in Parliament and in the media, while most Americans barely noticed.

Free trade became the ballot-box question for the next election, and Duffy ended up covering the beat for the CBC, guaranteeing him frequent spots on *The National* but with the challenge of making the dry negotiations into something interesting. In Washington, he covered a dramatic moment in the talks when Canada's mercurial negotiator, Simon Reisman, walked out. Duffy closed his piece with unattributed insider dope on why Reisman did it. He also covered the soul-searching within the Liberal hierarchy as the party decided to stake the next election campaign on a battle against the free trade agreement.

It was also a period of political scandal, which was grist for Duffy and his network of partisan informants. The Mulroney cabinet kept up a dependable record of corruption and resignations, including the departure of Duffy's old friend, defence Minister Robert Coates, who stepped down after a visit to a German strip club. John Fraser, the principled fisheries minister, resigned after contradicting

Mulroney about the "tainted tuna" scandal, and Sinclair Stevens, the minister of regional industrial expansion, left amid allegations of conflict with the interests of a family business. There would be another seven cabinet resignations over Mulroney's nine years in office, which the western Reformers condemned as evidence of yet more corruption in the capital. With all this going on and an election looming, Duffy's face showed up on the news almost every night, his reporting often based on apparently gold-plated access to political players. Viewers noticed it. So did television's money men, and one of the most successful of all, Douglas Bassett, would soon make a move.

Bassett was president of Baton Broadcasting, a major player in CTV, and owner of CFTO-TV in Toronto. It was the family business. His father John was a Canadian broadcast pioneer and millionaire station owner. Doug had designs on expanding Baton, winning larger audiences, and eventually consolidating CTV's far-flung affiliates into a more coherent and profitable corporate structure. Over time, he did all of that. But this was 1988, and Baton had only recently taken over CJOH-TV, the popular CTV affiliate in Ottawa. Bassett wanted to stir things up, and found willing allies at the station in news anchor Max Keeping and executive producer John Beattie. In late 1988, *Ottawa Citizen* TV writer Tony Atherton reported that Keeping and Beattie had long wanted to create an Ottawa-based Sunday political talk show along the lines of NBC's *Meet the Press*. Keeping and Beattie pitched the idea to Bassett, who quickly gave it the green light and promised the cash to keep it lit. Now they needed to find a host.

Keeping had met Mike Duffy in Halifax back in the 1960s, and the two had kept in touch. Atherton says that Keeping and Beattie agreed Duffy had the profile, personality, and contacts for the job. For Duffy, it was an opportunity to make more money, burnish the personal brand, and get off the treadmill of daily reporting. After a brief negotiation, a deal was struck, and Duffy announced his departure from the place he liked to call "The People's Network."

Duffy had made a lot of friends at the CBC, and there were many who were disappointed to see him go, if for no other reason than concern about losing his large and faithful audience. Duffy had also annoyed many, however, with his temperamental ways, which had begun to show up more and more often. There were spats with makeup artists and squabbles with producers who despaired of his casual approach to scripts. Duffy never worried about prosaic matters like scripts—he could wing it if he had to. He had also been near the top of the journalistic pecking order at the CBC for years, with seemingly few further options. Peter Mansbridge had become the main anchor, replacing the retired Knowlton Nash, while other contemporaries such as Brian Stewart and David Halton had landed coveted foreign postings, and young stars such as Wendy Mesley were getting some of the plum domestic assignments. Duffy told friends he was getting restless.

For fourteen years, Duffy had been a staff employee of a Crown corporation, a union member by default, who was paid an annual salary plus overtime. He had few tax deductions, no more than any other salaried worker. Not that he was just any old widget in the corporate works: the CBC's on-air personalities and top producers are regularly paid well over union scale, and Duffy was at or near the top of the wage list. But he was also an employee, with all that implies, and he had lots of bosses. At Baton, Duffy would have the chance to be his own boss through the creation of a company that, in effect, would rent Mike to the station. Mike Duffy Media Services was duly registered in 1988, and would become the vehicle for Duffy's broadcast and public-speaking ventures for the next twenty years.

The pay wasn't too shabby, either. The Baton deal would start him at $140,000 a year, made up of $65,000 in salary, a $70,000 "talent fee," and a clothing allowance of $5,000. By the third year of the contract, increases to the talent fee and clothing allowance would bring his total annual compensation to $153,000, plus five weeks' vacation and access to company staff benefits. And he could pursue other contracts that didn't directly compete with Baton, as long as he notified the company first. Not shabby money at all— about the same as a physician then earned and many times as much as the average Canadian worker. A national-level print reporter at that time might make $50,000 in a good year.

With the money set, next came a hurried campaign to get the new show designed, staffed, organized, and dressed up enough to put on the air. Duffy agreed to the deal in August 1988 and *Sunday Edition with Mike Duffy* would debut the next month from the CJOH studios in Ottawa. Duffy was no longer just a TV reporter; he was a network host and the principal of a new sole-proprietorship company. Mike Duffy Media Services bought a condominium in downtown Ottawa which would serve as his office and his home. Duffy intended to hire a small staff of "speechwriters and communications planners," who presumably would bid on government and private sector contracts. He admitted a few years later to a tax court that the speechwriting and media monitoring part of the business didn't pan out, but the basic Duffy offering, "consulting and writing for newspapers, radio and personal appearances by the company's principal...continued to grow." He landed some consulting work with Rogers Communications, and he figured Doug Bassett would need his advice as he worked the broadcast regulatory system to expand Baton. He also wrote columns for the *Sun* chain of newspapers. But that was all sideline stuff; Duffy's main vehicle was the new show.

Sunday Edition with Mike Duffy was first broadcast in September 1988. Although it went through format and cosmetic changes over the years, its staple offering was always Duffy interviewing or moderating panels of MPs and cabinet ministers, lobbyists and commentators. The show covered events from across the country and took a stab at top world stories, too. Its stock-in-trade, though, was news and analysis of Canadian politics, especially the big stories on Parliament Hill. Now styled editor-in-chief of *Sunday Edition*, Duffy and the show got by with a staff of four plus the host. The producers processed tape inserts and rounded up interviews; Duffy did the rest.

Duffy was in demand as a speaker, too, and his agency found him good-paying gigs across Canada. A typical appearance took place on November 10, 1988, ten days before the general election of that year, when Duffy spoke at a meeting of the Empire Club of Toronto. His speech was a mixture of one-liners and a rather bland message about how lack of trust in politics and politicians was corroding the democratic system. Of course, the many scandals of the Mulroney years had transformed parliamentary ethics into a political issue, and Duffy said he was growing ever more concerned about ethical lapses among politicians and how that affected popular perception of leaders. "Every time we run a story on the CTV *National News*—a story about government scandal and corruption—we get angry calls," he told the well-heeled Empire Club audience at the Royal York Hotel. "Not angry about the politicians' actions, but anger at why we have no good news to report." He cited recent public opinion polls that came to the unsurprising conclusion that Canadians were not inclined to vote for politicians implicated in fraud or conflicts of interest. "Eighty-two percent would be less inclined to vote for a candidate who had been accused of fraud in a business deal a few years earlier. Note the phrase 'accused of fraud'—not necessarily convicted of fraud." It was the kind of distinction Duffy himself would make in the years to come about allegations directed at him as a public office holder.

That wasn't the only telling part of Duffy's Empire Club speech, which he had entitled "A Conversation about Canada." By association, the famous political insider placed himself on the top rung of Canadian celebrity: "I sometimes hear my friends who work in theatre and films complain that Canada doesn't have a Hollywood star system. We do. Except the stars are our politicians. The political teams have their own stars, their own fans, and their own strategies. But unlike sports, where you can watch from the sidelines, in politics you can actually get involved."

Freed from the bondage of public broadcasting and the CBC's stifling rules and regulations, Duffy was now able to expand his business and social horizons. He intimated to friends that he was close to Prime Minister Mulroney and some of his cabinet heavies, such as the influential transport minister, Don Mazankowski. He was also on good terms with Progressive Conservative Senator Lowell Murray, a Cape Breton-born friend of Mulroney's since their university days at St. Francis Xavier. Murray, a constitutional expert, became an unelected cabinet minister, serving in three different posts under Mulroney while remaining in the Senate. He also lived in Ottawa, serving as a senator for Ontario. David MacDonald, a fellow Prince Edward Islander, Tory MP for Rosedale, and cabinet member, was another friend who could offer perspective on political events. Duffy didn't neglect to stay on good terms with senior Liberals either, especially those with track records going back to the Trudeau years. Mackasey and Dan MacDonald were gone, but Liberal heavyweights MacEachen and LeBlanc still worked out of the Senate. And John Turner had enough doubters in his own caucus to keep several reporters busy with rumours and dark muttering.

Sunday Edition kept Duffy off the road for most of the 1988 election, but the campaign brought viewers to the show, and where viewers went, advertisers followed. Mulroney's government was re-elected after a hard-fought campaign that the Duffy show exploited well. It was the kind of event that would keep *Sunday Edition* going for eleven years. But Duffy started to get a reputation as an impatient, even imperious boss. Over the years, he would go through a succession of producers and show staff, many leaving because they couldn't stand to work with Duffy any longer. Some of those people started talking to unsympathetic reporters, and they weren't being nice.

One of those reporters was Michael Bate, former editor of the print version of the satirical magazine *Frank* and still the Ottawa-based editor of the online edition. *Frank* chose Duffy as a target of particular scorn in a biweekly satire called "The Puffster," which mocked Duffy's celebrity ways and pretensions. In 1991, *Frank* named Duffy "Eyesore of the Year," complete with acidic commentary. Then, in 1995, *Frank* reporter Glen McGregor, later of Postmedia fame, suggested in a story that Duffy wasn't in North Carolina visiting Duke University on a fellowship, as he claimed, but at a fat farm. Bate hyped the story with an over-the-top head-line: "Mike Duffy: Fat-Faced Liar!" In 2012, Bate claimed in the *Toronto Star* that Duffy sued *Frank* for $600,000. That's when it got interesting. A mediation session in the spring of 1998 was going nowhere until a *Frank* lawyer asked Duffy about his many awards and honours. According to Bate, Duffy gave a bizarre reply: "I would like to have the Order of Canada before my mother dies. She's eighty years old. I've been nominated three times and three times the message has come from the Privy Council Office on the back channel that *Frank* is the reason you're not going to get it and *Frank* is the reason your mother is not going to see you win this award.... [This] makes my blood boil." Bate wrote that, after further questions, Duffy claimed his "back channel" was the prime minister himself, which opened the possibility of serving Jean Chrétien with a subpoena to testify. Duffy's case looked ready to founder, when the two sides agreed to an out-of-court settlement of $30,000.

As a postscript, Bate said Duffy called *Frank* in 2005 when he was having problems with his online subscription, and ended up passing on gossip he had picked up about Peter MacKay. Gradually, Bate claims, Duffy became a regular *Frank* source. And not just any old source: "a wellspring of gossip, promoting his Tory chums and attacking colleagues he disliked at CTV." The episode even came up in the Senate. When asked about Duffy's lobbying for the Order of Canada, his future Senate colleague Marjory LeBreton suggested it was improper for the prime minister to interfere in the Order's nomination process. And she would have known, since she had been in charge of patronage appointments in the Mulroney PMO. Bate now says the episode was typical of Duffy: "He never knows when to shut up," he told me. "He is his own worst enemy."

Duffy had set his sights higher anyway. According to multiple sources from that era of the Liberal government, he was angling for a Senate seat. Duffy had clearly signalled his desire for an appointment to the "taskless thanks" to Chrétien, whose people were ready for it. They had already heard that Duffy had approached Mulroney.

In fact, Mulroney had joked about it in public, at one point remarking that Duffy wasn't going to be satisfied with just a seat in the Senate, he wanted to be speaker. With the Tories out and the Liberals in, Duffy had let it be known he was keen on the Senate and would be happy to be part of Team Chrétien. Word went through the organs of the Chrétien government right up to the boss. A future antagonist of Duffy's, Prince Edward Island Liberal MP Wayne Easter, who served as solicitor general in the Chrétien cabinet, said in an interview for this book that Duffy had been working on fellow Islander Percy Downe, then Chrétien's chief of staff and now a senator. "He lobbied Percy Downe for it. He made it known that he was interested in a Senate seat." Easter's story was confirmed by two other former PMO staffers from the Chrétien years. For all Duffy's lobbying, Chrétien never saw fit to make the appointment. Later, when Paul Martin succeeded Chrétien after a bloody internal fight among the Liberals, Duffy transferred his affections to the new leader. A former Martin staffer told me that Duffy put out the word "that he would be proud to wear the red," the Liberal team colour.

Nothing happened on that front, either, so Duffy continued to toil away on *Sunday Edition*, booking well-known guests and keeping most of the talk to the subject of national politics. That was why people tuned in, and Duffy gave them what they wanted. He and his producers landed a succession of top political interviews, which really isn't as hard as it looks: politicians are always seeking opportunities to speak to the public and are usually quite willing to show up for a few more minutes of fame. And Duffy was a reliable, known factor. He'd ask the standard questions and sometimes challenge power, but didn't stray into his guests' personal lives. In that sense, his show was reliably old-school and it didn't court controversy. It covered the top stories and kept Duffy in the front ranks of the political beat.

In 1994, Duffy's long service in radio and television was recognized when he was named to the Canadian Association of Broadcasters' Hall of Fame. The CAB is the main lobby group for the broadcasting industry, representing mainly private stations and networks. The nomination cited Duffy's many accomplishments and awards, and noted he had been at the scene of some of the top stories over the recent decades. The accolades were pouring in, and some thought they were going to his head.

During this period, Duffy travelled back to the Island and was invited to speak to Charlottetown's tiny press club and its dozen or so members. One of those in attendance, interviewed for this book, said Duffy arrived carrying index cards with questions that the local journalists were supposed to ask him. Presumably, every question had a funny or profound answer that Duffy would use to entertain and edify his audience of lesser-accomplished scribes. More than one person in the room found that to be "a bit much" and walked out. But for the wider public, Duffy was a genuine Island celebrity, and he enjoyed the attention. At one point, the *Charlottetown Guardian* put out a cookbook with recipes from famous Islanders. The celebrity journalist sent in one of his mother's recipes for chocolate brownies, which he had dubbed "Duffy's Downfall."

In 1994 and into 1995, the broadcaster-businessman kept up a running battle with the tax department in a dispute over deductions he had claimed in 1990 for Mike Duffy Media Services. Years later, *iPolitics* reporter Elizabeth Thompson dug up records showing that Duffy had been told he couldn't legally claim $27,503 in expenses that Duffy said had been incurred for business reasons. Duffy appealed, and the dispute ended up in the federal tax court. In a statement filed for the case, Duffy described Mike Duffy Media Services as "a small Canadian knowledge-industry company operating on the cutting edge of the so-called 'new economy,'" and that disallowing his claims "puts Canada's position in this important field in jeopardy." The statement suggests that Duffy thought Baton had big plans for him, and that he had set up the company to provide both broadcasting and consulting services. He wrote that Baton required "detailed advice on the domestic political environment, the physical disposition of the cabinet and the CRTC [the Canadian

Radio-television and Telecommunications Commission, the federal broadcast regulator] as all have a bearing on communications policy and the licensing of future broadcasting and specialty channel undertakings." Duffy evidently saw himself as moving beyond the studio and into the backrooms of Ottawa political life. In concept, he was to be both a broadcaster and a lobbyist, giving his client Baton his insider's view of how federal regulations would affect the company's business and future plans. That didn't wash with the tax department, which relied on hard records to back up its case that Duffy was actually an employee of Baton's subsidiary, Nation's Capital Television Inc., the corporate entity that operated CJOH-TV. If he was an employee, he couldn't claim as many business expenses as those available to a truly independent subcontractor.

As he would later in the Senate affair, Duffy blamed it all on unclear rules and sloppy accounting. He maintained that, in the rush to get *Sunday Edition* to air, the contract had been hurriedly signed and had failed to reflect the status of Mike Duffy Media Services as a stand-alone company. He claimed that the 1988 contract, or letter of employment, "provides a distorted and incorrect picture of the relationship between the two entities" that failed to reflect "a unique response to a unique situation," which was the need to get a new television program to air in just a few weeks. He chided the revenuers for not understanding the way modern knowledge-based businesses worked: "rather than trying to force business to follow Revenue Canada's model, the department should be adapting to the changing economy."

After that bit of policy advice, Duffy concluded his argument with a rather grand quotation from author Isaac Asimov: "It is change, continuing change, inevitable change, that is the dominant factor in society today. No sensible decision can be made any longer without taking into account not only the world as it is, but the world as it will be." Stirring stuff, but the tax department is not known for its literary inclinations, and neither are the courts. The decision came down against Duffy's claim for more than $27,000 in deductions against income of $78,751, ruling that, for all intents and purposes, he was an employee of Baton and CJOH. The contract was for personal services, and he was now on the hook for the money he owed.

He also ran afoul of officialdom on the roads. In October 2000, after a well-lubricated flight, Duffy was driving away from the Ottawa airport when police noticed a car unable to negotiate a roundabout on the edge of the airport lands. The cops pulled Duffy over and demanded that he take a Breathalyzer. He blew over the legal limit. Duffy went to court, pleaded guilty to impaired driving, was fined $600, and had his licence suspended.

Duffy's lifestyle choices caused other bumps in the road. In 1989, he had been diagnosed with diabetes, which caused him to make a few slight adjustments to his lifestyle, including losing some weight. The memory of his father's death from a heart attack at age forty-eight also had to be on his mind. But he continued to enjoy his drinks and a good meal, often picking up the tab if accompanied by people he liked. The habit was an expensive one. During this period, he also underwent painful proctology treatment, which led to one of those unexpected turns everyone experiences at some time: he and his recovery nurse, Heather Collins, became attracted to each other. She would become Duffy's second wife, but even that didn't go as expected. His heart might have belonged to Heather, but it wasn't a healthy one. In 1992, as he was preparing to go to air with *Mike Duffy Live*, he experienced a mild heart attack. He ended up at the Ottawa Heart Institute, headed by famed heart surgeon Dr. Wilbert Keon, which fixed him and made him its ardent advocate. Brian Mulroney had appointed Keon to the Senate in 1990, and Keon would help welcome Duffy to the Red Chamber when it was his turn to ascend.

Heart problems don't follow human schedules, and Duffy's came at the worst possible time, three days before he and Heather were to be wed in a ceremony in her hometown, the Ottawa Valley community of Pembroke. Undeterred, Duffy arranged for the ceremony to be held in his hospital room with a party of eighteen friends on hand to witness it. Former CBC colleagues Peter Mansbridge,

Wendy Mesley, and Brian Stewart were there, and Duffy's old crony Hugh Riopelle presided over a parallel reception in Pembroke. In typical fashion, they arranged a video link with the hospital room.

The combination of diabetes, weight, and bad habits would catch up to him again. In 2007, experiencing fatigue and shortness of breath, he underwent open-heart surgery to bypass a blocked artery, again at the Ottawa Heart Institute, and this time he really had to heed the doctors. He told an interviewer later that year that he had cut his alcohol intake and was making an effort to build some exercise into his daily routine. He lost forty pounds and said he felt a lot better, especially for someone who had been battling a weight problem since his late teens. "I walk more. I pace myself more. I don't work as hard. I've reduced my intake of alcohol and I get more rest," he told *Innovation* magazine for a feature on heart health. Later, he would explain his Ontario health card by saying he needed to stay in close contact with the Heart Institute's experts.

Duffy's newfound interest in fitness, a mild one to be sure, even ended up as part of the shtick when comedian Rick Mercer visited him that year for "a day in the life of the most celebrated political journalist on Parliament Hill." Mercer opened the bit by saying, if you really wanted to know what was going on in Ottawa you didn't go to the Centre Block, "you go to Mike Duffy's house," his place on Morenz Terrace in Kanata. Duffy and Mercer sat on stools in the kitchen, sipped coffee, and made jokes. Duffy got interrupted by a fortuitous and likely staged phone call, purportedly with the scoop that Conservative MP Garth Turner was bolting to the Liberals. Duffy wouldn't reveal the source, but hinted broadly that it was Turner himself. He and Mercer then went downstairs and got aboard a treadmill and a stationary bicycle, where Duffy duly pedaled away, leaning over to show Mercer the scars from his surgical incisions. "It looks like a map of Prince Edward Island," Duffy quipped. Then they got into Duffy's car, which bore Ontario plates, and headed off to hear Stephen Harper at the Chateau Laurier Hotel. Harper was giving a rote speech about taxes, but he also gave

Mercer a clip, saying "I always like watching Duffy so I can find out what my cabinet ministers are thinking." Mercer and Mike then retired to Duffy's lair in the Hot Room, where they traded jests over what the Liberals were up to that day.

In 2004 Duffy moved on from *Sunday Edition* to host COUNTDOWN *with Mike Duffy*. The new show was launched on May 23, just as the campaign was getting underway for the federal election scheduled for June 28. The show was billed as "the program of record of the federal election campaign," and would feature "the top strategists from each of the major political parties, the country's most respected journalists, opinion makers and pollsters, celebrity guests and, of course, the people who make it all happen—the candidates." After the election, which reduced the Liberals to a minority government as the new Conservative Party under Stephen Harper surged, COUNTDOWN would evolve into *Mike Duffy Live: Prime Time*, his daily after-dinner show broadcast from the foyer of the House of Commons. It would serve as Duffy's main product until he moved on to the Senate. Some said, with justification, that it even helped get him there. And it paid the bills, even if it didn't become the vehicle Duffy thought it might, given his status at the top of the political reporting heap. With the host and his guests perched on chairs and the ornate doors of the Commons as a backdrop, the show became a regular stop for politicians and spin doctors, and it led to some memorable programming. And it was also where Duffy began showing his colours, although the first colour he showed was red.

As he had done with Chrétien in his quest for an Order of Canada, Duffy now courted Liberal prime minister Paul Martin for a Senate seat. According to one top Liberal, Martin came close to appointing him after Duffy told one of Martin's advisers about his willingness to wear Liberal red. But Martin would not be in office long and had other priority appointments to make to the Senate. Duffy didn't get the call.

After Stephen Harper came to power in 2006, Duffy's critics— and they were plentiful—started to notice a change in the celebrity journalist. Duffy had always tried to stay friendly with whatever government was in power. As one former associate put it: "Mike likes to suck up and kick down," meaning he's nice to the rich and powerful and scornful of those of lesser status. Some began to think he was getting a little too cozy with the Conservatives and a bit too eager to take the government's side. In 2007, he tangled with Newfoundland and Labrador's bombastic premier Danny Williams, who was battling Harper over offshore oil royalties. Duffy interviewed Williams from St. John's, suggesting that a campaign to oust the Conservatives could "end up backfiring" against Newfoundland's interests and lead to the province being cut off from federal spending. Later, as a Conservative senator, Duffy would describe Williams as "that whack job over in Newfoundland."

One night on the show, Mike dressed down Liberal strategist John Duffy over an online attack ad against the Conservatives that he felt had gone over the top. When the Liberal protested, Mike talked over him, saying he "would not be intimidated" and that he would do his job whatever the Liberals thought about it. Conservative bloggers picked up the episode not as illustrative of Duffy's pro-Harper bias, but as yet another example of Liberal arrogance.

Duffy's preference for blue really started to show in 2008, as the country prepared for its third election in just over four years. One incident stood out early in the campaign. Duffy was covering a local candidates' debate between Conservative foreign affairs minister Peter MacKay and Green Party leader Elizabeth May in the riding they were contesting in Nova Scotia. After the debate, Duffy criticized May's rhetoric. "I don't want to use the word off-the-wall, but some of it was pretty bizarre," he told his audience on *Mike Duffy Live*. He then solicitously asked MacKay whether it wasn't "difficult" for him to debate "someone who will never be in power and can promise the world and never have to back it up." MacKay knew a softball question when he saw one and took the high road, saying his approach in debates was just to stick with the facts. Duffy didn't realize that May was watching the friendly interview with MacKay, and when it was her turn to speak, she unloaded. Duffy's comments to her opponent "constitute a significant violation of journalistic ethics," she charged, because he had tried "to frame me as out to lunch." As Duffy shook his head in denial, May admonished: "You and I go back a long way. And I like you enormously. But I think that had to be called out."

Duffy and CTV were also starting to tire of each other. The network was paying him more than $250,000 a year, plus such perquisites as a membership to Ottawa's tony Rideau Club and car and clothing allowances. The clothing money came in especially handy: Duffy had developed an affinity for made-to-measure suits, which he ordered from Russell's, a high-end tailor in Montreal who dressed the famously fashion-conscious Brian Mulroney and whose suits ran to $3,000 apiece. Duffy also liked dinners at top Ottawa restaurants Hy's and Mama Theresa's and lots of wine, which some of his former colleagues say became a bit obvious on air from time to time. But Duffy found ways to spread around his cost of living; as one top CTV executive told me, "any drink, any meal, he expensed to CTV." His staff also tired of his antics. Television is a team activity, and even stars rely on a supporting cast to get the show to air every day. Duffy could be petulantly hard on his cast, and later, when he got into trouble, few would rise to his defence.

In the meantime, there was an election to cover—a bitter contest between Harper's Conservatives, Stéphane Dion's Liberals, and a determined New Democratic Party under Jack Layton. Duffy shrugged off the Elizabeth May *contretemps* and went about his coverage on *Mike Duffy Live*, coupled with his weekly spots on local CTV stations across the country. Soon, some among his combined audience of well over two million started to wonder whose side Duffy was on.

ELECTION 2008: L'AFFAIRE STÉPHANE DION

If you've got a PVR, set it on "record." This is going to be one you'll be talking about for days.

— MIKE DUFFY ON *MIKE DUFFY LIVE*, OCTOBER 9, 2008

ON THURSDAY, OCTOBER 9, 2008, FIVE DAYS BEFORE THE ELECTION, Stéphane Dion and the Liberal campaign rolled into Halifax. The cerebral former environment minister and author of the federalist Clarity Act had struggled all through the campaign. Dion had been a compromise leadership choice to start with, and many Liberals weren't convinced he could win an election. The party was still bruised by resentments from the Chrétien-Martin war, and Dion was also carrying its baggage from the sponsorship scandal, in which Liberal insiders and corrupt advertising firms stole millions from the federal government. His overtures to Green Party voters to cast their ballots strategically to block the Conservatives had been poorly received. Few Liberals believed they could win, but they were still competitive in the polls, nationally and everywhere east of Quebec. Lately, their numbers had even improved, and one top campaign advisor, interviewed for this book, said the Liberals cherished hopes of a strong showing.

They were getting help. In St. John's, Premier Danny Williams was running his noisy ABC—Anything but Conservatives—campaign to the Liberals' benefit. Dion had proposed a five-point plan to deal with the spreading financial and economic crisis, while Harper had made an uncharacteristically boneheaded comment by laughing off the crisis as a buying opportunity in the stock market. The East Coast should have been friendly territory for Dion, and mostly it was. But the visit occasioned one of the strangest incidents in the 2008 campaign, one in which Mike Duffy played the key role and which Christopher Waddell of Carleton University's School of Journalism later called "the most controversial journalistic decision of the campaign."

Liberal campaign staff had made arrangements for TV interviews during Dion's Halifax stop, and had scheduled a set-piece speech at noontime attacking the Conservatives' handling of the economy. The interviews were set for late in the afternoon, right before Dion's departure to the next campaign stop in Montreal. Global had booked a slot, as had CTV Atlantic. Local TV stations relish these "one-on-ones" between political figures and their anchors, and they are a campaign staple for all the parties. Professional politicians see them as an easy hit because local TV interviewers are generally far more accommodating than the national breed, although they hate being characterized that way. In Halifax, the CTV Atlantic interview would go to its anchor and biggest in-house celebrity, Steve Murphy.

In the Maritimes, Murphy is as well known as Duffy, although far less notorious. A likable veteran newsman, by 2008 Murphy had anchored *CTV News at 6*, the network's popular dinnertime regional newscast, for fifteen years. The show was an institution; for most of those years, CTV's audience in that time slot was larger than all its local competitors combined. The formula was straightforward: news mixed with feel-good features and weather programming. It had enough hard news to satisfy the basic needs of public affairs consumers, but rarely strayed into investigative journalism or probing reports on social issues. Murphy could ask tough questions, and often did, but he also had a Duffy-like way of seeming deferential to those in power but less so with those on the outs. Being nice to powerful figures made it more likely that they and their ratings potential would come back to his show.

Duffy was also a regular staple on *CTV News at 6*, showing up every Friday from Ottawa to give his insider's views of political stories, updates on what Maritime MPs were doing, and his trademark name-dropping commentary. Duffy and Murphy would banter their way through five or six minutes of program time in chatty familiarity. It was "Duff" and "Stephen," suggesting an off-camera friendship between them which was more apparent than real—they knew each other, but they weren't close.

Going into the Dion interview, the Liberals had every expectation they'd get fair treatment from CTV Atlantic and that it would be a routine campaign stop in a friendly part of the country. Instead, the day's interview and the fallout from it would be a kind of journalistic black swan that affected the course of the national campaign. The interview was set for about 4 P.M., an hour before Murphy was to do a live news update from the station in Halifax's North End. A room at the Delta Barrington Hotel downtown was prepared and a portable lighting kit set up. CTV was using two cameras, so as to record Murphy's questions as well as Dion's answers. That much was traditional television news.

But, by the election of 2008, a lot that had been traditional about Canadian campaign coverage had changed. Most prominently, the networks had abandoned their decades-old practice of sending three-to-four person teams on the road, from writ to vote, with all the major party campaigns. Costs had escalated sharply in recent years, and now ran into the hundreds of thousands of dollars for each team assigned to each leader. It was also galling that network money helped to subsidize the campaign by paying for their seats on the plane. With the economic crisis biting into advertising revenues and budget cuts rattling many newsrooms, the networks had to find ways to pare costs. At many campaign events in 2008, all the networks agreed to be represented by a single pool camera, provided according to a rotation. The camera operator, a sound technician, and a producer would gather the material and distribute it to the rest of the media. Anything they shot or recorded was fair game for everyone.

On this day, the pool camera was operated by a shooter from Radio-Canada, who would record Dion's interview with Murphy and another with Global News. The presence of that camera played an important part in what was to happen over the next three hours. CTV Atlantic had taken the prudent step of sending along Peter Mallette, a thirty-year TV veteran, to keep everything moving and to supervise the all-important tape relay back to the station. According to a sequence of events prepared later for a Canadian Broadcast Standards Council investigation into the incident, Global began its interview at 4:10 local time. At 4:20, Murphy took over for CTV. Almost as soon as the interview began, there was trouble, all of it recorded by both CTV cameras and the pool cam. It started when Murphy noted that Dion had said in his speech earlier that day that Stephen Harper had no vision for the battered Canadian economy, then looking as if it might go hard aground like those of most Western countries. Dion nodded assent to that, then some kind of cognitive fault line opened up between the two men, sitting a metre apart in comfortable chairs. A transcript of the interview prepared for the Broadcast Standards Council hearings illustrates how widely the fault yawned as Murphy asked the twisted question that would lead to the clip of the day, a bonanza for the Conservative war room, and, quite possibly, Mike Duffy's elevation to the Senate.

MURPHY: Monsieur Dion, the economy is now the issue in the campaign and on that issue you've said that, today, that Mr. Harper's offered nothing to put Canadians' minds at ease and offers no vision for the country. We have to act now, you say. Doing nothing is not an option. If you were prime minister now, what would you have done about the economy and this crisis that Mr. Harper has not done?

DION: If I would have been prime minister two and a half years ago?

MURPHY: If you were the prime minister right now.

DION: Right now?

MURPHY: And had been for the last two weeks.

DION: Okay, no. If I'm elected next Tuesday, this Tuesday, is what you are suggesting?

MURPHY: No, I, I'm saying if you, hypothetically, were prime minister today.

DION: Today.

MURPHY: What would you have done that Mr. Harper has not done?

DION: I would start the 30/50 plan that we want to start the moment that we'll have a, a Liberal Government. And the 30/50 plan, uh, the 30, in fact, the plan for the first 30 days, I should say, the plan for the first 30 days once you have a Liberal Government. Can we start again?

MURPHY: Do you want to?

MALE VOICE OFF-CAMERA: Sure.

DION: [*looks at someone off-camera*] Yeah?

MURPHY: I'm okay to start again.

DION: Yeah. Because I think I been [*sic*] slow to understand your question.

MURPHY: Sure.

DION: I don't think it will be good.

MURPHY: Well, I'll repose the question.

DION: Yeah.

MURPHY: [*looks to others off-camera*] Is everybody okay with that?

DION: The question is "If you are prime minister today?"?

MURPHY: Yeah. Okay?

MALE VOICE: I'm recording.

DION: Okay.

MURPHY: Monsieur Dion, good of you to come again.

DION: Thank you, Steve.

MURPHY: Monsieur Dion, you've said today that Mr. Harper has offered, uh, nothing to put Canadians' minds at ease during this financial crisis and you go on to say that he has no vision for the country. You say we have to act now. Doing nothing is not an option. So I'd like to begin by asking you if you were prime minister now, what would you have already done in this crisis that Mr. Harper hasn't done?

DION: I can't, I don't understand the question. Because, are you asking me to be prime minister at, at which moment? Today or since a week or since two weeks or since—

MURPHY: No. If you, if you were prime minister during this time already.

DION: We need to start again. I'm sorry. If I was the prime minister starting when? Today? If I was the prime minister today?

FEMALE VOICE OFF-CAMERA: If you were the prime minister when, since Harper's been prime minister.

DION: But, yes, two years and a half ago.

FEMALE: At any given time.

DION: Two years. Two years and a half ago.

FEMALE: What would you have done differently between, between the time that Harper's been there to change things.

DION: Yeah, but if I have been prime minister two years and a half ago, would [*sic*] have had an agenda. Let's start again.

MURPHY: Okay.

[*Female off-camera laughs*]

DION: We'll go there.

MALE VOICE OFF-CAMERA: I'm still recording.

MURPHY: Monsieur Dion, thank you for coming.

DION: Thank you, Steve. Let's start again, I'm [*laughs*].

[*Female off-camera laughs*]

MURPHY: It's a good job that tape is cheap.

DION: But, but give me, give me a first date where I'm prime minister that I can figure out what, what is your question is about [*sic*].

MURPHY: If you were prime minister of Canada today, what would you have done by now that Stephen Harper has not done about this economic crisis?

Eventually Dion offered an answer, the torture ended, and the interview moved on to other topics. When it finished after 4:30 local time, Murphy and Mallette had to dash back immediately to the CTV studios, where Murphy had to do the live news update at the top of the hour. There clearly was concern in the Liberal team about how Murphy and CTV had interpreted Dion's difficulties. Mallette says now that "Dion's people knew that it was explosive." A staffer approached him and asked whether CTV intended to use the retakes. "You're not going to put that on air, are you?" she asked. The Liberals said, and CTV doesn't deny it, that Mallette offered them some kind of assurance about the retakes. "No worries," is what he said as he was leaving the hotel. Today, Mallette doesn't blame the Liberals for thinking the tape wouldn't be broadcast. "If you had heard that, you would have likely thought there is no way that is going to end up on TV."

Heading back across town with Murphy in a taxi, Mallette sensed he was mixed up in a major news event. "I was sitting in the cab with Steve and my heart was beating right out of my chest," he said. "I knew we had an explosive piece of tape that was going to change the election." He also knew what he had said to the Liberals. "I was very conflicted about it. I knew I had said 'no worries.'"

From the cab, Mallette called his boss, CTV Atlantic's executive producer Jay Witherbee, to tell him they were on their way back to the station and about the unusual start-and-stop beginning of the interview. He asked Witherbee to be ready to view the tape. After a maddening traffic delay, Murphy and Mallette arrived at the station and went straight into an editing suite with Witherbee. For Mallette, it was an extraordinary situation, dealing with a potentially controversial story at a key moment in a federal campaign. "I had never been involved with anything like that before in my life," he recalled. Witherbee decided to kick it up the line and called Toronto to speak to CTV News president Robert Hurst, himself a veteran political reporter. But Hurst was tied up in a meeting. The minutes were ticking by, and when they did get him on the phone, Hurst didn't waste time over the decision. According to Mallette, "Bob Hurst said 'This is an election, everything is on the record.'"

Mallette, Witherbee, and Murphy talked over what they had captured on their tape. They had been influenced by the Liberal campaign staffer's attempt to intervene. They agreed with Hurst that the false starts were legitimate news. After all, what candidate could presume to lead a country if he couldn't understand the household language of most of its citizens? And they were concerned about the pool camera. What if CTV held off showing the restarts but the rest of the media picked them up?

CTV News at 6 ran the entire tape, including the stumbling retakes. Viewers were outraged and wasted no time letting them know. "From the moment the tape went to air, the phone started ringing. There were dozens and dozens of calls. As far as I know, there was only one who supported us," says Mallette. Worse, the viewers blamed Murphy personally. The biggest complaint wasn't even on a journalistic issue. "It's just not the Maritime way of dealing with people" was the common theme.

According to CTV's interpretation, if Dion didn't understand the question it was his own fault. The network later published a detailed letter from Hurst, defending its actions and setting out its version of the event. It was clear that Dion had had difficulty understanding Murphy's question. There was some uncertainty, raised by the Liberals themselves, whether Dion had a slight hearing problem. Dion himself said he had no trouble hearing Murphy—that wasn't the issue. The mixing of tenses—"if you were prime minister now, what would you have done"—seems to have been what threw him off, along with fatigue after many pell-mell weeks of travel and campaigning. CTV would also claim that it was unusual to allow restarts once the cameras were rolling, although many other TV news professionals dispute that. When an interview is being conducted in a controlled environment, with time to do it right, most networks allow interviewees latitude, especially if he or she is speaking a language other than their mother tongue.

It's clear now that Witherbee's decision to send the tape up the line to Toronto was a fateful one. This was an unusual situation because of the sensitivity of the election campaign and the story's potential impact so close to voting day, but also because of traditional Canadian sensitivities over language issues. English-speaking politicians are rarely criticized in the francophone media for their poor French, which raises a potential double standard in *l'affaire* Dion-Murphy. You could be prime minister of all Canadians with only adequate mastery of French, but your command of English had to be no worse than Jean Chrétien's. To this day, that seems to be CTV's view. Although Witherbee now calls it "the darkest day of my professional career," the participants still stand by their decisions and insist that CTV's treatment of Dion was fair and journalistically sound in every respect.

In Ottawa, Duffy and his producers saw the Dion tape as soon as it was uploaded into CTV's Gateway system. Under his direction, they fashioned their own version of it, which had significant differences from what went to air in Halifax—differences that would come under the critical eye of the Broadcast Standards Council. Opening *Mike Duffy Live Prime Time* about two hours after Murphy's version ran, a grinning Duffy promised his viewers they were about to see something that would have a huge impact on the campaign. From his set-up, viewers might have thought they were going to hear about some cataclysmic event that had taken place, rather than just a video of a politician fumbling a question. Duffy began the segment with an accolade for the Harper government's handling of the banking and financial crisis, then got right into what he was really interested in—the stumbles of Stéphane Dion.

"Well," said Duffy, "the Harper Conservatives got some good news today and it wasn't just the World Economic Forum, which rated our banking system as the best, the most secure in the world. This good news came in the form of a devastating reminder of Stéphane Dion's struggle with the English language. We'll have the tape in just a few moments. If you've got a PVR, set it on 'record.' This is going to be one you'll be talking about for days."

What the Duffy show ran was very different from the content on the regional show, which included the full interview with the retakes, but also Dion's answers to the rest of Murphy's questions. Duffy didn't bother with any of that. Instead he ran just the series of misunderstandings and restarts, with the camera left mostly on Dion as he struggled to answer. Duffy called it "the tale of the tape," and ran it several times during the show. There was nothing about the economy, Afghanistan, or the environment, just Murphy asking convoluted questions and Dion misapprehending him.

After the Dion tape had rolled, Duffy turned to a panel of MPs who were on hand to discuss the day's news. One of them, Liberal Geoff Regan of Halifax, suggested that Dion had hearing difficulties and that CTV was mocking a physical impairment on Dion's part. The transcript illustrates Duffy gave short shrift to Regan's attempt to defend his leader.

DUFFY: We were more than generous in giving him, I think, three or four chances. And he comes up with this? And then you tell me we're making fun of his physical impairment?

REGAN: That's not what I said, Mike.

DUFFY: Give me a break.

Duffy then turned for comment to Conservative MP James Moore, who was sitting in a studio in Vancouver. Predictably enough, Moore suggested strongly that the campaign was about who was most fit to govern, Dion or Harper. The implication was that the Liberal leader's problems with English made him unfit to be prime minister. Moore, a veteran campaigner and senior minister under Harper, made it clear that the CTV tape played very well in the Conservative Party campaign script.

"We saw the full clip there unedited," Moore said. "I guess people can make their judgments about it...but the choice is between Stephen Harper and Stéphane Dion in terms of who Canadians want to be the prime minister of this country. Who has a plan, who has a track record, and who has the capacity to lead Canadians through a difficult international economic time. And I think Stephen Harper clearly is the right man to lead this country." Duffy asked the third MP, New Democrat Joe Comartin, what he thought. Comartin, sensing this was an area best handled with discretion, steered around the question, and the discussion turned to other campaign issues.

On the sidelines, reporter Stephen Maher, then of the *Halifax Chronicle Herald*, sat waiting to go on air in a reporters' panel. Maher, who sat next to Duffy in the Hot Room, says now that he was nervous enough about going on national television, but overhearing Duffy's treatment of Dion, he really started to sweat. He wrote later that "CTV was right to air the clip, since Dion wanted to be prime minister, but I thought Duffy's take on the interview was way over the top. He treated it like the biggest gaffe since Robert Stanfield fumbled a football." In fact, Duffy had done just that, likening Dion's stumbles to the famous photograph of Stanfield's bobbling a pigskin at a Canadian Football League game. Maher's conclusion: "Duffy was in the tank for the Tories because he wanted Harper to appoint him to the Senate."

Duffy then moved on to a segment with two of CTV's highest-profile reporters, Craig Oliver and Tom Clark. Duffy started by asking Clark, "How are the Liberals explaining this Dion language problem?" Clark said the senior ranks of the Liberal campaign were furious at what they regarded as "an appalling breach of journalistic ethics" by CTV after Mallette's assurance that the false starts would not be aired. The Liberals planned to take their complaints to senior management at CTV. "They're going to have some conversations, I would expect, with your bosses and my bosses, Mike, about all of this," Clark said. That didn't slow Duffy down a beat. He suggested the producer on the scene, Mallette, didn't have the authority to tell the Liberals the retakes wouldn't be shown on air. He was making no apologies. "It's one thing to say...we'll let you start again, but clearly it wasn't because somebody coughed or had to blow their nose or sneeze," Duffy said loftily. "It's because of something much more important. And when you're dealing with someone who wants to be prime minister of Canada, this is not a laughing matter."

Duffy's treatment of the Dion tape hit the campaigns like a bomb. In his book *Harper's Team*, former Harper advisor Tom Flanagan called the botched interview a "windfall" for the Conservative campaign, and noted that Harper himself seized on the incident: "Indeed, Harper goosed the publicity by personally drawing it to the attention of journalists travelling with his leader's tour. It was risky for the prime minister to intervene this way rather than letting a surrogate carry out the attack, but it ensured maximum publicity." That is an understatement. The Conservatives thought the event so important that they put Harper's plane down in Manitoba so the media could file on Dion's bad moment.

Some go even farther. A top CTV journalist told me that "the whole incident was manipulated by the Harper PMO. Duffy must have tipped them off." The Liberals, meanwhile, flew to Montreal, headed for a campaign event in suburban Laval. Only then did they hear what Duffy had done with the tape. "No question it had a huge impact on the campaign," one senior Liberal told me. "Our tracking polls told us we were headed toward a hundred seats. We went straight downhill after that night."

Not surprisingly, other major media organizations picked up the story, a fact CTV emphasized in its argument before the Broadcast Standards Council, but they could not agree about CTV's decision on the retakes. Raging debates broke out in newsrooms across the country, where journalistic lapses are matters of obsessive interest. That just added to the weight news organizations gave the story, promoting the controversy to front-page news. Duffy's bosses were hearing about it all right, but they had been central to the decision and were no more ready to back down than Duffy was.

By the next night, Murphy had had twenty-four hours of strong reaction ringing in his ears, much of it aimed directly at him. He was being called biased, a Tory hack. He seemed abashed during the regular *Friday Politics* segment with Duffy, calling it "a difficult decision and certainly one that many viewers did not agree with." Duffy said through a thin smile that his contacts were telling him otherwise and viewers had lauded CTV for putting the whole story to air and not holding anything back. "It's in the public interest that everybody know everything," he said. He then tossed off the controversy by saying, "To me, that's yesterday's news, let's move on. There's a lot more news to cover today."

Murphy pointed out that the Liberals had been making gains in the public opinion polls in the dying days of the campaign, a fact well reported in the national media. Duffy laughed that off, replying that former prime minister Jean Chrétien was appearing that night for the Liberals in Toronto, and, mocking Chrétien's *québécois* accent, talked about the party's internal troubles. He announced that the Conservatives were promising funding for a harness racing track in Summerside and finished with a flourish, suggesting that one of the Island's most respected Liberal MPs, Wayne Easter, was about to be knocked off in the election four days hence. Harper himself was coming to the Island to support Easter's Conservative opponent, Mary Crane, "who all the locals tell me is within an inch of beating Wayne Easter."

Easter, however, ended up winning handily, and Duffy's critics used the comment as more evidence of his Tory tendencies. The tape certainly worked well for the Conservatives, who took it to social media. An anonymous YouTube poster using the handle "Jiminalberta" uploaded the material with the title, "Stéphane Dion screws up again, and again and again." More than 165,000 people viewed it.

When it reviewed the incident months later, the Broadcast Standards Council came down hard on CTV and especially Duffy, calling his actions "an unfair and improper presentation of news, opinion, comment and editorial, contrary to the rule established in Clause 6 of the [Canadian Association of Broadcasters] Code of Ethics." That rule mandates the principle of "full, fair and proper presentation of news, opinion, comment and editorial [as] the prime and fundamental responsibility of each broadcaster."

The council criticized CTV for its heavy emphasis on the false starts as the central news element of the interview, calling them not newsworthy but "very common, even absolutely routine." It noted that the rest of Murphy's interview dealt with substantive issues: the economy and the Liberals' economic plan, Dion's call for a carbon tax, and the bloody Canadian military mission in Afghanistan. "That is where the substantive meat was, not in the restarts," the council wrote. It questioned whether CTV was more interested in "the stumbles, the whoopses and the mis-starts" or in the significant political issues raised in the rest of the interview. It also noted that it was standard practice for a responsible producer to make decisions about false starts on the scene. For the Dion interview, Mallette was a senior producer and Murphy was the program's de facto managing editor, and there is no doubt about their seniority or authority over material going into CTV News at 6.

Clearly, the council wouldn't have been so critical if not for the way Duffy handled the tape on air. It's also possible that, were it not for the Duff's gleeful treatment of Dion's difficulties, he would not have been appointed a Conservative senator ten weeks later. All these years later, Liberals are still angry about Duffy's treatment of Dion. Instead of the hundred or so seats they thought they might win, they ended up with seventy-seven. "It's where the tide turned finally against us," says a Liberal advisor who was travelling with the leader. "It came at a critical time in the campaign, and it just killed Stéphane Dion."

When the Conservatives realized what they had in the Dion tape, their war room, aiming for maximum impact, put out the word to as many news organizations as possible. And when Duffy was appointed to the Senate a few weeks later, some top Ottawa insiders weren't the least bit surprised. Many felt that he had already crossed the line between journalism and partisanship, one he had tiptoed along for years.

DUFFY GOES TO THE SENATE

So I thought: what the heck, this is a sure deal.

— SENATOR-DESIGNATE MIKE DUFFY, DECEMBER 23, 2008

ALTHOUGH IT'S NOT POSSIBLE TO DRAW A DEFINITIVE LINK BETWEEN Duffy's savage treatment of Stéphane Dion and his appointment to the Senate, it's safe to say it didn't hurt his chances. On October 14, 2008, Harper's Conservatives managed to eke out another minority win, and the prime minister wasn't taking any chances on losing control in the Commons and getting knocked out of office. There was already muttering among his opponents about teaming up to defeat the Conservatives on a confidence vote, then stepping in to approach the Governor General to turn over power to a Liberal-NDP coalition supported by the Bloc Québécois.

As Christmas approached in that chaotic, depressing year of 2008, Harper, trying to keep the Opposition dogs at bay, seemed determined to create some new senators to strengthen his hand in the Upper Chamber. Duffy's name appeared in a newspaper speculation piece along with other possible appointees. Duffy noticed, of course, and he and Heather talked it over. Duffy, who has told several different versions of how he was appointed, would claim later that he wasn't all that interested in a Senate seat—remarkable considering how much he had thought about it over the years. Then on Saturday, December 20, the phone rang at the house in Kanata. It was the prime minister and, according to Duffy, he wanted to know what Duffy thought about the state of the Senate. Duffy claims he advised the PM to "fix it or kill it." If Harper was posing a skill-testing question, he got the right answer. After all, wasn't one of his avowed goals to reform the Senate and make it better? His next question: would Mike "Senator" Duffy consider becoming Senator Mike Duffy? The moment had arrived. For Duffy, it was vindication for all those years toiling in journalism, his lobbying of previous governments, and the painstaking creation of the "Old Duff" legend as Ottawa's ultimate insider. It was a chance finally to join the club.

The telephone discussion with Harper instantly became the stuff of the Duffy auto-legend. His supposedly reluctant decision was the kind of yarn Duffy cherished because it fit perfectly into the myth he had nurtured so carefully over the years. He would tell the story every chance he got—how he had to be coaxed, just a bit, by the most powerful man in the country to take a job in the Red Chamber and do something important for the country. The way he described it, the new appointees would be part of Stephen Harper's band of hardy reformers to bring about lasting change—not to kill it, but to fix it. On a more personal level for the soon-to-be senator, it was a chance, as he put it, "to go from an observer to an active player on the field."

True to form, before the official announcement, Duffy had a hard time keeping it to himself. Postmedia columnist and former Hot Room seatmate Stephen Maher recalls that it wasn't long after the campaign that Duffy "excitedly told me he got a Senate vetting call. He was due to speak with the prime minister. I told him he should ask Harper to appoint him as an independent." That wasn't going to happen, but Maher recalled that "he seemed thoroughly delighted to finally make it into the chamber of taskless thanks."

On a cold, blustery Friday night in December, the star summoned some of his Mike Duffy Live staff and a handful of his frequent on-air guests to a soirée at Hy's Steakhouse, a now-defunct media and political hangout two blocks from Parliament Hill. Hy's was all dark wood panelling and plush seating, where you could enjoy a delightful glass of Cabernet Sauvignon for $19 and a steak for $50, all the while seeing and being seen. The get-together was hastily organized, so the only show regulars who could make it were former Liberal minister Sheila Copps, Greg MacEachern, a Liberal consultant originally from Cape Breton, and Greg Weston, a canny old Ottawa hand and then a political columnist for the *Toronto Sun*. Duffy had also invited some producers and staff from CTV and his show. The host soon proposed a toast in which he waxed on philosophically, mostly about himself. He also mentioned not having "a real pension," at which Weston and MacEachern looked up. An experienced political spinner himself, MacEachern realized, as he puts it now, "we were being pre-spun." Weston muttered to MacEachern: "He got it. He's in the Senate." Weston's political antennae proved to be finely tuned.

On December 22, Harper announced he was appointing Duffy, Patrick Brazeau, Pamela Wallin, and fifteen others to the Senate, all as Conservatives. Such announcements, author Claire Hoy wrote in his 1999 book on the Senate, *Nice Work*, were like a "first-class passage to patronage paradise." After all the years of joshing about it, after all the broad hints, after thousands of TV shows, Duffy's call had finally come. His self-created persona as the ultimate insider, the player, the small-town boy who walked with the powerful and influential would no longer be just a personal legend; it would be real.

There are good reasons to conclude that Harper's real agenda wasn't about Senate reform at all. Major constitutional change was not a practical political objective for the Conservative minority government in 2008. Nothing had evolved on that front since the twin Tory failures over Meech Lake and the Charlottetown Accord back in the Mulroney days. Not only that, but Harper seemed to have a deep aversion to matters constitutional. He wouldn't even meet the premiers as a group on routine issues such as the economy, evidently fearing that, locked up together in a conference room somewhere, they would transform into scavengers looting the treasury while ensnaring Ottawa in yet more expensive programs. Harper had seen it happen to his predecessors—how dealing with the provinces had entangled Trudeau, Mulroney, and Chrétien.

Trudeau had burned bridges to get his made-in-Canada Constitution, alienating francophone Quebecers for a generation and making it difficult to elect Liberals in that seat-rich province. When his turn came, Mulroney put his personal prestige and all his political capital on the line for the Meech Lake Accord, building a coalition with Quebec nationalists—the *beau risque* that would explode in his face in the form of the Bloc Québécois. His decision "to roll the dice" on Meech Lake led directly to the destruction of the Progressive Conservative party, a lesson not lost on Harper or other astute observers like Chrétien. As prime minister, Chrétien chose not to pussyfoot around with troublesome political elements in Quebec, but took on the nationalists directly with Stéphane Dion's Clarity Act, which aimed both to set up a rigorous test for any province seeking to secede and to fire a booming legal-constitutional shot across the bows of the separatist movement.

Still later, Harper, newly chosen as the first leader of the new Conservative Party of Canada, was watching when Paul Martin convened a first ministers' conference in September 2004 to talk about health care, eventually granting most of what the provinces wanted at the cost of multiple billions. With the provinces, demand always seemed to follow demand, and Harper wasn't inclined to play along. Saying yes could be dangerous to the treasury as well as to Harper's philosophical preference for a minimalist federal government. But saying no also supplied political fuel to the premiers, as Danny Williams had proven in the scrap over offshore oil revenues and as every Quebec premier had known, going back to Confederation. Harper wanted nothing to do with any of it, so if there was to be any type of reform in the Senate, it would have to be cautious and incremental so as not to trigger formal constitutional discussions. Without the political horses on Parliament Hill and absent any type of consensus among Canadians, making the Senate elected or equal was not in the cards.

Harper's eighteen appointments that December had far less to do with Senate reform than with deflecting an immediate political threat in the arena where the prime minister did have cards to play: the House of Commons. Harper was plainly worried about talk of a potential coalition to topple his minority government. Although he had pledged not to make appointments to the Senate, he feared that an ungodly coalition of Stéphane Dion's Liberals and Jack Layton's New Democrats, with the connivance of Gilles Duceppe and the separatists in the Bloc Québécois, would seize power from the Conservatives and steal a democratic election from Canadians.

Harper's public reasoning was straightforward: he and his party had been elected fair and square, and only he had the legitimate right to make the appointments. Constitutionally, his argument was bulletproof. The political optics weren't great, but the decision belonged to him as prime minister and not to what he liked to call "a coalition elected by nobody." It follows that, if the appointments were to be political, Harper expected partisan fealty. A news release from the PMO made that crystal clear: "The incoming Senators have all pledged to support eight-year term limits and other Senate reform legislation," the statement said. "Each incoming Senator has also declared his or her unwavering commitment to support Canadian unity and oppose the coalition." Oddly, none of the new star appointments mentioned term limits when their turn came to talk about their new incarnations as senators-designate.

If Mike Duffy appeared to be a non-partisan appointment, or at least one without formal ties to the Conservative Party, it was clear he was being appointed as a Conservative, would be a member of the party's parliamentary caucus, and would be expected to toe the party line. Most of the other Harper appointees had strong Conservative ties as fundraisers, party activists, or former candidates, but the two broadcasters, Duffy and Brazeau, an aboriginal activist, seemed to be off that script—or, at least, that was how they were portrayed publicly. On the day the appointments were announced, it was all sweetness and light and the humble acceptance of a high honour.

The youthful Patrick Brazeau, at thirty-five one of the youngest ever appointed to the Senate, smiled broadly when he told a television interviewer that he didn't need any Duffy-like coaxing from the PM. "I was in shock and probably for the first time in my life, I was speechless for about ten seconds," he said. "But once that ten seconds went by, I certainly accepted the prime minister's offer." At his age, and absent significant reform of the institution itself, Brazeau potentially could serve in the Senate for forty years. Over that time, he might earn more than $5.5 million even if he never got another pay raise, and after that collect a plush pension until the day he died. There was no mention of any eight-year term in his appointment, and legally he wasn't bound to it. Under the circumstances, it's surprising it took him ten seconds to consider the offer. Later, journalists would discover that Brazeau went right out and purchased a vacant lot in Chertsey, Quebec, for a bit more than ten thousand dollars. With that, he met the constitutional requirement of owning at least four thousand dollars worth of property in the province he was to represent.

For her part, Pamela Wallin told CTV, her former network, that she took longer to think it over. "I spoke to the prime minister ten, twelve days ago, so I have been thinking about it," she said. Unlike Duffy, Wallin had been out of journalism for years and already had a track record in public service, having been appointed by Chrétien Canadian consul-general in New York. Like Duffy, she was also a star public speaker, commanding thousands of dollars in fees at gigs across the country. Because of her celebrity status and diplomatic experience, she had been asked to sit on several corporate boards, including Bell Globemedia, owner of the *Globe and Mail* and CTV, as well as Oilsands Quest Inc., Porter Airlines, and Toronto wealth management firm Gluskin Sheff + Associates. Most directorships are part-time jobs that pay a superb day rate plus travel and other expenses, and all are excellent networking opportunities. Wallin never claimed she needed convincing; she just wanted time to think it over, if only to make sure nothing in the rules prevented senators from serving on corporate boards or earning money from their regular professions. There wasn't—almost every senator has a little something on the side.

Duffy not only accepted right away, but he immediately began dramatizing the momentous event of his appointment, as ever in the mould he had created for himself as the unlikely Islander who rolled with the big guys. In a CTV interview the day after the appointments were announced, he said that hearing himself described as "Senator Duffy" was "still a little strange," but he allowed as how "I'll get used to it." Over the next few days, in interviews with the media from whose ranks he had just graduated, it would become clear why the appointment was such a triumph. It vindicated his claim to insider status and fit the myth he had created for himself. It's also clear that, right from day one, he saw the Senate as a retirement vehicle—something to do after his regular career ended and still get paid. No wonder he called it "a sure deal." No more hustling for stories, no more driving down long winter highways to speaking gigs, and no more daily show deadlines. Just a nice, steady paycheque until age seventy-five from an employer that would never go bankrupt, and after that an excellent pension and benefits for life.

It was also over those next few days, even before he was sworn in as the Conservative senator for Prince Edward Island, that questions began to be raised about his legitimacy. With public news of his appointment less than twenty-four hours old, the first critical stories appeared, a piece in the *Charlottetown Guardian* among them, raising the issue of where he lived. But Duffy wasn't going to let a few naysayers slow him down as he made the media rounds, including an appearance on CTV's *Canada AM* with host Beverly Thomson. He allowed as how he had reluctantly permitted himself to be drawn into the Senate.

"When this thing first came up," a slightly raspy Duffy told Thomson via a remote feed from Ottawa, "when that first newspaper story ran, my wife, my lovely bride Heather, said, 'if they did call, what would you say?' I said, 'well, I'd say no.' And then I thought about it and thought it about and I said, you know, I'm two and a half years away from retirement, and I ran into a couple of our former colleagues who had recently retired and they're just desperately unhappy because they're not busy enough....I thought 'oh dear, I don't want to go there. I want to still be challenged.' So I thought, what the heck, this is a sure deal, and it's going to be a lot to do and hopefully represent the people of PEI well."

Thomson evidently felt compelled to bring up the delicate subject of whether Duffy was actually an Island resident, as required by the Senate's eligibility rules. "There have been a few questions about your ability to represent PEI because, while you have a place there..." Thomson began, but Duffy cut her off.

"There's one story in the *Charlottetown Guardian* [that] the former [Progressive] Conservative leader of PEI Pat Mella had wanted the job," he said, referring to the ten-year MLA, former provincial Tory leader, and cabinet minister. She had also co-chaired the Conservative election campaign on the Island, and many senators had been created out of appreciation for similar services. But Duffy wasn't showing any love for his fellow party member and Islander. Instead, he drove in the knife while embroidering his own personal legend as a powerful and respected political insider. Duffy claimed that Mella's brother had "sent me an email and said 'you have lots of influence in Ottawa. Would you put in a good word for Pat with the prime minister, to get her the job?'"—as if television hosts had anything to say about Senate appointments. "I didn't put in a word with the prime minister for anybody and I didn't apply for the job myself. She applied, she didn't get it, she's bitter. That's the only negative comment that I've picked up."

In fact, *Guardian* reporter Teresa Wright had rounded up several comments on Duffy's appointment, and from her coverage it appeared that, on the Island, the applause for his elevation was distinctly muted. "Duffy's appointment to PEI's vacant seat has a number of Islanders questioning how someone who spends the majority of his time in Ottawa will represent Islanders in the Senate," she wrote. Wright did quote a disappointed-sounding Mella, but also another senior Island Tory, Patrick Ross, who said he was surprised that someone who had lived away for thirty-seven years could be appointed as one of the Island's federal representatives. He suggested Duffy would have to acquire a year-round home on the Island, if for no other reason than to reacquaint himself with local issues. Political scientist Peter McKenna at the University of Prince Edward Island also said he was surprised Duffy got the call: "I think that there were Islanders with connections to the Conservative party who were probably more deserving," he said.

Mild though these first-day notes of skepticism were, they were enough to ignite the new senator, who turned out to be highly sensitive to criticism for someone who had spent so many years around media and politics. "I didn't go looking for [the appointment]," he told Wright with some asperity. "I didn't apply. The prime minister called me. That was his judgment....He knows I'm from the Island, I talk up the Island, I'm always proud to say where I'm from. I keep track of Island and Maritime issues. I have a place in Cavendish and I'm home several times a year. I'm not from Mars, I'm from 11 Villa Avenue."

A few days later, Duffy had a similar encounter with Sarah Fraser of the local CBC-TV station. Again, he told the story of how Harper had called him, not the other way around, and how the prime minister had persuaded him that he was just the kind of guy he needed to shake things up in the Senate. Fraser commented that Duffy and the Senate had been mentioned together often, but Duffy reacted with his best aw-shucks routine, as if it were no big deal for a player like him. "People have said, ah, Senator Duffy, Senator Duffy, for years—it's been kind of a running joke, and I've always brushed it off because it didn't strike me as being something that I'd really want to do." But, as he had told Thomson, he was facing retirement, and when he got to thinking about it, the Senate gig sounded pretty sweet. "When the call came, I thought, 'this is a lifeline for me. Because this will give me something to do that's important, that is giving back to the community, and that is active to the degree that you want to be active.'" In other words, the perfect part-time retirement gig.

He also didn't forgo the chance to take another shot at his putative rival for the seat. "Can you imagine if Prime Minister Harper had appointed Pat Mella or some other retired politician, they'd be saying 'look, once again, Harper—just another pork-barrel operation just like the Liberals.' Instead, he tries to do something different, and here you have Conservatives [saying] 'oh this is terrible, blah blah blah.' You can't win!" Fraser smiled, but as the interview was ending, she, too, raised the residency issue, which had already become the subject of kitchen-table talk around the Island. She asked whether Duffy planned "to be living here now." His answer combined defensiveness and the willingness to slap at anyone who seemed ready to criticize.

"Uh…of course, um, you know, as much as any MP or senator," he replied, before getting off a parting shot at another of his perceived critics. "I saw some professor the other day in the paper—I'll just leave it at that—saying that you have to be an Islander, you have to live here 183 consecutive days. It's not possible. MPs and senators are expected to be in Ottawa, in Parliament when it's sitting. It's the law. You couldn't be [here] 183 consecutive days. I don't know what law school that professor went to." In fact, that professor, David Bulger, went to some pretty good schools, including Dalhousie and the University of Toronto. He had taught courses in constitutional law at the University of Prince Edward for many years, and it was his educated opinion that Duffy didn't live on the Island and therefore could not be an Island senator.

In a follow-up story in the *Guardian* by the pesky Wright, Bulger would lay out his argument, based on the Constitution and Canadian electoral law. "What it comes down to is: does he have to be a resident in the province at the time when he's appointed?

Some of us, and I am one of them, would argue yes." Senate seats are based on geography, so it made no sense to appoint a senator who wasn't resident in the province he represents. And it was probably unconstitutional. Although senators aren't elected, Bulger cited the federal Elections Act, which is the only statute related to Parliament that contains a definition of residency. Bulger summarized it as, "if you work in one place and you live in another, then where you sleep is your residence—and Mike Duffy sleeps in Ottawa."

Bulger did at least offer some advice on a way out of the problem: Duffy could simply take up residence in Prince Edward Island. And there is evidence that, at some point in the appointment process, Duffy did tell the prime minister or his people that he would indeed move to the Island. Certainly, the PMO seemed to be under that impression. Harper's people put out word that Duffy would be living in Charlottetown, in a home jointly owned with his brother. But that never happened. In fact, property records obtained for this book show that Duffy was co-owner along with his brother Peter of his mother's house in Charlottetown, and that property was sold in 2011. When he did stay in Charlottetown, the senator bunked out at the Great George Inn, an upscale condo-hotel development with some of the finest accommodations in the city.

Still, Duffy wasn't particularly worried about where he lived, for good reason. On January 6, 2009, Duffy asked Senator Marjory LeBreton, the government leader in the upper house, to clarify the rules on residency. According to Duffy, she replied with a two-page email stating that senators decide that question for themselves: "Given that the Senate is the master of its own house in terms of the qualifications, it is also right to assume that they, the Senate, can define precisely what residence constitutes. And the Senate has done that." Duffy would take this email as *carte blanche* to deem 10 Friendly Lane in Cavendish his primary residence, thereby making him eligible for about $23,000 a year in housing expenses.

Three days later, on January 9, Duffy joined the other new senators to be sworn in to office in a dignified ceremony in the

Red Chamber, presided over by another distinguished former journalist, Governor General Michaëlle Jean. According to tradition, new senators are expected to feign reluctance as they are escorted into the chamber by two senators of their choosing. Duffy, who had already had some practice feigning reluctance, picked senators LeBreton and Wilbert Keon for escort duty—two people who had played a role in his life before unelected politics. The three walked arm-in-arm into the packed chamber as Harper looked on with undoubted satisfaction. After all, the prime minister had gone a long way toward ending Liberal dominance of the Senate and had built in a buffer in case the unholy trinity of Dion, Layton, and Duceppe tried anything funny. He had brought aboard a useful fundraising attraction, and it wouldn't be long before Duffy would be sent into the field to meet donors.

Several friends advised Duffy, however, to stay out of the unseemly political side of his new job. His old pal and later nemesis, Robert Fife of CTV, told me he tried to warn Duffy against getting too deeply into the partisan mire. "I told Mike to find some good cause and to work on that. Stay out of the political stuff, if he knew what was good for him. He didn't listen."

Stephen Maher also gave him similar advice, only to see Duffy become a willing member of the Conservative attack team. As Maher put it, "Duffy embraced his new role with unbecoming partisan fervour." Duffy, in fact, became such a willing voice in the chorus that, in 2010, Harper would sing his praises for a piece in *Broadcaster* magazine, calling him "one of my best and hardest working appointments." What he didn't know was that he had also admitted a new kind of trouble into his caucus.

SENATOR DUFFY

You are beneath contempt. I follow all the rules.

— SENATOR MIKE DUFFY TO A REPORTER, NOVEMBER 6, 2009

AS A NEWLY MINTED SENATOR AND MEMBER OF THE CONSERVATIVE caucus, one of Duffy's first duties was to attend a "boot camp" for new senators, a briefing laid on by government leader Marjory LeBreton, the new chair of the powerful Standing Committee on Internal Economy, Budgets and Administration—also known as the Internal Economy Committee—David Tkachuk, and some of the Senate's administrative officials. The idea was to go over the rules and procedures that new senators have to know, along with information about setting up and running offices, hiring staff, and managing their time in the Senate.

Postmedia reporter Jordan Press quoted an unnamed senator in 2013 as saying that travel expenses were also on the agenda for the briefings, although apparently not the rules on primary and secondary residences. Tkachuk told the new senators that it was okay to carry on their various outside activities, including corporate and volunteer boards. But he says they were told not to charge expenses for third-party activities to the Senate. Tkachuk also told the rookie senators that partisan activities were part of their job description, and suggested it was legitimate to bill some of those expenses to the Senate. Later, that advice was changed to make it clear that partisan activities had to be "related to the work of the senator or the Senate." The rule change, which Wallin and Duffy later claimed had been applied retroactively, went into effect in 2012. By then, both senators had become veteran fundraisers with gigs all across the country and appearances at campaign events for the Conservatives during the 2011 election campaign. Sorting out which trips were for legitimate Senate business and which were "purely partisan" would later give auditors headaches.

The new senators were then assigned offices. Duffy's was in a good location in the Centre Block, just two doors down from Senator Carolyn Stewart Olsen. The rookie senators were also handed business cards emblazoned with the ornate symbols of the Senate and little red lapel pins that identified them as members. There was committee work to do and, given his potato-province heritage, Duffy was posted to the agriculture committee. But the real job, hinted at by Tkachuk at rookie camp, was to get out there and raise money for the Conservatives and, wherever possible, slag off the government's antagonists.

On January 29, less than a month after he was sworn in, Duffy got to do both. He showed up at a meeting with provincial Tories in the Charlottetown suburb of Winsloe. The Island's Liberal premier, Robert Ghiz, had recently aligned himself with Newfoundland's fiery Danny Williams in a squabble with Harper and Finance Minister Jim Flaherty over the federal equalization program. Ottawa wanted to impose a cap on the growth of equalization payments, which would take $20 million out of annual provincial revenues, a substantial sum for the cash-strapped Island government.

Duffy didn't think Ghiz should be getting too close to the firebrand Williams, who had mobilized Newfoundlanders against the Conservatives, resulting in the shutout of the Tories in the province in the 2008 election. He suggested that Ghiz had gotten into bed with Williams on the equalization dispute, and when "two men" get in bed together, "one is going to get the shaft. I can assure you it won't be Danny Williams." The comment didn't get good reviews from Islanders, even from the Tory faithful there for the Duffy show. A few days later, *Charlottetown Guardian* reporter Wayne Thibodeau reached Duffy in Ottawa, but the senator brushed off the criticism: "I think people are pretty easily offended if they're offended by that," he said.

A couple of days later, in his maiden speech to the Senate, the unrepentant Duffy resumed his attack on the two East Coast premiers who had the temerity to stand up to Harper and Flaherty. He adapted a quote from disgraced US vice-president Spiro Agnew to disparage Williams, whom he counted among "the nattering nabobs of negativism on the East Coast," always demanding too much from federal Ottawa. "I was disappointed," he went on, "to see that our dynamic young premier in Prince Edward Island, Robert Ghiz, has climbed into bed with the premier of Newfoundland and Labrador, and honourable senators know what a grotesque scene that is. Do honourable senators know what happens when two politicians climb into bed together? One of them comes out on top, and I am afraid that when one is in bed with Danny Williams he will come out on top, and I would hate to see where that will leave PEI in the end." It was bad enough that Duffy had used the implied image of sodomy in a party meeting, now he had used it again in Senate debates, where it was dutifully recorded in Hansard.

Duffy's maiden speech wasn't all partisan slashing. He reeled off some funny lines about his own background on the Island, and about his grandfather, the Liberal MLA and speaker in the provincial legislature who eventually, "like many good Liberal lawyers," was elevated to the bench. He spoke about his own "spotty" academic record and his career in journalism. In keeping with the "Old Duff" legend, he also made sure to talk about his personal relations with the powerful and influential, emphasizing how close he had been with John Diefenbaker, whose image as a populist oddball was being rehabilitated by the Harper Conservatives. "After I arrived here,

Mr. Diefenbaker would frequently call me and invite me to his office for coffee," Duffy reminisced. He said the Tory lion had even called him the day before he died in 1979 and they'd had a forty-five minute conversation, validating yet again the idea that the great men of Canadian politics consulted Duffy and valued his views. Of course, Duffy also had lavish praise for Harper, who had "the judgment and courage" to be a great prime minister and "an economic action plan that I believe is right for these troubled times. Despite the bleating of a few, this economic action plan does more for more people in more parts of Canada than any budget in my memory." At one point, Duffy highlighted the fact that his two grandfathers had supported opposing parties, his maternal grandfather being a Tory. Hansard for that date records Senator Marcel Prud'homme as suggesting Duffy join the Senate's independents. Duffy laughed it off.

In reaction to the speech, public objections erupted on the Island, in Newfoundland and Labrador, and in the Senate itself. In Charlottetown, Premier Ghiz accused Duffy of choosing partisanship over the interests of the province he represented. "Mike Duffy said he wanted to be a senator from Prince Edward Island. I would hope that he would act like one," he grumbled. And that was just what he said publicly. Sources interviewed for this book say Ghiz was furious at what he saw as backstabbing by a fellow Islander. If Duffy was to represent the Island, then Ghiz felt he should fight for every dollar due his supposed home province. Williams, rarely given to understatement, accused the prime minister of pulling Duffy's strings, and said the senator's remarks exemplified "the nasty, vindictive type of mentality of Stephen Harper and Flaherty."

Even though Duffy wasn't sorry for his comments in Winsloe, his tone changed, just a little, in the Senate. On February 5, he rose to offer words that sounded somewhat apologetic: "Honourable senators, if the metaphor I used in my speech on February 3 was offensive to some members of this chamber, I withdraw the metaphor." He didn't withdraw the remark or mention what he said in Winsloe; he merely suggested that it was other people who had the problem, not him. Still, it was close enough to an apology, and Speaker Noel Kinsella didn't take it any further. Duffy might have made a political point, but, as it turned out, the only lasting damage was to the senator himself. A few years later he would need a big favour from the Ghiz government, and his words would come back to haunt him.

If his maiden speech had been unremarkable other than for a few nasty lines, it soon became clear that Harper had not chosen Duffy merely to speechify in the Red Chamber. At the party's bidding, the new senator was soon packing his bags for the road and a series of Conservative fundraisers that would bring big dollars into the party war chest. As so many Conservative and Liberal senators had before him, Duffy would raise money for his party while drawing a stable salary from the Canadian people.

From the Conservative point of view, there was some urgency to raise cash. Harper still led a minority government, which meant an election could happen any time. The parties might all be exhausted from three elections in four years, but Harper was not dropping his guard, and he was determined to keep the campaign coffers topped up. That elusive majority was almost within reach, and a cash shortage was not going to keep him from calling an election when the time was right.

Harper's former chief of staff from the Canadian Alliance days, Tom Flanagan, has written about how keeping the war chest full was always a basic party rule, on which Harper insisted. Flanagan wrote in *Harper's Team* that, as soon as one campaign ended, the fundraising would start again. The party never relaxed its pressure on donors—its massive databank on members and other voters enabled year-round fundraising from the party's committed core. Road shows were also popular, and that's where Duffy came in. As expected, Duffy proved to be a popular draw for riding events right across Canada, and over time he appeared at more than thirty of them. It's no coincidence that the majority of those were in Ontario, the key electoral battleground that helped Harper and the Conservatives get over the top and obtain a majority in 2011.

Duffy eventually would speak at party fundraisers in every province except Saskatchewan, where Pamela Wallin was helping stock the coffers, and hostile Newfoundland and Labrador.

A typical fundraising event took place in Wendover, Ontario, on March 21, 2009, in support of Pierre Lemieux, MP for Glengarry-Prescott-Russell, a riding that had been a Liberal stronghold. Duffy was the star attraction at a $100-a-plate dinner at the local community centre. The evening featured Highland dancers and a projection screen flashing pictures of Stephen Harper, former Ontario premier Mike Harris, and modern Conservative luminaries such as Chuck Strahl, Rona Ambrose, John Baird, Stockwell Day, and Peter MacKay. Incongruously, Governor General Jean's image also appeared. Lemieux and Duffy posed for photos with supporters "and shook hundreds of hands," according to the local community newspaper, the *Review*. Then the senator rose to orate. *Review* reporter Philippe Morin called the speech "explicitly partisan," but it was really the "Why I am a Conservative" speech he had been giving around the country. In it, Duffy extolled the virtues of Conservative prime ministers down through history and made jokes about the party's opponents: "What's the difference between a member of the NDP and a Liberal? About five hundred dollars worth of suit material." He heaped praise on Lemieux for his success in getting federal money for the riding. It was a performance that would be repeated, with local variations, many times in many towns.

In June 2009, Duffy acted as master of ceremonies for a major public event in Cambridge, Ontario, with his boss, the prime minister. Surrounded on the stage by supportive Conservatives, Duffy asked deferential questions designed to let Harper expound on his recession-fighting Economic Action Plan. But the prime minister's presence at Duffy's gigs was the exception, not the rule. Mostly, the senator was on his own, driving or flying into towns to be met by thankful local candidates or riding members and taken to a church basement or school auditorium for the evening's show. He called them gigs, just like any performer in any travelling road show. While laying out his admiration for the party of Sir John A. Macdonald and John Diefenbaker, he would make sure to heap oleaginous praise on his current boss, whom the Conservatives' legend writers were casting as the linear descendent of the great Tory statesmen of the past. "As the Prime Minister said...the Conservative Party is Canada's party," Duffy would say in many towns to many party members. It became like a stump political speech, but delivered by a man who'd never had to win votes for himself.

Still, the history lessons and comedic monologues made Duffy a known quantity to Conservative riding associations. The crowds laughed and cheered his ribald, entertaining, and decidedly partisan speeches and got out their cheque books. At every event, Duffy would pose for pictures and sign autographs, often staying well after the formal part of the evening to bask in the adulation of his public. This was even better than broadcasting. On TV, the fans are out there in the electronic ether. In politics, they are right there, at the end of a handshake. Even better, Duffy could say what he wanted because he didn't have to worry about the sensitivities of advertisers or network managers. Being unelected, he didn't have to stay on the good side of voters either. He could be the party's class clown and attack dog all rolled up into a single cufflinked, avuncular package.

For those who couldn't make it in person to fundraising events, the party developed specialized appeals. Duffy was drafted into helping with new forms of custom content the party had devised. The Canadian Press reported that Duffy was recording and distributing "personalized video messages from the Conservative party in which he called the recipient by their first name and invited them to fill in a survey. An interactive, online application allowed people to provide their names so Duffy could appear to hail them, as well: 'Hey Susan, it's the Old Duff here.'" He would then ask for a donation to help the party fight the good fight against the Liberals, New Democrats, environmentalists, scientists, "media elites," or anyone else who needed to be fought.

It turned out that the Senate wasn't exactly retirement after all, and Duffy was finding it tough to keep pace with the demands on his time. Later, when he got into trouble over expense claims, he would complain that there was too much paperwork involved and he couldn't stay on top of it. Early on, just six months after his appointment, Duffy struck upon a way to get everything done and paid for, keep him organized, and maybe even pick up some extra cash while he was at it. Why not get himself named to the federal cabinet?

It wasn't an unprecedented idea. Senators had served in cabinets under many prime ministers, and not just in the olden days— Marjory LeBreton was a member of the Harper cabinet as government leader in the Senate. But senators mostly got appointed to the cabinet when the party that won an election got skunked in some part of the country. In the absence of MPs in the region, a senator would get the call. Recent prime ministers, including Pierre Trudeau, Clark, and Mulroney, had all put senators in their cabinets to fix such gaps. Harper, too, had appointed Michael Fortier as minister of public works in 2006 before he was even installed in the Senate—in effect, naming someone to the cabinet right off the street, then putting him in the Upper Chamber. Senators have even become prime ministers, as Conservatives John Abbott and Mackenzie Bowell did while sitting in the Senate.

If it wasn't all that unusual to have a senator in the cabinet, it didn't usually happen simply to facilitate the fundraising efforts of the ruling party or to satisfy the ego of a rookie parliamentarian. Nevertheless in May 2013, CBC News reported on a four-year-old email exchange in which Duffy appeared to lobby for a cabinet job or some other mechanism to compensate for "my expanded role in the party." The emails from July 2009 indicate he had been lobbying Senator Irving Gerstein—the millionaire president of Peoples Jewellers, head of Conservative Fund Canada, and top Tory bag man—for help managing his busy fundraising schedule. "I suggested they make me a min without portfolio, so I get a staff, car and more resources to deal with the pr fallout etc.," the email says.

It's not clear who was at the other end of the correspondence because that part of the email was blacked out, but Duffy evidently was rebuffed, because he never made it to the inner circle. In fact, Duffy's email says that Gerstein "laughed and said he didn't think THAT was within the realm of the Cons fund." The other tangible benefit of elevation to the cabinet, although it isn't mentioned in the email exchange, would be a tidy pay increase. Junior cabinet ministers get an extra $57,000 a year over their regular pay as MPs or senators, as well as extra staff, a car and driver, and other perquisites, not to mention a boost in political clout. Even Duffy could see that appointment to the Harper cabinet was a long shot, and he later told friends he'd been kidding all along. Yet, in the emails, he asked his adviser whether he should lobby Senator LeBreton or even appeal to the prime minister himself: "Should I request a one-on-one with Stephen?" he queried. "To what end?"

Failing a cabinet appointment, maybe there was some other way Duffy could be compensated for his extra time and effort. Perhaps "the Cons fund [could] hire my private company, and I [could] use the cash to hire additional staff to assist with these gigs?" That idea wasn't taken up either. Foreshadowing trouble to come, Duffy's correspondent urged him to keep his Senate accounts and Conservative expenses well separated. He was to maintain contact with Gerstein, and expenses related to the fundraising road show should be sent directly to the party, "so you don't get in trouble or run out of points"—a reference to the sixty-four travel points, each equivalent to a return trip, to which each senator is entitled every year. "Don't take a credit card, just expense to them," the email urged, referring to the Conservative Party.

When the cabinet-seeking emails were made public at the height of the scandal in 2013, reaction among Conservatives was quick and it was savage. LeBreton, scrummed in the Senate foyer, poured scorn on the idea that Duffy would ever have been appointed to the Harper cabinet as she had been. "It's ridiculous. The idea that the prime minister or anyone would pass over elected members of the House of Commons and name Mike Duffy as a minister? It's so ridiculous it's not even funny. It's totally bizarre." And she was quick to distance herself from the idea of negotiating with Duffy about a cabinet seat. "There isn't a chance of a snowball in hell of this ever happening," she said, adding "and I never spoke to him about it." While her quotes were certainly colourful, LeBreton ignored the fact that she, an unelected senator, was a cabinet member and, in an earlier iteration, had been minister of state for seniors. In any case, when Harper shuffled his ministers on July 16, 2013, LeBreton was left out of the mix, and the Senate role in the cabinet ended, at least temporarily.

But that was all far in the dark future. In the meantime, Duffy kept busy during his first years in the Red Chamber. He had a good attendance record during debates and question periods, but he seemed bored by the committee work that is such a big part of a parliamentarian's life in both the Senate and the House of Commons, and he missed about half of the committee meetings he was scheduled to attend. Not surprisingly, Duffy's extracurricular activities were his central focus. Around the time he was lobbying for a cabinet position and for help with his travel expenses, he flew to Prince Edward Island to talk up the Conservative government's response to the continuing economic crisis. The *Guardian*'s Teresa Wright reported on a speech he gave in August 2009 to a Rotary Club function in Charlottetown in which he claimed that "your federal government is moving heaven and earth, literally, to protect Canadians from the economic downturn." Duffy told the no doubt deeply grateful audience that "you will receive millions more in federal spending on everything from a new Summerside raceway to the Confederation Centre and literally hundreds—that's right, hundreds—of projects in between."

Challenged later about his apparent promise making, Duffy denied that the speech had been political since he hadn't mentioned Harper or the Conservative Party directly. Appearing on Ottawa radio station CFRA with journalist Michael Harris, he accused the

Guardian of spinning the facts to make him look bad, and compared it to a recently discredited story in the *Telegraph-Journal* in Saint John about Harper's only pretending to take Holy Communion while attending the Catholic funeral of former Governor General Roméo LeBlanc in New Brunswick. It was like "Wafergate or the virus or something," Duffy told Harris. "It's creeping across provincial borders...the Charlottetown paper can't just report the news. They've got to make it up." After that blast from Duffy, Wright told me, Conservative bloggers bombarded her with abuse.

Perhaps mindful of his onerous workload, sometime in 2009 Duffy hired an old friend from the CTV days, Gerald Donohue, to give him some help. Donohue and Duffy had worked together at CJOH, and Donohue had gone on from technician to a job in human resources. He had retired with a disability in 1997, but he had also registered a private company, Maple Ridge Media, although it had been dormant. His wife was listed as the company's president and his son was a director.

According to RCMP documents filed in October 2013, Donohue later told investigators that, when Duffy was appointed to the Senate, "he asked Donohue if he would work for him as a consultant, conducting research and providing advice. Donohue, who had never been a consultant in the past, agreed." Donohue also said he didn't receive any money from the contracts, although it seems clear from the Senate's documentation that the money did go to his company. According to an RCMP audit, the first contract with Maple Ridge Media covered the period from February 23 to March 31, 2009, to provide "editorial services," speechwriting, research, consulting, and the like. Duffy paid for the contract using the office expense allocation that was set aside for every senator. For the five-week period, Maple Ridge Media was paid $10,000, a figure the RCMP would later consider to be pretty rich considering that Donohue told them "he did not produce any tangible document, report, or work product." Instead, Duffy would call him from time to time and ask him to dig up information on a given topic, such as "the aging population" or an unspecified "heritage project" that Duffy had in mind. "Duffy would call him with a subject, such as obesity, or being a Conservative, and he would do internet research on the topic and provide advice or an opinion," the RCMP concluded. "Though his job description included speech writing, Donohue never did speech writing for Duffy, or any other kind of writing." His reports to the senator were given over the phone—Donohue told the police he had never even been in Duffy's office.

Still, it worked out as a great arrangement for Maple Ridge Media and its successor company, ICF Ottawa. Duffy's office budget paid out almost $65,000 to the two companies over four years. It was the largest single contract, by far, in Duffy's office expense list, accounting for more than half of his annual spending. The size of the contracts relative to the rest of Duffy's office expenses would become a matter of key interest for the RCMP's investigators. They also wanted to know where the money went.

Duffy was getting around, and it was being noticed on Parliament Hill—and not only by friendly Conservatives. In November 2009, New Democrat MP Peter Stoffer released a caucus report that looked at the costs of twenty-seven Senate appointments Harper had made to that date. He was using figures prepared by the NDP research office, which pays particular attention to senatorial spending and maintains spreadsheets with all the information it can collect; every chance the NDP gets, it fires a dart into the Senate's fleshy flanks. Stoffer, a famed constituency MP and a popular figure on the Hill, figured taxpayers were on the hook for $177 million when one added up all the salaries, benefits, pensions, and related costs of maintaining just the senators Harper had appointed over the previous year. Stoffer argued that a lot of the work senators do could be done more cheaply and efficiently by others, such as elected MPs. His report concluded that Senate expenses were far too high and, in passing, it mentioned Duffy's $44,000 in travel claims over a three-month period that year. Duffy took deep offence at this, and his outrage led to one of the strangest incidents of that fall's sitting of Parliament. It would happen on both live television and via email, where Duffy's BlackBerry would get him in trouble, not for the first time and not for the last.

Bruce Cheadle is an experienced and respected national affairs reporter for The Canadian Press, based in the Ottawa bureau. On November 6, Cheadle was covering the Stoffer report as a fairly routine story but decided to look a little more deeply into Duffy's expenses. Late that afternoon, a Friday, Cheadle sent Duffy an email requesting a comment on Stoffer's numbers. He didn't hear back and wasn't sure whether Duffy had anything to say or not. The reporter didn't know that the senator was busy getting ready for an RCMP Mess Dinner in Charlottetown, a black-tie event with some of the Island's leading citizens. The CBC News Network's *Power and Politics* show had better luck. Producers managed to reach Duffy on the Island, and he agreed to appear in a segment with Stoffer, moderated by host Evan Solomon.

Duffy showed up at the Charlottetown location in a tuxedo, as if he had dressed up fancy for a scrap. Solomon started by asking about the report, and Stoffer went over the numbers but didn't mention Duffy's name. The MP explained why he objected to what he felt was a waste of public money. From Charlottetown, Duffy called the report "bafflegab" put out purely for political reasons. He had obviously prepared a counterattack, because he brandished his BlackBerry and read off Stoffer's expenses, which he claimed were similar to his own. How could Stoffer say his work as an MP was any more important than Duffy's role in the Senate "listening to Canadians?" The report was all a partisan scam, he said, produced to help the NDP win a federal by-election a few days hence in Nova Scotia, where he predicted they would get "trounced"—which they did, with Conservative Scott Armstrong winning the seat vacated by maverick Tory Bill Casey, one of the few Conservative MPs ever to stand up to Harper.

Stoffer tried to respond, but Duffy talked over him, repeating the scam allegation. When Solomon intervened and the New Democrat got a turn to speak, he admonished Duffy for his rudeness. "A good

Maritimer listens to others," Stoffer scolded, but that didn't slow down the senator. Duffy turned his attack on Cheadle's Canadian Press report, which had shed unwanted light on his spending. He called the story unfair and accused the news agency of falling for an NDP publicity stunt. For a guy who felt he had been appointed to help bring a softer light to the hard-edged Conservatives, he showed himself pretty quick to the attack. He called Stoffer "a backbencher and a faker," and insisted his senatorial expenses were every bit as worthwhile to Canadians as Stoffer's. "Mr. Duffy, I would have thought you would have had a thicker skin than that, but I guess I was wrong," Stoffer responded before counterpunching with effect. As an elected Member of Parliament, he said, he had to defend his expenses to voters back home, while Duffy answered to no one except the prime minister who appointed him.

After the show, Duffy emailed Cheadle asking what he wanted. Within a couple of minutes, Cheadle asked for a telephone number where Duffy could be reached. He got no reply, presumably because Duffy was toasting the Island's Mounties at the Mess Dinner. But at 12:20 A.M. the next morning, the senator got out his BlackBerry. "How did you like my response to Stoffer? No wonder u are hiding. Let's see CP defend ur biased reporting." Cheadle replied the next morning, saying he did see the televised confrontation with Stoffer, which he called "interesting." He asked for details on Duffy's expenses travelling to Conservative Party functions around Canada. Duffy riposted that Cheadle had fallen for Stoffer's stunt, and wrote, "I have spent the day telling [Canadians] about your failings." The reporter replied with one last attempt to get Duffy to answer his questions on expenses and his travel to Conservative Party fundraisers. The final line of his email went straight to the vulnerability Duffy felt about the legitimacy of his Senate seat: "Although you represent PEI, I believe your full time home is in Ottawa. Is this correct?" Duffy's response would make its way into that day's talk on Parliament Hill and open a window into his sense of senatorial entitlement. "You are beneath contempt. I play by all the rules," he wrote, and signed off with "–30–," the traditional ending of a news story dating from the era of telegraphy.

Times had changed since Duffy's heyday in the journalism business, and overall, the reporter-turned-senator didn't like what he saw. Perhaps his increasingly dim view of his former profession was coloured by the venomous relationship between the Harper Conservatives and the news media. In keeping with his newfound ultra-partisanship, Duffy selected his former profession as a subject of particular scorn. Speaking to fellow Conservatives at an event in Amherst, Nova Scotia, in the spring of 2010, Duffy claimed that journalists were being trained to be antagonistic to conservatives. He said journalists were taught leftist, radical ideologies in university, specifically through the teachings of left-wing American thinker Noam Chomsky. It wasn't like the good old days, he said. This was something new and ugly, not like the journalism he had practised just a year or two before. "When I went to the school of hard knocks, we were told to be fair and balanced. That school doesn't exist any more," he said, ignoring the fact that "fair and balanced" is precisely the motto of the unashamedly conservative Fox News network in the United States.

Duffy then claimed that the University of King's College School of Journalism in Halifax and similar programs across Canada taught the craft using radical theories about media and politics. "Kids who go to King's, or the other schools across the country, are taught from two main texts," said the senator. The curriculum included manuals in "critical thinking" and Chomsky's *Manufacturing Consent: The Political Economy of the Mass Media,* a controversial 1988 analysis that has been taken up as a favoured text of the radical left. Chomsky concluded, among many other things, that the media had evolved into propaganda institutions which shared a common purpose: to promote state and corporate control over society. Critical thinking, at its most basic, teaches students to analyze facts to help them decide which ones are true. To Duffy, they were loony ideas that had politicized journalism. "When you put critical thinking together with

Noam Chomsky, what you've got is a group of people who are taught from the ages of eighteen, nineteen, and twenty that what we stand for, private enterprise, a system that has generated more wealth for more people because people take risks and build businesses, is bad," Duffy told the no-doubt appreciative crowd of Conservatives. If that was what they were teaching in the universities, it's little wonder the party couldn't get a fair shake from the media.

The senator's foray into academic discourse might have pleased his media-skeptic fellow Conservatives, but it didn't get him far beyond that. Kim Kierans, who at that time was head of the King's journalism school, thought the senator was way off base. Critical thinking was taught to help students evaluate content, Kierans told the local *Metro* daily in Halifax. It wasn't political but analytical. Kierans, who has been around King's since the early 1980s, said she had never seen Duffy on the campus, and wondered where he was getting his information. Her students read Duffy's remarks, and they decided to fight words with words. "After this story hit the pages of *Metro*, the students at King's were appalled at Duffy's remarks," Kierans says now. "Unknown to me they pooled their own money, went to the King's bookstore and bought a copy of collected writings of Chomsky. They apparently all signed it with a message that he should remember to do his research before speaking, and they sent it to Mike. He never responded."

In the Senate, Duffy was often in his seat, but his interventions were rare, mostly tributes to dead or retiring politicians or small points raised during speeches by other senators on issues of the day. Duffy had not done well in his own run-in with the tax man in the 1990s, and several of his interventions dealt with taxation. In 2010, he lauded a change that would make it easier for foreigners and non-residents to donate property in Canada and obtain favourable tax treatment. He noted, perhaps mindful of his own status in Prince Edward Island, that "there is a lot of non-resident land ownership right across Canada, but especially along the north coast of PEI in so-called Anne's Land," where Duffy's own summer abode was located.

It was also in 2010 that the prime minister made some changes to the PMO that would have a major impact on Duffy, especially when the expenses scandal started to build. In September, Harper announced that Nigel Wright would take over as chief of staff, replacing Guy Giorno. Almost unknown to Canadians outside Ottawa circles, the position of chief of staff to the prime minister is one of the most powerful positions in the government. The chief runs the PMO, which had become immensely more powerful under Harper and which oversaw every aspect of public policy and government operations. Just as important, the PMO also controlled the day-to-day political operations of the Harper machine, as well as all media relations, every government statement, every news release, program, and policy. Almost every word that emanated from the Canadian government was vetted by the PMO's vigilant staff and managed by Wright, who, according to all accounts, was a man of enormous personal capacity and moral rectitude. He was a fitness fanatic, running the equivalent of a half-marathon every morning before work. He was a member of the Anglican Church, a graduate of the University of Toronto and Harvard University law schools, and, before joining the PMO, had been managing director of Onex Corporation, a $6 billion conglomerate with interests in businesses across North America. He was a wealthy, generous, and sensitive individual who was respected even by the Harper government's opponents. He had been an early supporter of the Reform Party and the Canadian Alliance, the first director of Conservative Fund Canada, and was one of the most trusted operatives in the conservative movement.

Then, as Canada celebrated the collective high of the 2010 Olympic Winter Games in Vancouver, Duffy was again featured prominently in a Conservative fundraising campaign. He appeared with Harper and other Conservatives such as Senator Nancy Greene Raine, the former Olympic champion skier, in videos promoting "our strong leader." In them, Duffy declaims that "we Conservatives are champions in our own right," partly because Sir John A. Macdonald had been a Conservative. In separate feel-good ads paid for by taxpayers and salted throughout the television coverage of the Games, the Harper government applauded its own economic policies. The "Olympic media blitz" ended up costing $5 million. Critics said the campaign was pure Conservative propaganda.

And that was just the start. The Harper government was still in a minority position, and an election was right around the corner. From the end of the Olympics until the spring of 2011, Duffy and the rest of the Conservative fundraising apparatus kept up a frenetic pace. The party money machine was the most refined and effective in Canada, making brilliant use of its large base of generous core supporters. It was directed by Senator Gerstein, and had at its core a database of potential donors going back to the party's Canadian Alliance forerunner. It used social media, email, and telephone contacts produced by its voter identification software to reach out effectively to those donors, often in response to events in the news. Anything that seemed even remotely like a move by the would-be "unelected coalition" sparked an email from Conservative Fund Canada to its thousands of grassroots supporters asking for cash to fight the Liberal-NDP-Bloc foes.

It wasn't all just technology and outreach. The fund and individual Conservative ridings could also rely on star power to bring in the bacon—names like Pamela Wallin and Mike Duffy, who crisscrossed the country drumming up donations. That in itself was seen as an unfair advantage by the New Democrats, who had no senators. They complained that Liberal and Conservative senators were able to roam the country using subsidized travel and salaries while fundraising and campaigning for the two old-school parties. Added to the take from the road shows, the Conservatives were well funded when the opposition parties in the House banded together on March 25 to defeat the government on a confidence vote, sparking a spring election. It was time to hit the campaign trail for the decisive election of 2011.

Later, records would show that Duffy appeared in seventeen ridings—mostly in the Maritimes and Ontario—during the five-week campaign, plumping for candidates that included Joe Oliver, Harper's minister of natural resources. Some of those records also appear to show him collecting a Senate per diem of $86.35 while he was out on the campaign trail, which was out of bounds even under the permissive rules of the day. Whether or not they were legitimate claims eventually would become part of the RCMP investigation into Duffy's expenses.

A typical 2011 election event for Duffy took place mid-campaign in Nova Scotia with Conservative candidate David Morse, a former provincial Tory minister who was trying to defeat popular Liberal Scott Brison in the Annapolis Valley riding of Kings-Hants. Morse had planned a day of mainstreeting with a popular former candidate, Dr. Bob Mullan, but as they were getting set to go, he found out Duffy had been dispatched by the party "to help out." Like many Nova Scotians, Morse was a fan of Duffy's television persona, so he agreed to change his schedule to accommodate the senator. Morse and Mullan were supposed to start early in the town of Kentville, but were asked to wait thirty minutes because Duffy had to record some campaign advertising at a local radio station. "We waited a half-hour, then forty-five minutes, then an hour. Finally he got finished and we headed out," Morse told me. "We barely got started when someone said we had to be in Wolfville for lunch." So they jumped in the campaign minivan and headed the twelve kilometres down the road to Wolfville's lovely old Blomidon Inn. "We had a nice lunch, but time was passing by and I was anxious to get going," says Morse. "Just as we were getting ready to go, the manager came over and asked whether we wanted to have dessert. Only one hand went up. Guess who?"

So there was another thirty-minute delay while Duffy enjoyed one of the Blomidon's sweet delicacies. With candidate Morse getting ever more anxious, they paid the bill and, finally, hit Main Street in the university town. They shook hands with voters along the main drag and, as campaigning politicians are wont to do, went into a Tim Hortons to engage with the electorate's double-double and donut segment. The Timmy's crowd is a particular favourite of the Conservatives, and things went swimmingly. "It was great, Mike was shaking hands and signing autographs," says Morse. "People were getting their pictures taken with him. Then the manager came out and said, 'who wants to try our delicious new ice cream treats?' and we lost another half an hour." All in all, not much got accomplished that day, but Morse, ever the gentleman, says "it was nice having Mike with us for the day."

Morse lost the election to Brison by eleven hundred votes. But the election itself was a triumph for the Conservatives and for Harper, who now had the double majority in the Commons and Senate that he so craved. Like other senators, Duffy had done his part, and victory seemed to encourage him to wade even deeper into the partisan mire that his friends Fife and Maher had warned him about. He got into print for suggesting that Liberal leader Michael Ignatieff was mentally ill, asking, "Is he a multiple personality disorder or something? What is he?" He also questioned the intelligence of PEI premier Robert Ghiz, and said he'd never live up to the example set by his late father, Premier Joseph Ghiz. Green Party leader Elizabeth May was laughed off as "Bucky the Beaver."

Yet Duffy's comments might not have been that far outside the embarrassing norm of modern political discourse. Years of minority governments and the collateral damage of four elections in seven years had driven the partisan debate to new lows of disdain and disrespect. Duffy had been appointed to the Senate supposedly to soften the Harper government's pugnacious image, yet he ended up barking with the Conservative attack pack.

Duffy's newfound influence also appeared to be going to his head. Liberal MP Wayne Easter said he'd had a friendly relationship with Duffy for many years, often appearing as a guest on *Mike Duffy Live* and, until the Stéphane Dion fiasco, had always considered Duffy to be a fair journalist. Duffy's cottage is in Easter's Prince Edward Island riding, and he would sometimes show up at constituency ice cream socials to hobnob with the common folk and trade gossip with the local politicians. Easter has a picture of Duffy at one of those events on the wall of his parliamentary office. He says Duffy changed after he went to the Senate and drank the Conservative Kool-Aid. "Relations were good until he became a senator," Easter says now. "After that, a Liberal became the enemy. He became more and more partisan. It was cruel, I couldn't understand it at all. It was a shame."

Easter is also a long-time and enthusiastic support of Charlottetown's Confederation Centre of the Arts, the undisputed world champion in plays and musicals about *Anne of Green Gables*. Easter said he was at the gala opening of one of the annual *Anne* shows, when Duffy showed up late with two unexpected guests, demanding to know "who let him [Easter] in" and that his friends be seated with the official party. Informed that the seats were all taken, Duffy told Centre officials that he had a pipeline to federal funding agencies and to the federal cabinet. If they wanted Ottawa's help with capital improvements, they better fix him up. "I've got [Heritage Minister] James Moore on my speed dial," Duffy told them, brandishing his trusty BlackBerry. The Confederation Centre people scrambled to fix up the senatorial party, if only to avoid a scene.

Back in the Senate, Duffy rose in 2012 to sing the praises of Harper, Finance Minister Jim Flaherty, and the Conservative budget of that year, and to slam environmental lobby groups which claimed charitable status while criticizing the Canadian oil sands industry. Duffy suggested that some of those groups were fronts for competing corporate interests in the United States. When a senator intervened to ask whether Duffy had any concerns about the effect of the budget's cuts to programs such as employment insurance in Prince Edward Island, Duffy took the partisan route. His target, not surprisingly, was a Liberal from the Island.

Liberal MP Lawrence MacAulay was stirring up fears among his constituents, Duffy said. "One of the really damaging things that goes on in our region of the country is the fear-mongering by members opposite. The member for Cardigan is an old friend of mine, but you can tell when an election is coming. He runs around

Prince Edward Island saying they are going to cancel the ferry. Guess what happens? They do not cancel the ferry, and then he says, 'Oh, they did not cancel it because I spoke up.' Recently, when he raised this canard, the Minister of Transport reported that the member for Cardigan had never written a letter to Ottawa making representations." The next day, Liberal senator Percy Downe of Prince Edward Island shot holes in that claim, producing a series of letters MacAulay had written on the status of the ferry, including correspondence with the minister of transport. Details, details.

When Duffy finally did make a foray into what some might consider a nation-changing idea, he chose a controversial topic, especially one for a senator from Prince Edward Island. In November 2012, Duffy joined forces with two other Harper senate appointees, Stephen Greene of Nova Scotia and John Wallace of New Brunswick, to propose a political and economic merger of the three Maritime provinces. Maritime Union is a hoary old political topic in the East, predating Confederation. It gets revived every few decades, but has never caught on among Maritimers, and not just because they're averse to change. Its benefits have never been demonstrated. The idea of gaining a unified voice of 1.7 million citizens has appeal, but it is offset by the dangers it presents to the influence of Acadian and aboriginal communities and the prospect of even more infighting over jobs and money.

This time, the Maritime Union proposal had come with some weighty intellectual support. Donald Savoie, a renowned New Brunswick author and academic, suggested that the Maritimes could no longer afford the status quo of three separate provincial governments and all of their expensive apparatus. Savoie, who had served as an advisor to Brian Mulroney and to New Brunswick premiers Frank McKenna and Shawn Graham, said the three tiny provinces were facing challenges across the economic spectrum and had to become more self-sufficient. A political union would help achieve that through economies of scale and would augment the region's pitiful store of clout in Ottawa.

Duffy embraced Savoie's comments, taking the media lead in this new, unexpected push for a Maritime Union. He compared the purchasing power of a unified Maritime province to that available to big-box retail chains, which bought in bulk to realize savings for consumers. He criticized the Atlantic premiers for not insisting that petroleum pipelines be extended all through the region, and lamented the "patchwork quilt" of energy projects that included a billion dollars to refurbish the Point Lepreau nuclear plant in New Brunswick and the proposal for a subsea cable to bring Labrador hydro power to Nova Scotia. Apparently forgetting that the Harper government supported the subsea cable and had promised to back its financing, Duffy questioned the wisdom of "a massive project that will put a huge debt burden on our kids and their kids." He called for a "grassroots movement" that would push for more efficient government across the region and a gradual approach toward political union.

It was predictable that the idea wouldn't go far, and Duffy's sally into the swamps of parochial Maritime politics turned out to be little more than a one-day wonder, getting more serious treatment in the Toronto papers than in those in Halifax or Fredericton. That might have been because the senators proposing it—Greene, Preston Manning's former chief of staff and a Reform party pioneer in the East, and Wallace, who ran unsuccessfully for the Conservatives in 2006 in Saint John—were virtually unknown to ordinary Nova Scotians or New Brunswickers. But in Prince Edward Island, with a better known and more combative supporter in the person of Duffy, this new outbreak of Maritime Union talk immediately became controversial. Easter said he was "incensed" that a senator "who's supposed to be representing" Prince Edward Island was "encouraging our demise." In the provincial legislature, Liberal deputy premier George Webster said he was "shocked and dismayed." True to form, Duffy took the criticism personally and gave back as good as he got.

Duffy went on local CBC Radio in Charlottetown to talk up the idea of Maritime Union and settle some accounts. When asked what it would take to make union happen, Duffy portrayed it as a matter of political will. "People have to start taking forceful leadership action. This requires leadership," which was a fine point for debate, but Duffy couldn't leave it there. "When you hear somebody like George Webster get up in the legislature this afternoon and attack me for trying to find a way to make our economy better for people...it sounds to me like George Webster is afraid of losing his own job." The unelected parliamentarian carried on, immune to irony, by saying the region of 1.7 million people was overgoverned with 155 members in three provincial legislatures. The number actually was 134 at that time, but for Duffy, that wasn't the point: people like Webster wanted to preserve the status quo to maintain their own plush positions. "It appears to me the politicians should put the people first...and their own jobs second...that's called leadership, that's called having courage. Put the people first and their own jobs second."

As it turned out, the national media didn't stay interested in Maritime Union very long either. Pretty soon their attention turned to a non-policy aspect of Duffy's role in the Senate: his expense claims. And that, not Maritime Union, would become the defining event of Duffy's Senate career.

UNRAVELLING: TROUBLE IN THE RED CHAMBER

An absurdly effete body, nothing but a
political infirmary and bribery fund.

— GOVERNOR GENERAL LORD DUFFERIN, 1874

THE SENATE IS AS CANADIAN AS POTHOLES AND HOCKEY PUCKS, A PART of politics since Confederation and an institution created in compromise among regions of the new country. Ever since 1867, there have been arguments over whether it is proper for a democracy to be ruled, even in part, by unelected parliamentarians. And since those horse-and-buggy days, the Red Chamber has been a repository for political hacks and an endowment for life for friends of the governing parties. It has always had lots of lawyers and business people among its members; after all, somebody has to stick up for the poor downtrodden corporate interests of the land, like the banks and the railroads. Many of the lawyers and magnates of the Upper Chamber have also carried the part-time designation of bagman or fixer, people who served the parties of the day and helped to enrich their coffers. What the Senate has not always contained is a lot of determined servants of the public good.

As early as 1874, Governor General Lord Dufferin called it useless, and in 1886 Sir Wilfrid Laurier complained that it was "not responsible to anybody whatever." At the birth of Canada, the first Senate mainly consisted of graduates of provincial upper chambers, commonly known then as legislative councils. But given that the Fathers of Confederation wanted the new Senate to be modelled on the British House of Lords, its members would be appointed by the federal government of the day. Canada's first prime minister, Sir John A. Macdonald, made sure that Canada's first Senate had a majority of members from his Conservative Party. So it would go over the decades and generations, prime minister to prime minister, each seeing the value of appointing faithful party servants to the Upper Chamber where they could use public funds to pursue partisan affairs. In that sense, it's the longest-running public subsidy to political parties in Canadian history. Senators and their corporate connections were useful on a number of levels: they could act as conduits for information to and from the business community, they could cheerlead for legislative measures that helped their constituencies, or oppose measures that worked against them. So it should be no surprise that all attempts at reform—at eliminating conflicts of interest, improving account-ability, or making the Senate elected—have failed in no small part because reigning governments have seen no value to themselves in making changes.

During its existence, the Senate has seen many eruptions of scandal, both serious and small, but little has ever been done about it. Corporate directorships have always been commonplace among the well-connected senators, but given the Senate's permissive rules, it's rare that their business dealings have got them into any real trouble.

There was a scandal during the Roaring Twenties when the Beauharnois Power Company tried to bribe its way into a series of exclusive rail and power-generating contracts. Working with a trio of senior senators, the company's president raised $864,000 for a secret Liberal Party slush fund, and the company's interests provided $750,000 to Mackenzie King's Liberal campaigns in 1925 and 1926. For the times, those were titanic figures—the average annual salary for a teacher was $1,800 and a qualified machinist made 30 cents an hour. Few working people were able to make any kind of significant donation to a political party, so corporate fundraising was the preferred method of financing national political machines. Back in the day, senatorial connections were useful for fundraising campaigns among corporations. More recently, large donations have been banned, so money has had to come from a wider range of small donors; that's where the likes of Mike Duffy and Pamela Wallin found their usefulness to Stephen Harper and his Conservatives.

Senators have run afoul of the law and of the rules of Parliament many times over the years, but until the expenses scandal of 2013, rarely had they been accused of defrauding the Senate itself. That might simply be because the Senate is self-governing and has always kept an eye patch handy for indiscretions on office expenses or travel claims. The honour system on which the internal business of the honourable senators is based has served it well, but it pays little heed to modern standards of accountability. The few attempts over the years to change that invariably have been foiled by senators who argued that the Senate should not be answerable to federal bean-counters.

One notorious scandal involved Hazen Argue, a New Democrat-turned Liberal, MP-turned senator, and unelected cabinet minister. Argue had tried to get his wife elected in a suburban Ottawa seat and committed Senate office staff and resources to a nomination campaign. She lost, but there were complaints about the senator's use of public funds. He had even used $3,000 worth of Senate cab chits to help in the campaign. The auditors who were commissioned to look at Argue's bills went back eight years and found thirty-five fraudulent claims and another thirty-five that weren't backed up with documentation. The Senate asked the RCMP to investigate and, in November 1989, Argue became the first senator in Canadian parliamentary history to be charged with a criminal offence directly related to misuse of Senate funds. The Crown laid five charges of theft, fraud, and breach of trust over Argue's use of Senate resources for his wife's Liberal nomination bid. Later, he was also charged with fraud and uttering forged documents related to his travel expenses. Argue would argue that he had "done no wrong," and pleaded not guilty. He faced years in prison if convicted, but he never got his day in court; by 1991, he was suffering from terminal cancer, and the Crown set the charges aside "for humanitarian reasons." Argue died in October of that year.

The Argue case never turned into the defining legal and criminal test that it might have been had Argue's health not failed. If it had gone ahead, the case would certainly have turned on the rules and regulations governing the Senate's regime of self-regulation for itself and its members. Twenty years later, when Duffy, Wallin, Harb, and Brazeau were called to account for their use of expenses and Senate resources, they would all claim that the Senate's rules either permitted their use of public funds, or that the rules were too vague to allow for enforcement, or that their office administrators had failed to keep them in line. The Argue case would have provided legal precedents for the history-minded Senate to consider as it dealt with its problems in 2012 and 2013 and beyond. But that didn't happen. The Senate certainly took one step that would echo many years later. As it would in 2013, every attempt was made to keep the matter within the shadowy boundaries of the Internal Economy Committee.

Argue wasn't the only senator to test the patience of Parliament and Canadians. Teamsters Union boss Ed Lawson, named by Trudeau to the Senate as an Independent in 1970, was a pinkie-ringed, foul-mouthed wheeler-dealer of organized labour's old school. For him, the Senate was icing on the cake of a very lucrative career. He added his Senate salary of $50,300 plus an $8,200 tax-free expense allowance to a Teamsters paycheque that in 1984 was worth $300,000 a year, more than that of the president of the United States, and he was flying around in a private jet. He was also no fan of parliamentary democracy—at least not of participation in it. Senate records indicated that Lawson missed 1,111 of 1,379 sittings, an absentee rate of 80.5 percent. When he was criticized, he threatened defamation suits against such critics as Preston Manning, who made a fuss over his overlapping but profitable interests. Of course, Lawson said the Senate should pay his legal fees. But nobody ever laid a glove on the cunning Teamster-senator. He declared himself a Liberal in 2003 and served his full term, retiring in 2004 at age seventy-five as the second-longest serving member of the Senate.

Before Lawson, there was Liberal Andrew Thompson, whose attendance record was so bad that he became known as "the Senator from Mexico," where he whiled away the winters as other parliamentarians toiled in frigid Ottawa. Appointed by Lester Pearson in 1967, Thompson was said to have the worst attendance record of any senator, showing up for only fourteen days in eight years of sittings. Thompson thought he had figured out how to get around the rules. Claiming more or less perpetual illness, he would show up for a day or two at the beginning of each sitting to qualify for his salary and benefits. Then he would vanish. After reporters tracked him down in his sun-drenched getaway in Baja California, Mexico, the Reform Party called attention to Thompson's bad example by hiring a mariachi band and serving burritos in the Senate lobby. The publicity stunt was absurd, but Thompson was booted from the Liberal caucus by Jean Chrétien, and the Senate voted to strip him of his privileges and perks. When Thompson refused to return to Ottawa to explain himself, his salary was suspended; then, in 1997, his office and other privileges were removed. He finally resigned on March 23, 1998, almost two years earlier than his scheduled retirement date, but he was still entitled to an annual pension of $48,000.

Then there was former Progressive Conservative Senator Eric Berntson, appointed by Brian Mulroney in 1990 and convicted in 1999 of collecting more than $42,000 in fraudulent expense claims during his days in the Saskatchewan legislature and the cabinet of Premier Grant Devine. He was just one of several Saskatchewan Tory MLAs and party staffers who were swept up in a massive expense fraud investigation during the 1990s that sent several of them to jail. Berntson had been one of the most powerful politicians in Saskatchewan, a key figure in Conservative politics and a colleague of David Tkachuk, who as chairman of the Senate's Internal Economy Committee in 2013 would play such a significant role in the Duffy matter. Berntson was known for his confrontational style, and even after his conviction he defiantly told reporters, "as far as I'm concerned I did nothing wrong." He, too, resigned before being expelled, and kept his pension and benefits.

Mulroney appointee, lifelong friend, and close political ally Michel Cogger spent nine years fighting influence-peddling charges arising from his corporate-government dealings. Cogger was charged with corruption for accepting $212,000 from a Quebec businessman who was trying to flog translation software to the federal government. He was acquitted in 1997, but the Supreme Court of Canada overturned the acquittal. He was convicted in a second trial in June 1998, but he appealed and won a discharge in 2001. By then, he had already resigned from the Senate, but, like the others, retained his pension and benefits.

The list of misbehaving senators continues. Conservative Pierre-Hugues Boisvenu was accused of a conflict for arranging a job in his office and extra perquisites for a woman with whom he was having an affair. Boisvenu denied wrongdoing, but quietly dropped the affair, and the woman moved on to other work in the federal government. Liberal Rod Zimmer resigned from the Senate in August 2013, citing health problems, after briefly becoming notorious for the antics of his twenty-three-year old wife, Maygan Sensenberger, who had been arrested after a drunken incident on an Air Canada flight to Saskatoon. While the seventy-year-old Zimmer was cast as the victim of his spouse's intemperate behaviour, it cast a poor light on the judgment of a senator who was old enough to know better. Later in the year, the *Globe and Mail* reported that Zimmer's expenses were being referred to the Internal Economy Committee, but by then he was already gone. On June 14, 2013, former Liberal senator Raymond Lavigne was sent to jail for breach of trust and fraud over his expense claims. He had been charged originally in 2007 and ejected from the Liberal caucus, but he managed to collect his salary, benefits, and office expenses while his case wound through the courts. By the time he found himself in prison, Lavigne had already resigned from the Senate, but resignation before expulsion meant he still qualified for his $79,000-a-year pension.

So the Senate has a history of unsavoury affairs going back almost to Confederation. It has never been a popular institution with Canadians, who were mostly indifferent, few seeing value in an unelected chamber of sober second thought. On the other hand, political parties saw great value in the Senate. Ontario Senator David Smith organized federal campaigns for the Liberals and Alberta Conservative Doug Finley did the same for the Conservatives. It wasn't easy to draw lines between Senate activities and those that were strictly partisan because, after all, the Senate is by definition a partisan institution. But most thought it to be merely irrelevant until some senator looked like he was enjoying too much the entitlements to which he was entitled.

Mike Duffy's claim to Prince Edward Island residency and the Senate seat it legitimized might have been the subject of public skepticism from the day he was appointed, but years went by before anything tangible came of it. He carried on in the Senate and with his party fundraising activities, brushing off the occasional critic who questioned his residence qualifications or expenses. One of his critics back on the Island, Premier Robert Ghiz, told the CBC that "I thought he was an Ontario senator," but jabs like that just came with the turf. The Harper government had lots of adversaries, and its standard responses were to counterattack with whatever dirt could be dug up, or to ignore them completely. When it works, scornful disdain allows problems to fade into the woodwork as long as they aren't too serious. Counterattacking, however, with researchers going through whatever they can find out about the party's tormentors, is more expensive and time consuming. In public, it's politely called "caucus research"; among practitioners, it's very impolitely known as "rat fucking." All parties have them, and their products are on display every day in Question Period and through leaks to journalists. Now, Liberal and NDP "researchers" were getting to work on the Duffy matter.

The senator still seemed complacent about his critics, and his default response was simple disdain. After all, he didn't think he had a serious problem, either about his status as a senator or his expenses. Duffy held that line from the day his appointment was announced until early 2011, when Auditor General Michael Ferguson and a team of flinty-eyed numbers people started going over the Senate's books. They didn't set out to dredge up scandal. The auditor general's mandate is to ensure that government departments, agencies, and programs have the resources they need to get the job done and that the resources are managed properly. When the auditors identify a weakness, the department or agency is expected to respond with proposals to fix it. There is one important distinction: under the ancient doctrine of parliamentary privilege, the Senate is autonomous and has the power to make up its own rules. It's still subject to the occasional review by the auditor general, but the ordinary rules used in government departments don't apply.

For the Senate audit, the first since 1991 to examine the expenses of members, Ferguson assigned a team of nine professionals under the hands-on direction of Assistant Auditor General Clyde MacLellan, a Maritimer and seventeen-year veteran who had worked for Deloitte earlier in his career. Assistant auditors are responsible for specific parts of federal operations, and "all the agents of Parliament" fell under MacLellan's mandate. The report his team came up with in June 2012 provided insight into how the Senate was managed and how its chain of accountability was supposed to work. The Senate costs taxpayers $93 million a year, so the audit was not inconsequential, but it did have significant limitations. It wasn't mandated to drill into detail about individuals or their claims and, following the auditor general's usual practice, it didn't name names.

It's important to understand how the rules of parliamentary privilege affected the initial audit. In formal terms, the Senate, through its administrative arm, invites the auditor general to review its operations—the auditors can't just show up and demand to see the Senate's books. Parliament is the ultimate authority in the land and, constitutionally speaking, answers to no one, not even the Queen. Like MPs, senators are self-administered, in the sense that they make their own rules and oversee compliance among themselves. But the Senate has many quirky customs. Even its Question Period, committees, and debates are run differently from the House of Commons. Liberal George Baker, the longest-serving parliamentarian, says, "they don't even follow Beauchesne"—the basic rule book for parliamentary procedure in Canada—"they just do whatever they want."

Although some tentative reforms had been made, payments to members of the Red Chamber at that time were made according to the honour system, which put the onus on senators to conduct themselves ethically and to respect the rules governing the use of public money. It also meant that, by definition, if a senator deemed his or her expenses to be appropriate, they were. If a senator said he or she lived in a certain place, then, under the Senate's rules, that is where they lived. That made it difficult for the Senate's bureaucrats to say precisely which claims were appropriate and which ones weren't. The bureaucrats in Senate administration, through the clerk of the Senate, report to the Internal Economy Committee. This fifteen-member body is supposed to reflect the political composition of the Senate, so senators from all parties are eligible for membership; in practice, it is run by the majority party; at that time Harper's Conservatives.

The full committee met regularly and had authority over "all financial and administrative matters respecting the Senate, its premises, services and staff, and Senators." Day-to-day operations, however, were run by a steering committee of three senior senators—two Conservatives and a Liberal—which, until the expense scandal broke, managed to keep a low profile. The chair of both the full committee and the steering committee was Conservative David Tkachuk of Saskatchewan, a Mulroney appointee who has been in the Senate since 1993. A lifelong political operator, Tkachuk learned the ropes under Premier Grant Devine in the 1980s, a period tainted by an expense scandal in the provincial legislature. Tkachuk was never accused of wrongdoing, but twelve Tory MLAs and senior staffers— including Tkachuk's pal, the aforementioned Eric Berntson—were charged with expense account fraud. Investigators determined that some $837,000 had disappeared, some of which was found later in caches of thousand-dollar bills stuffed into bank safety deposit boxes. Court testimony revealed that the money had been funnelled through shell companies to MLAs who spent it on Hawaiian vacations and fancy horse-riding tack. Some of the accused politicians went to jail, and Devine himself was expelled from the provincial Progressive Conservative Party, which later folded and disappeared from politics. Survivors of the Tory meltdown later combined with like-minded conservatives under the banner of the Saskatchewan Party.

On the steering committee, Tkachuk was aided by the reliable Carolyn Stewart Olsen, a New Brunswick Conservative who had been Harper's press aide in the Alliance days and then director of communications in the Harper PMO. She is known as one of the Conservative true believers, someone who puts partisan interests and loyalty to the leader above all else; it was during her time running media relations at the PMO, for example, that relations with the Press Gallery became so toxic. The third member of the steering committee was Liberal George Furey, a Newfoundlander appointed by Chrétien in 1999. The full committee has authority over "all financial and administrative matters respecting the Senate, its premises, services and staff, and Senators." In practical terms, the three-member steering committee got a lot of the work done and it would prove to be a central, if opaque player in the scandal as it gained momentum during 2013.

The auditor general's people looked at the books, but they didn't examine every piece of paper. Instead, they sampled documentation from the Senate's spending and drew conclusions. They didn't identify any smoking guns or directly point to anything Canadians would later associate with scandal or fraud, but what they did find proved significant, even when stated in the mild bureaucratese of the auditor general. "Some expense claim files did not contain sufficient documentation...to explain the intended purpose of the transactions," the report read. "For example, a Senator who, in addition to a primary residence, owns a secondary residence in the National Capital Region is reimbursed a flat rate for each day that the residence is available for the Senator's occupancy. Annually, the Senator must provide proof that he or she owned the secondary residence throughout the year. In two of the seven cases we tested, we found insufficient evidence to determine whether the Administration had ensured that the Senator had complied with the policy."

It is now known that one of those two cases involved Senator Pamela Wallin, but the auditors gave no names and singled out no senators for criticism—that would be up to the Senate. The auditors probably could have gone deeper if that had been in their mandate, but their 2012 report makes clear that "we did not audit Senators' expenses or the work of their offices....[W]e tested individual transactions processed by the Senate Administration to determine whether they complied with the Senate's policies and directives." Without accusing anyone of doing anything wrong, the auditors were pointing to gaps in the record about who spent money on what. "Because some of the expense claim files do not always contain sufficient documentation, it is difficult for the Administration to clearly conclude that expenses are appropriate," they wrote.

The auditors did go one more important step further, recommending that Senate administrators "should bring to the attention of the Internal Economy Committee any cases in which the Administration believes that required documentation is not sufficient to clearly demonstrate that expenses are appropriate." For Duffy and the others, that was where the trouble really started. Constitutionally, the Senate is not part of the government nor is it subject to the Treasury Board's rules. But for political reasons, the Senate can't thumb its nose at a report from the auditor general, and it had an unwritten obligation to look deeper into the expense swamp than it might have otherwise. The Senate said it was taking steps "to clarify the types of documentation required to demonstrate that expenses are appropriate." Eventually, it would come up with a list of documents required to establish residency. Not all of Duffy's would fit the bill.

It took a while for all this to percolate in public opinion and in the backrooms of Parliament, but it was clear that more scrutiny of Senate expense claims and residency payments was coming. In November 2012, CTV aired a Robert Fife piece questioning where Patrick Brazeau lived, pointing out that he had been paid expenses for a second home in Gatineau while claiming that he lived in Maniwaki, outside the magic one-hundred-kilometre circle around Parliament Hill. Fife's story suggested strongly that Brazeau lived in Gatineau, which raised questions about whether he had a legitimate claim to the housing expenses, and Senator LeBreton announced that the Internal Economy Committee would look more closely at Brazeau's expenses. A couple of weeks later, *Ottawa Citizen* reporter Glen McGregor, a Duffy antagonist from his days writing for *Frank*, reported that Duffy had claimed more than $33,000 in secondary-housing expenses, "even though he is a long-time Ottawa resident."

McGregor also published part of a testy email exchange with Duffy in which the senator insisted that "I have done nothing wrong, and am frankly tired of your B.S." Duffy got some backing on that statement from his colleague Tkachuk, chair of the committee reviewing those very expenses. "When you travel to Ottawa, you get expensed for living in Ottawa. In his case, he has a home here, so he would charge off whatever the daily rate is," Tkachuk told McGregor, adding that, under the honour system, "Your primary residence is what you say your primary residence is."

Three weeks later, on December 6, the committee announced it would carry out the auditor general's recommendations to determine "whether all senators' declarations of primary and secondary residence are supported by sufficient documentation" and to dig deeper into some of the gaps in the paper trail the auditors had identified. The committee said senators would be expected to provide a provincial health card, driver's licence, and something on paper showing where they were registered to vote. Later that month, Duffy moved some of his banking business to a Prince Edward Island address, which the RCMP later would find suspicious. McGregor's story noted that Duffy and his wife, Heather, were both registered with Elections Canada in the riding of Carleton-Mississippi Mills, which includes Kanata.

The request for documentation was significant in that Duffy, Brazeau, and Wallin all claimed that's when the rules were changed without notice and applied retroactively. That wouldn't wash with the public or even with some members of the Senate. The then-Liberal leader in the Senate, James Cowan, insisted that the rules were similar to those used elsewhere in government or in private business: you claimed only legitimate expenses, and you signed for them. "The problem wasn't with the rules. They were perfectly clear to most people," Cowan says. Two Senate staffers would review each claim, and if there were questions, the forms would be returned for more information. The rules on residence were also clear, says Cowan, since about 95 percent of all senators had properly identified their primary homes. The requests for driver's licences and the rest "were clarifications, examples of what is okay and what is not okay. As a senator, you make the call."

Parliament broke for the 2012 Christmas recess, but the questions came flaring back as soon as business resumed, and for good reason. On February 4, 2013, PEI health minister Doug Currie revealed that Duffy had applied for a provincial health card back in December, right after the Senate said it would require one as part of the documentation needed to establish a second residence. Duffy's office had called repeatedly from Ottawa, saying the matter was urgent and asking the minister to intervene and expedite the request. Currie, whose Liberal government had taken many shots from the Conservative senator, told Duffy's people that the senator would have to wait in line just like anyone else applying for a health card. It usually took two to three months. "Express service for a senator is not something we would do," a senior Island official told me. The official, who wasn't authorized to discuss the Duffy matter by name, told me there was no agenda to trip up the senator, but he did acknowledge that relations between Duffy and the Ghiz government were uneasy, to say the least.

The next day, the CBC cited public records to report that Duffy was not eligible for a preferential property tax credit reserved for full-time Island residents. To qualify for the credit, you have to spend at least 183 days a year in the province, a period Duffy later said was impossible given the demands of his job in Ottawa. At this point, with questions arising about Wallin and Brazeau as well, media attention was growing by the hour. The issue was starting to dominate the political talk shows and was getting a lot of traffic on social media.

Then, a day after the tax-records story broke, one of the strangest scenes in the entire Senate expense saga occurred. Duffy's now-famous "kitchen exit" became part of the lore of the Senate scandal for the image it left of a famous former journalist dodging cameras over legitimate questions about his expenses. And it raised the profile of the Duffy story right across the country.

On February 6, Duffy was in Halifax for a speech to the Maritimes Energy Association, which represents East Coast energy producers and service firms. According to one of the organizers, Duffy was first approached the previous October "because of his support of energy projects, particularly Energy East [pipeline] and the fact that he was from PEI." The association contacted his office, which referred its call to Duffy's fee-for-service speaker's bureau. "We ended the conversation there," according to Barbara Pike, the association's chief executive officer and herself a former journalist. The group then booked Nova Scotia premier Darrell Dexter and Kathy Dunderdale, premier of Newfoundland and Labrador. But less than a month before the event, Dunderdale backed out, "so I went back to Duff and sent him an email asking him to get us out of a jam. He agreed," says Pike. The association paid for his airfare, hotel room, and expenses, which Pike said were pretty standard for a visiting speaker. "We did not pay Duff a speaker's fee. It was gratis," she says. And the speech promoting various regional energy schemes was well received. "It was a great speech and he received a standing ovation from the crowd of 250 to 300," Pike recalls. "His remarks were not reported....[T]here were six camera crews and a dozen reporters who sat at the back of the room and talked through the whole speech."

Duffy's speech might not have been newsworthy, but he got the media's attention when he referred to the importance of regional energy projects, jobs, and economic development, in contrast with "other less important issues." The journalist-turned-politician then waved a red flag at the assembled media pack with an off-the-cuff remark: "Who would have known there would be such interest in the question of offshore development and energy?" he asked, to laughter from the room. Looking toward the back where the reporters lurked, he added: "I look forward to reading your full and analytical reports in the media tomorrow." It came off like a dare to the reporters to challenge him. The journalistic pack had already annoyed several guests at the event, roaming the hallways and crashing a private reception. Hotel managers asked Pike whether the media should be excluded from the speech, but both she and Duffy said they should be allowed in to cover it. It was after the speech that events went sideways.

At the end of the evening, Duffy was approached by hotel security again and asked whether he wanted to take an express elevator to his floor. Pike says "it was discussed that security could go to the main elevator and hold it for him to make it through the media. His concern was for the people milling at the back of the room and in the foyer. He agreed to go through the back entrance, although he did not know it was a food staging area. When he ducked out, cameras and reporters literally shoved people aside running through both entrances. More than a few members [of the association] called later to say they were roughed up."

The media's behaviour aside, published images of Duffy high-tailing it through a kitchen as a hotel security man tried to block the cameras left the impression of a senator with something to hide, and more than a bit arrogant to boot. As he brushed by the cameras and reporters, the former celebrity journalist told a CBC reporter: "You should be doing adult work. Write about energy." It was the kind of comment that would put his face right back on the front pages. One of the NDP researchers working on the Senate scandal told me that, "after the kitchen incident, interest in the case just shot up. It was a key event, huge. We started getting calls from all the networks." In the Commons the next afternoon, New Democrat MP Charlie Angus seized on Duffy's kitchen exit to attack Harper's Senate appointments. "It's like Senator Come From Away is on the lam," Angus said to raucous laughter from the Opposition benches. "What do Mike Duffy and Anne of Green Gables have in common? They're both fictional residents of Prince Edward Island."

Then, on February 8, faced with the auditor general's observations about the Senate's genteel approach to accountability, the Internal Economy Committee voted to send the Senate's expenses to the Deloitte accounting firm for an independent review. It wasn't to be a full audit, but a good hard look at the books by private sector professionals, who would then file separate reports as they saw fit. It turned out they reported on Duffy, Mac Harb, Patrick Brazeau, and later Pamela Wallin. Their work shed a lot of light on the spending habits of the four senators and brought unwanted attention to people at the highest echelons of the Conservative government. The Deloitte reports eventually would identify who owned the dirty laundry cluttering up the Senate cloak rooms.

Meanwhile, following the auditor general's recommendation, the Senate's director of finance and procurement, Nicole Proulx, also started digging deeper into her files. She gathered up Duffy's travel expense claims, his per diem claims for maintaining a second residence in Ottawa, and some other documents and electronic records. From that information, she prepared a summary which concluded that Duffy made forty-nine claims for per diems to which he was not entitled and got paid for twenty-five of them, simply because the Senate's administrators didn't know that Duffy was away from Ottawa on those dates. Deloitte's bird dogs figured that out by analyzing Duffy's mobile phone records. Later it would become clear that, even after the Internal Economy Committee's examination, the Deloitte review, and a parallel internal Senate administration review, no proper forensic audit had been done— each review built on the one before it, and each found new pieces of evidence. Eventually, the RCMP would go over all of that same ground when it took on a full-dress audit in search of evidence of fraud and breach of trust.

According to well-informed sources, Duffy felt the scandal train was bearing down on him even though in his mind he had done nothing wrong and the Senate had unfairly changed the rules. Any problems with his travel expenses were minor, he felt—certainly nothing criminal or anything that would threaten his Senate seat or party affiliation. But his attempt to get the Island health card suggests he knew he might be vulnerable. Duffy also found himself pressured by powerful colleagues in the Conservative caucus to "take one for the team and for the prime minister," as Duffy put it, quit protesting and just pay up, which would make the problem go away, for everyone. That pressure was to build relentlessly in the weeks to come.

Months later, details emerged which shed more light on what was happening that February week during the murky talks that led to Duffy's bailout. Postmedia reporter Jordan Press used access-to-information laws to obtain visitor logs from the Langevin Block, seat of the PMO. The logs revealed that Duffy, Tkachuk, and Gerstein all visited the Langevin building that week, for reasons that have not been explained. Duffy was there on February 11, three days after the Internal Economy Committee sent his expenses off to Deloitte. His meeting with unidentified Langevin officials lasted fifty minutes. And those weren't the only meetings among top Conservatives at the building that day. The logs show that the Conservative House leader, Peter Van Loan, Conservative MP Scott Reid, and caucus chair Guy Lauzon were also there, accompanied by Senator Claude Carignan. A former mayor of St-Eustache, Quebec, and a defeated Conservative party candidate, Carignan would be named Government leader in the Senate after LeBreton stepped aside at the height of the scandal.

The next day, February 12, Tkachuk and Gerstein both visited the Langevin Building. Jordan Press spoke to Tkachuk, who confirmed he met with Nigel Wright to brief him on the Senate audit. Tkachuk denied there was any discussion of a plan to have Wright finance Duffy's repayment. The logs show that Tkachuk visited an unidentified official in Room 204, the prime minister's private, high-security boardroom, for about twenty minutes. After Tkachuk left, Gerstein arrived in the same room and met with at least two other officials, both unnamed in the logs. One of the PMO officials left after an hour, but Gerstein stayed until 4:30 P.M. The logs thus place three of the four central players in the Duffy case in the PMO within three days of the decision to bring in Deloitte to go over the books.

Although we don't know what transpired in those meetings, or even who was there from the PMO, they do seem unusual in terms of timing, if nothing else. According to the logs, the visits on February 11 by Duffy and February 12 by Tkachuk and Gerstein were the only times any of the three were signed in as visitors to the Langevin Block in the four-month period between January and April 2013. And they occurred as media coverage was intensifying and public awareness of the scandal was growing. People were talking about it, and not just on the political shows but also in the hockey rinks and donut shops of the nation. It also seems significant in terms of how Duffy reacted to the imminent Deloitte audit. He refused to cooperate from the start, so it's reasonable to ask whether something he gleaned from his Langevin Block meeting might have convinced him there was nothing to gain, and potentially much to lose, from playing ball with the auditors.

Sometime during this period, Duffy also handed over calendars, office diaries, travel records, and other documentation to Wright, a fact that would emerge only months later when the RCMP got involved. While the Deloitte auditors puzzled over the records they did have and were being refused cooperation from Duffy, Wright apparently had stacks of pertinent information at hand, which raises questions about whether the prime minister's top staffer knowingly withheld information from the audit.

We know now that Duffy was at the centre of the federal government apparatus on a key date in the expenses affair. What isn't clear is whether Duffy was there to plead his case or was summoned to be told what was expected of him. But we do know what happened next. Duffy tried to sort the matter out with the one man who might still be able to help him: Stephen Harper.

On Wednesday, February 13, the prime minister spoke at the weekly Conservative caucus meeting in the Centre Block. According to one account, he told his MPs and senators that, if there were any inappropriate claims out there, they should be repaid. After all, Harper had said many times over the years that he was going to clean up Ottawa and end waste and abuse of public money.

He didn't mention Duffy or any other parliamentarian by name, but Duffy decided he had to do something. After the meeting, he approached the boss.

We don't have an independent record of what took place in that conversation, but spokesman Andrew MacDougall gave the PMO's version: "Following a caucus meeting, Mr. Duffy approached the prime minister in the caucus room regarding the situation with his expenses....The prime minister was adamant that he should re-pay any inappropriate expenses." Officially, that was the only time the two men spoke about the expense controversy or the political problems the senator was causing for the Conservative Party. Later, Duffy would say that Wright was also there and that it was much more than a quick chat.

Contrast the prime minister's brush-off of Duffy with his treat-ment of Pamela Wallin later that same day. Not long after the caucus meeting, he told the Commons that he had looked into Wallin's ex-penses and that everything was just fine. He told Opposition leader Tom Mulcair that, "in terms of Senator Wallin, I have looked at the numbers. Her travel costs are comparable to any parliamentar-ian travelling from that particular area of the country over that period of time....The costs are to travel to and from that province, as any similar parliamentarian would do." The prime minister's comments evaded the central question about Wallin, which wasn't about whether her expenses were higher or lower than others, but whether they were legitimate public expenses at all.

Harper's statement, which later proved to be at variance with the facts, set off alarm bells among his minions. As a member of the steering committee, Stewart Olsen knew better than almost anyone else what the audits were revealing and how hard it had become to keep the scandal under wraps. In fact, Wallin's expense reports had been the first to raise red flags for the Senate administration. Stewart Olsen heard the prime minister speaking and made a panicked call to the PMO, warning him off saying anything else that sounded like an endorsement of Wallin or any other senator.

Whether or not the details already had been sorted out on a deal to rescue Duffy, events moved along relentlessly. On February 14, the day after Duffy's direct appeal to Harper after the caucus meeting, the Internal Economy Committee took a step that would change the course of the entire Senate story: it decided to include Duffy's filings in the material it was giving to Deloitte. From that day on, nothing in Duffy's life would be the same. For the first time, his expenses would be given a thorough review, which was significant enough. Beyond that, the committee's decision suggested that the Conservative power trust was losing patience with its star fundraiser. According to reliable sources, Duffy was by then facing intense pressure to do something to take the load off the prime minister and the party. They wanted him to pay back whatever he owed "for the good of the party," whether or not Duffy agreed he was in the wrong. That did not sit well with the senator, who felt that any admission of wrongdoing would come back to haunt him. He hit upon a fateful recourse: take the matter to Nigel Wright. That step would have far-reaching significance for Duffy, the Senate, and, eventually, the prime minister himself.

On February 20, according to a report by Robert Fife at CTV, Duffy emailed friends to say that Wright had "worked out a scenario" to bail him out with "cash for the repayment." It's still not clear if that scenario was worked out during the Langevin Block meetings. But we do know that Duffy had already handed Wright a binder full of information on his expenses, including calendars, receipts, and photographs of the renovations he had carried out on the cottage on Friendly Lane. (Wright later turned that binder over to the RCMP.) Fife now says that the February 20 email, which he read, is the key to the allegations connecting Duffy and Wright, and that provoked the intense interest of the Mounties when they waded into the case a few weeks later. The allegation of a promise to pay cash in return for cooperation from Duffy would be at the centre of the police case in the months to come. Later, Wright's lawyers would provide investigators with "hundreds of emails" from that period, along with Duffy's big binder.

In the meantime, Deloitte would go over Duffy's books, whether or not the senator played along, examining the rules about residency, living expenses, and travel claims, and the Senate records for the eighteen-month period between April 1, 2011, and September 30, 2012. And Deloitte was the logical choice: the same Deloitte office, two blocks from Parliament Hill at 100 Queen Street, also audited the books for Conservative Fund Canada, overseen by Gerstein and formerly managed by Wright. This, of course, is the same fund that Duffy had helped to enrich with his many appearances at fundraisers around the country and which he tried to tap when he needed help with his expense claim troubles.

Just sending the books to Deloitte must have been disturbing enough for Duffy, who insisted he had followed the rules as he understood them. But it wasn't as though the storm clouds had only suddenly appeared—Duffy knew about the Senate probe of his colleague Brazeau's claims and all about the stories questioning his eligibility to represent Prince Edward Island. Deloitte's people asked for an interview and access to Duffy's files. The senator declined both requests, and Deloitte never did get a chance to ask him any questions. That meant parts of the Deloitte report are incomplete, even though the information was available; unknown to the auditors, Wright had it. Deloitte also had problems with the rules, just as Duffy and some of the others had predicted. The accountants concluded that, because the criteria weren't spelled out precisely, it was impossible to establish the facts about a senator's primary residence, so they were unable to pin down whether Duffy was living in bucolic Cavendish or suburban Ottawa. Duffy would rely heavily on this uncertainty, telling reporters on several occasions that the Deloitte report cleared him of any wrongdoing.

Ambiguities aside, Deloitte did some good detective work. Based on records from Duffy's Senate-issued mobile phone and his government American Express card, the accountants were able to confirm the senator's location on 94 percent of the days covered by the review. Deloitte concluded that Duffy spent 54 percent of his time in Ottawa and 30 percent in Prince Edward Island, and only 8 percent of his time on the Island was outside the summer holiday period, when the Senate was adjourned. Nevertheless, Duffy identified the cottage in Cavendish as his primary residence, and he claimed both the cost of maintaining the house in the National Capital Region and per diem expenses.

Deloitte also determined that, when the Senate did set out some criteria for establishing the location of a primary residence, Duffy still met only one of the four proofs required: a Prince Edward Island driver's licence, which he had applied for the day after his Senate appointment was announced back in December 2008. He didn't have an Island health card, his income tax address was in Ontario, and he didn't produce a signed statement or other proof of where he had voted. Travel claims were a separate matter, but among other revelations about his movements and expense patterns, they shone new light on how Duffy used the houses in Cavendish and Kanata. Deloitte determined that, in both 2011 and 2012, he had driven to the Island in June, at adjournment, and returned to Ottawa in September, and had claimed for mileage and travel expenses for all the trips, specifying the date of each leg and what it cost him to go from his "primary residence" on the Island to his "secondary residence" in Ottawa.

Although much has been made of the Deloitte report and the RCMP's use of it in its investigation, the accountants didn't reveal anything the Senate didn't already know if it had cared to look. All the significant information Deloitte cited came from the Senate's own records. Senate staff knew that many of Duffy's claims had been rejected as inappropriate, and they probably had held their noses while approving others. The Internal Economy Committee had a good idea of what was happening, too, both from the administrative records and from the further research of its administrative staff. That the committee knew more than it was saying became significant later, when the RCMP drew links from Wright's payment to Duffy's public declaration that he was paying back the money and to the "amended" committee reports into Duffy, Brazeau, and Harb. The RCMP was struck by the fact that the reports seemed to go so hard on Brazeau and Harb and so easy on Duffy. It is this link that would prove key to the RCMP's allegations against both Duffy and Wright: that money exchanged hands to confer a benefit on a public official.

With Deloitte breathing down his neck, the Senate no longer providing a shield, and no joy from his appeal to the prime minister, Duffy was feeling more isolated by the day. He asked for direction from senior Tories and even from the PMO, in the person of communications director Angelo Persichilli, and the message was that he should simply pay the money back. Persichilli, who soon left the PMO and was appointed a citizenship judge in Toronto, told CTV that he was "urging him to give the money back, but as a friend," not on orders from above. Months later, Robert Fife would report that he had seen emails in which senior Conservatives pressured Duffy to pay back the money and help the party. The emails suggested that Wright and senators Tkachuk and Carolyn Stewart Olsen were working on a solution for Duffy, one that would make the problem go away. The two senior Conservatives denied they were part of the pressure on Duffy, but with qualifications. "At no time did we have knowledge of Mr. Wright's payment to Senator Duffy before it was reported publicly," the two senators said in a prepared statement. "Anyone who suggests that we were aware of Mr. Wright's payment to Senator Duffy before it was reported publicly is lying." But that wasn't actually what Fife reported, which was that they had put on pressure, not done the deal making between the senator and the chief of staff.

In an interview, Duffy told another CTV reporter that, "when the process is finished, Canadians will find, as the independent auditors at Deloitte found, that my expenses are not meritorious of criticism." And on February 22, with Deloitte combing through the books, the Opposition and news media raising more questions every day, and his own party keeping up the pressure, Duffy broke the logjam. The senator was on one of his occasional winter visits to the Island, staying in his usual digs at the Great George Inn in Charlottetown. He called the local CBC-TV station and announced that he wanted to make a statement. The call was cryptic, but the staffers were intrigued and invited him to come in. He would be interviewed by supper-hour host Bruce Rainnie.

According to people who were there, Duffy arrived at the CBC station on University Avenue with Heather and long-time aide Mary McQuaid. They walked up to the front door but then withdrew to their car, parked in the CBC lot. A series of lengthy phone conversations followed. We now know Duffy was talking to the PMO and lawyers for the Conservative Party, discussing what he was to say. But that wasn't clear at the time. The calls went on so long that CBC staffers were coming in to the newsroom to make sure Rainnie and the producers were aware that Senator Duffy was outside in a car. The producers started getting antsy, but the senator kept everyone in suspense as the calls continued. Finally, with minutes to spare, Duffy came through the door. He was ready to talk.

What the audience saw that night was Duffy in his characteristic role as the Old Duff. He buttered up Rainnie by saying how great it was finally to meet him in person and that he watched the show all the time. Rainnie didn't fall for that, mostly because he had met Duffy several times over the years and the two had chatted at a recent public event. Duffy wanted the time, Rainnie reminded him. What did he have to say?

It turned out the senator had a lot to say, most of it scripted by the Prime Minister's Office. He called the expense uproar "a major distraction from the important work that I'm trying to do for Prince Edward Island," which was keeping him away from "a lot of exciting projects on the go." He acknowledged there was public pressure on him. "Everywhere I go people are talking: 'Well, where do you live, what's it all about?'" he said, sounding more than a little frustrated. "It's become a major distraction." Then came the news: "My wife and I discussed it and we decided that in order to turn the page and put this behind us, we are going to voluntarily pay back my living expenses related to the house we have in Ottawa." The talking points were set out: he wasn't admitting anything, but was paying the money back. It was a distraction. Those lines would be heard many more times from the Conservatives, including from Harper himself.

At that time, Duffy's expenses were believed to be around $40,000, and Rainnie asked him to clarify the figure. Duffy knew way more about the amount than he was willing to say. "Whatever it is...ah, the accountants, you know...we're going to pay it back and until the rules are clear, and they are not clear now, the forms are not clear and I hope the Senate will redo the forms to make them clear, I will not claim a housing allowance." Rainnie then aimed a question at the heart of Duffy's insecurity about his Senate seat. "Is that an admission that you're not an Island resident?" he asked, to a quick denial from the senator. "No it has nothing to do with residency in PEI. I'm an Island resident and I'm entitled to be a senator. I've met all those requirements."

To Duffy, publicly and in private to his inner circle, it was still just an accounting matter. He admitted on air that he "may have made a mistake" in filling in forms related to his primary residence, but "rather than go through months and months and months of an audit, we've got important work to do. So my wife and I talked last night and I said, let's just get this off the plate." Duffy insisted that the system was at fault, that there was "no formula and no rule" for determining primary residence. Much had been made about the 183 days per year defined in Prince Edward Island's resident and non-resident tax regulations, but that was a provincial law, nothing to do with the federal Senate. "That 183 days doesn't apply," he insisted. "There is no number of days in the Constitution, so there is no formula, there is no number." Duffy was paying the non-resident tax rate, essentially double what full-time Island residents pay, but suggested it was almost out of the goodness of his heart. "That isn't because of the lack of time I spend on PEI. That's tied in with the PEI tax system. That's why I pay that and given the state of the province's finances I'm happy to pay double to help them get out of the hole." Still, Rainnie said, people were complaining about the expense mess, on the Island and across Canada. Was Duffy close to resigning? The senator threw up his hands. "Not at all, no, no, no no, no. No." Had it not even crossed his mind? "No, no, no, no, no, no, no....Not at all, no."

The senator then managed to add another layer of confusion to the question of where he lived. He talked about living in Charlottetown during the winter, not at the place in Cavendish, and suggested that was a routine option for Islanders who live in rural areas but might need medical care. And, like many others, he stayed at the Great George Inn. "I'm surrounded by people who live in the country, and move in to the Inn of Great George. It's practically full of people, a lot of people who live in the rural areas and want to live near the hospital in case they have a problem, and of course our winter weather is not exactly conducive to getting to the hospital in a hurry." Many Islanders would question that, since few can afford to stay in rented digs in Charlottetown during the endless Island winter, no matter what their medical problem.

By the end of the interview it was clear that, most of all, the senator wanted to make sure his reputation as a genuine son of the Island and good old boy remained intact. When Rainnie asked why he had called the CBC to issue his statement, the reply came right from the old pre-scandal Duffy script: "I hope it reassures Islanders and Canadians that the Old Duff, the Duff they've known and trusted, would never do anything wrong. I would never knowingly fiddle anything. And I hope that as a result of this conversation that people will have a better understanding. I live at the shore three months of the year, I live in town in the winter. My job's in Ottawa. My heart's in PEI."

Unfortunately for Duffy, it doesn't matter where a senator's heart is or whether the heart is even healthy. Even if the definition tends toward the vague, what matters is that a senator is supposed to be "resident in the province for which he is appointed." Whether or not he paid back the money didn't address that issue at all. What was at stake was Duffy's job, paycheque, and pension plan. If he wasn't "resident in the province," then he might not have a seat at all. In a few months, the deal worked out in mid-February, the one Duffy says he accepted so reluctantly, would make him face that fear.

The Young Duff. Mike Duffy in 1979, an emerging star on CBC Television and already showing an affinity for made-to-measure suits.

1

Duffy shooting a "stand-up" during the 1980 election campaign. For a script, he often used notes scribbled on a piece of paper and laid on the floor. His pause to look down at the script became a trademark move.

At the 1983 Progressive Conservative leadership convention in Ottawa. Brian Mulroney became leader and a year later, prime minister. It wasn't long before Duffy was lobbying Mulroney's people for a Senate seat.

Prime Minister Stephen Harper after an appearance on Mike Duffy Live *from the foyer of the House of Commons. Harper rarely gave television interviews and getting him on the Duffy show was considered a coup.*

Duffy on the floor of the Senate with Senator Irving Gerstein, the top Tory fundraiser, in 2009. Duffy helped raise big money for his adopted party.

C

Duffy's cottage on Friendly Lane in Cavendish, P.E.I. Duffy claimed it as his primary residence, but it appeared to be empty during the winter months.

Senator Duffy makes a mocking salute to reporters at an event in Halifax in February 2013. A few minutes later he was seen escaping the room through a hotel kitchen to avoid questions about his expense claims.

D

In July 2013, the Canadian Taxpayers Federation commissioned a ten-metre Duffy balloon with money bulging from a briefcase as a publicity stunt to highlight the Senate expense scandal.

Nigel Wright, Harper's former chief of staff. His $90,000 payment to Duffy became the subject of scandal and an investigation by a special unit of the RCMP.

At the height of the scandal, Duffy had to walk the gauntlet of cameras and reporters outside the Senate.

F

Senator Patrick Brazeau leaves the Senate after his expulsion from the Conservative caucus in February 2013. He was later suspended from the Senate along with Duffy and Wallin.

Senator Pamela Wallin leaves the Senate after facing allegations that she too had misused her Senate living and travel expenses. She denied any wrongdoing, but like Duffy and Brazeau, was suspended.

As the Senate scandal enveloped the Conservative government, cartoonist Michael de Adder depicted Harper being dragged underwater by his most infamous appointee, Mike Duffy.

THE SENATOR, THE STAFFER, AND THE $90,000 CHEQUE

It is clear the public controversy surrounding me and the repayment of my Senate expenses has become a significant distraction to my caucus colleagues, and to the government.

— SENATOR MIKE DUFFY, MAY 16, 2013

IN OTTAWA, THE RAINNIE INTERVIEW HIT LIKE A BOMBSHELL. DUFFY'S startling news would go directly to the supper-hour political shows and be subjected to instant analysis. Ordered to get the word out, Duffy made his way across Charlottetown to the Delta Hotel to do a similar interview with CTV. By then, the stress was showing. The *Guardian*'s Teresa Wright saw the senator on television, jumped in her car, and made for the Delta. She arrived as the senatorial entourage was leaving and asked for an interview, but was brusquely waved off. Aide Mary McQuaid told Wright the senator was "too busy" to talk to her. "I thought it was strange, they had never treated me like that before," Wright said later.

If Duffy thought he could ease the pressure by snubbing the *Guardian*, his sensational revelation emphasized how serious a problem his claims were. It also represented a personal defeat. He had tried with all his might to resist the demands to "take one for the team," partly because his lawyers felt that paying the money back would imply wrongdoing. Now, he would be forced to do it anyway. The CBC interview was the first clear statement by the senator that he intended to pay back the money he had claimed for the "second home" in Ottawa. At some point during that stressful day, and according to the plan worked out with the PMO, Duffy wrote to the chair of the Internal Economy Committee, Senator David Tkachuk, telling him he had "filled out the forms in good faith," but "may have been mistaken." He intended to "repay the housing allowance that I have collected to date" and wanted to know what the total tab would be "to settle this matter in full." What wasn't clear was where the money would come from. Duffy would later tell Robert Fife that he had arranged a bank loan, a line that had been worked out for him by the PMO.

From the contents of the February 20 email about the "scenario" developed by Nigel Wright and as reported by Fife and later documented by the RCMP, it now seems clear that, by the time Duffy appeared on television on the Island, the immediate money problem had been substantially solved. Wright's lawyers later told the RCMP that Irving Gerstein had been approached and was okay with paying off Duffy's bill from Conservative Fund Canada accounts before he realized how much it would cost. When it turned out to be $90,000, not the $30,000 or so that had been suggested, Gerstein balked. Wright would identify Gerstein as one of the top Conservatives who were aware of the arrangement to bail out Duffy, which makes perfect sense: Gerstein is close to Stephen Harper, who appointed him both to the Senate and as head of Conservative Fund Canada. Opposition critics would take that close connection as more reason to doubt Harper's claim to be out of the loop about his team's effort to bail out Duffy.

With pressure building in the Commons and in the media, the PMO went over to the offensive. On February 27, the day Tkachuk confirmed to Duffy the total figure of $90,172.24 to "settle the matter in full," the prime minister rose in the Commons. What he said fit with the deal worked out with Duffy: "All senators conform to residency requirements. That is the basis on which they are appointed to the Senate and those requirements have been clear for 150 years." The prime minister, by implication at least, was affirming that Duffy's Prince Edward Island seat was legitimately held. Considering what was going on in the PMO conference rooms in the Langevin Block, in the Senate, and in party back channels, that was a telling comment. It suggested that the prime minister felt the situation was under control. Perhaps, as his defenders would claim, there was no need for him to be involved at all. In any case, Harper could argue that the honour system allowed senators to deem themselves resident wherever they wanted. But to say the rules had been clear for 150 years was a stretch—more like, open to interpretation for a century and half. There had always been a property requirement and a rule that "he shall be resident in the province," but documentation was required only after the changes in 2012. The current rules certainly had not been spelled out at Confederation.

A few days later, on March 1, Senator Marjory LeBreton took a similar line to argue that Duffy's claim to a seat was perfectly legitimate, even if her explanation seemed oddly put. "There is no doubt that senators that sit in the Senate, by way of the declaration of qualification, qualify to sit in the Senate." Translating that later, she told the CBC "Senator Duffy maintains a residence in PEI and is qualified to sit in the Senate."

Even so, problems were piling up for the senator for Prince Edward Island-Cavendish. Deloitte was demanding information and face time, the Internal Economy Committee seemed indifferent to his complaints of unclear rules, and his image was getting badly smeared.

The party was helping, at least with his legal fees. On March 4, Duffy's lawyer, Janice Payne, sent an invoice to Conservative Party lawyer Arthur Hamilton at the firm Cassels Brock for more than $13,000 in legal services. That was another fact of which the prime minister was either unaware or not forthcoming. It would only become public much later, in the Senate's mad month of October.

Meanwhile, Duffy's lifeline was being put together in the form of a cash infusion from Wright. It took a couple of weeks to sort out the details, but the deal was made. The conditions included a promise by Duffy to pay the money over to the government immediately and to stop talking to the media. On March 25, a bank draft for $90,172.00 was transferred from Wright to Duffy's Ottawa lawyer. The next day, Duffy moved the money to the Senate, apparently by cheque, but there's confusion over that. The Senate said the cheque went to the Receiver General for Canada, but the Receiver General's department had no record of a cheque from Duffy. According to Postmedia, a press line was sent down from the deputy minister's office saying that "any payment by Senator Duffy would have been remitted directly to the Senate and subsequently deposited by that institution into the Government's bank account. Receiver General is not in possession of this information." Still, the money was moved somehow, and there should be paper on it somewhere. The Privy Council Office, the bureaucratic arm of the PMO, told the CBC's Greg Weston that it didn't have a single document relating to the scandal, not about Wright, not about Duffy, not even about Mac Harb. Weston and other inquiring journalists were told the information "does not exist." Evidently, no one asked Wright, because he had lots of documentation. There was a paper trail all right, just not one to which the Harper government would admit.

The deal done, Duffy tried to declare the matter closed. His attorneys informed Deloitte that, since their client had paid back what was allegedly owed, there was no purpose in cooperating with the auditors' research—Duffy would decline all further requests for information from Deloitte or for an interview with its audit team.

But it wasn't closed; Duffy and the Harper government had bought themselves only a couple of weeks of quiet.

The interlude was soon over. On April 16, Duffy and Tkachuk met to talk over the problem in what the latter described as "an informal chat." Others saw the meeting much differently. The Canadian Press reported that Tkachuk had given Duffy a briefing on what was going on behind the scenes in the Deloitte audit process. That same day, the Deloitte team met with senators Tkachuk, Carolyn Stewart Olsen, and George Furey, the steering committee of the Senate's Internal Economy Committee, to give them a first official look at how its research was going. Deloitte told them it appeared Duffy had claimed per diems for working in Ottawa in January 2012 when he was actually in Florida. That night, Duffy and Tkachuk met for another "informal conversation" in which, as Tkachuk told *Maclean's* reporter Aaron Wherry, he suggested Duffy "better straighten this out and get...organized." Two days later, Duffy again wrote to Tkachuk, saying he might have made some errors on the expenses for his Florida vacation and offering to repay anything owed. He had discovered that he had "inadvertently charged...per diems for several days when...not in the National Capital Region," blaming the oversight on a temporary staffer in his office. He then issued a statement saying he had repaid the money, although it wasn't clear when. "I am a man of my word," he said. On April 20, Duffy told Tkachuk that he was willing to meet with the Internal Economy Committee to discuss his situation, but he wasn't prepared to play ball with Deloitte. By then it was too late. The auditors were already forming conclusions.

The back-and-forth between Duffy and Tkachuk, with Wright, LeBreton, Stewart Olsen, and a team of PMO staffers working offstage, is a key factor in the expense scandal story. The Conservatives were intent on keeping the matter as quiet as possible, and that included the Internal Economy Committee's reports on Duffy, Harb, and Brazeau issued on May 9. The committee went very hard on Harb and Brazeau, stopping just short of alleging criminal wrongdoing. But in its Twenty-second Report, on Duffy, the committee blandly noted that he had paid the money back and that his expense claims would be monitored for a year. Later, the RCMP would find the wording significant because it suggested an improper arrangement between Duffy and Wright, worked out in secret meetings involving the Conservatives Tkachuk and Stewart Olsen and without the agreement or even knowledge of Furey, the only Liberal on the committee. Furey, who declined to be interviewed for this book based on advice from Senate lawyers, told colleagues he was furious about being excluded, and it was his anger that led to accusations of a whitewash. The Senate's Opposition leader, James Cowan, wanted the matter pursued by the police, but the motion was turned down by the Conservative majority.

More questions would be raised when Wright's lawyers told the RCMP about the side arrangements in the deal to pay off Duffy's expense bill: pay back the money immediately and keep quiet about it, and in return the Senate would "go easy on him" in its report. The allegation that Tkachuk and Stewart Olsen worked behind Furey's back to whitewash the Twenty-second Report would loom significantly in the RCMP's case against Duffy and Wright. Paying off a senator was one thing. Conspiring to keep it secret was another. Manipulating an official Senate report was something else again.

With the release of the reports on the three senators on May 9, Deloitte's audits were disclosed and immediately posted online. Now, Canadians could read the reports and draw their own conclusions. They didn't like what they saw, and public anger was reflected in the harsh media coverage that ensued. Later that day, Duffy posted a statement on his personal website. It had the style of a Government of Canada news release and was place-lined Cavendish, PEI. In it, Duffy claimed that the Deloitte report had vindicated him because it described the Senate's rules as opaque and unclear. He also suggested he was the victim of an innocent misunderstanding about what he was allowed to claim as legitimate expenses, and as soon as he realized something was wrong, he had moved right away to fix it. Furthermore, according to his interpretation, Deloitte had identified only one inappropriate claim, for $1,050.60 for expenses during the vacation trip to Florida, which he had already paid back. Even so, he was paying back more than $90,000, which "covered all of the expenses I was paid as a result of having to maintain two residences; one on Prince Edward Island, another in Ottawa." Most of the information wasn't new, other than the amount, which was more than double what had been rumoured.

In short, Duffy wasn't accepting blame for anything worse than sloppy bookkeeping. "When I discussed these issues with my wife in February, we came to the conclusion that repaying the ninety-thousand was the right thing to do, regardless of the outcome of the audit that was to come. It was the right decision then, and it is the right decision now," the statement said. His expenses "were claimed in good faith," and he hoped Islanders would see it that way. "I can only effectively represent the people of Prince Edward Island if I have earned their trust and respect....I am honoured to serve the people of my home province, and with the actions I have taken, I feel confident I can look them in the eye and assure them I am doing so with integrity." He also tried to close the door on future questions: "With these matters now dealt with, my focus going forward will remain: to be the most effective representative I can be for my fellow Islanders."

That would not be easy. Less than a week later, on May 14, in a story that became by far the most explosive turn of events in the Senate scandal to date, Fife reported on *CTV National News* that Wright himself had cut the cheque that allowed Duffy to repay his expenses. The day before the story ran, Fife had asked Duffy where the money came from, and was told in an email that "[t]he Royal Bank helped me....I dealt with my bank personally. Nigel played no role." That version of the repayment stood up for less than twenty-four hours. Fife quoted a "senior PMO official" who said that Duffy didn't have the $90,000 and refused to borrow it, partly because he was worried that Heather would get stuck with a debt should something happen to his wonky heart.

That wasn't the only untruth emerging from the Conservative ranks. Party insiders told other media that Duffy and Wright were friends from the Mulroney days, when Wright was a junior PMO official, and that Wright wrote the cheque to help out an old pal. But, as Wright's lawyers would later tell RCMP investigators, the two men were anything but old pals. Wright is a marathon-running fitness freak, a regular churchgoer, and Harvard-educated boy wonder. He had made millions as a Bay Street dealmaker. He and Duffy had almost nothing in common except their allegiance to Stephen Harper. Fife's story not only took the scandal in a whole new direction, it also suggested that something far more sinister than sloppy accounting had taken place. Linking the senator, the payment, and the prime minister's chief of staff brought the scandal out of the Red Chamber and into the centre of the PMO. Wright was Harper's most senior operative and spoke with the authority of the prime minister. He is true Conservative Party blue.

On May 16, with Fife's revelations raining smoking wreckage on the cover story and a link now made to the PMO, Duffy's phone rang in Cavendish. According to his version of the conversation, Senator LeBreton and Ray Novak, the prime minister's devoted principal secretary, presented an ultimatum: resign from the Conservative caucus or the Internal Economy Committee, with Tkachuk and Carolyn Stewart Olsen pulling the strings, will vote him out of office. Play along, LeBreton told him, and you can keep your Senate seat. Still protesting, but to no avail, Duffy had no way out. The senator issued a statement, in wording that the prime minister would recycle many times in future weeks:

> It is clear the public controversy surrounding me and the repayment of my Senate expenses has become a significant distraction to my caucus colleagues, and to the government. Given that my presence within the Conservative caucus only contributes to that distraction, I have decided to step outside of the caucus and sit as an independent Senator pending resolution of these questions. Throughout this entire situation I have sought only to do

the right thing. I look forward to all relevant facts being made clear in due course, at which point I am hopeful I will be able to rejoin the Conservative caucus.

Yet Duffy's claim to be following the allegedly vague and unspecific rules of the Senate was unravelling a bit more with each passing day. A knowledgeable source says that, by then, Duffy was speaking darkly about a "set-up by the PMO" that was part of Harper's supposed agenda to abolish the Senate or at least severely clip its wings. Duffy had also made demands, which the PMO resented but approved. He had spoken to Tkachuk, who at first seemed supportive, but who then stood by and let him sink. He had approached Gerstein, who wanted to help but wasn't prepared to shell out $90,000. He had been defended by Marjory LeBreton, who said Duffy had a right to his Prince Edward Island seat, but after he was out of the caucus she wanted his head. We know Duffy spoke at least once with the prime minister himself. The Langevin Block visitor logs also show that he spoke to an unnamed official, now known to have been Wright, in the PMO for almost an hour. And we know communications with Wright led to the controversial bailout cheque and a tangled skein of PMO emails discussing how to manage the Duffy problem.

Now, Duffy seemed determined that, if he were to go down, he would have company, telling friends that, if charged, people high up in the Conservative Party would be called to testify to what they knew. It didn't take long for the first to fall, and it was Wright himself. The prime minister defended his top aide for four days, then suddenly changed his mind. On May 19, he accepted Wright's resignation from the PMO "with regret." Conservative MP Pierre Poilievre, a go-to mouthpiece for Harper on the political talk shows, sent out a tweet that would sound very hollow as the months went by: "Saddened to hear of Nigel Wright's departure. He is an honourable man, and great Canadian."

Before too long, Stewart Olsen herself came under scrutiny for her expense claims. The *Huffington Post Canada* website reported that the senator, whom Harper appointed in 2009 to represent New Brunswick, had lived in Ottawa for her first two years in the Red Chamber. Digging through Senate records, reporter Althia Raj determined that Stewart Olsen, who had done so much to pressure Duffy and others and who was operating as the prime minister's whip hand in the upper house, had claimed $63,594 in travel and living allowances during that time. Indeed, she had been living in Ottawa for twenty years at the time of her appointment, and it was only two years later that she established a permanent residence at Cape Spear, New Brunswick. Raj reported there was evidence Stewart Olsen had claimed more than $4,000 in per diems for days the Senate wasn't sitting and she had no committee meetings or other official business. "I will absolutely repay immediately, if my staff...if we made an error in claiming per diems," she told Raj. Later, she issued a statement contradicting what she had told the *HuffPost*: "I have reviewed these claims with the Senate finance administration and they have found nothing improper."

Other senators had problems justifying their expenses and figuring out where they lived, but it still had little bearing on Duffy's situation. The man who had tended to his image so carefully for so many years by now had fallen drastically in public esteem, particularly in Prince Edward Island. As the scandal led the news across Canada in the spring of 2013, a Charlottetown radio station ran a "Do ya a Duffy" promotion, offering to pay off the debts of callers to a limit of $20. Charlottetown retailers reported brisk sales of "Stuff the Duff" T-shirts over the summer tourist season. The Canadian Taxpayers Federation, normally a staunch supporter, showed up across from Parliament Hill with a giant inflatable Duffy balloon. One hand of the air bag held a briefcase overflowing with cash, while the other hand was held out for more. The taxpayer group planned to tour its creation around Canada to draw attention to the Senate scandal's Prince Edward Island poster boy. The task wouldn't be difficult—Canadians were well aware of Duffy's plight, including a team of investigators from the Royal Canadian Mounted Police.

THE OTHER
THREE

[B]eing an official of the Senate of Canada, did commit breach
of trust in connection with the duties of his office.

— RCMP DOCUMENT ALLEGING WRONGDOING BY
SENATOR MAC HARB, JULY 25, 2013

DUFFY HAD TROUBLES, BUT HE WASN'T ALONE. SENSATIONAL, DAMNING
reports emerged about senators Pamela Wallin and Patrick Brazeau,
and investigations revealed a disturbing pattern of residence claims
by Liberal Senator Mac Harb. Some observers predicted that having
Harb, Brazeau, and Wallin—in fact, the entire Senate—under
suspicion would simply "spread the muck" and take the pressure
off Duffy, but Canadians didn't see it that way. As facts emerged
about Harb's unusual land deals in the Ottawa Valley, with the
RCMP's allegation that Brazeau "never lived in Maniwaki" despite
claiming expenses for a second home, and details coming to light
of Wallin's criss-crossing the country on the public dime, public
disdain for the Senate deepened.

The four senators enveloped in the scandal could not be more different in background or qualification to sit in the Upper Chamber. Duffy and Wallin had been famous broadcasters and Conservative sympathizers, while Harb, a former Ottawa MP, had nothing on his resume but Liberal politics. Brazeau was an aboriginal politician who echoed Conservative views in his criticism of mainstream indigenous leaders. Harb had been in the Senate since 2003, Brazeau and Wallin were sworn in on the same day as Duffy in January 2009. But with the publication of police investigative documents, first relating to Duffy, Harb, and Brazeau, and later Wallin, their differences were overcome by their common involvement in the ethics crisis.

Patrick Brazeau: Young, Ambitious, Troubled

Patrick Brazeau came to the Senate by a roundabout route: through the rough and ready world of aboriginal politics. An Algonquin from the Quebec town of Maniwaki, 135 kilometres from Ottawa, Brazeau was born on Remembrance Day 1974. As a boy, he wasn't legally considered aboriginal—his grandmother had married a non-native man and was therefore banned from living on-reserve or claiming aboriginal status. When Canada's notorious Indian Act was amended in 1985, status rights were returned to aboriginal women, including Brazeau's grandmother, and Brazeau officially became Algonquin only at age eleven. In 2009, he told the Senate that, "in the eyes of the non-Aboriginal population I was too Indian, and yet in the eyes of the Indian population I was not Indian enough, because I lived off-reserve."

In 1994, after an indifferent academic career and a series of short-term jobs, Brazeau landed a position with the Congress of Aboriginal Peoples, an umbrella organization representing off-reserve First Nations and Métis people. In 2005, Brazeau became a vice-chief on the day his mother died of cancer. The following year, he won election as head of the Congress and soon adopted the title of national chief, to the irritation of the hereditary chiefs in the reserve-focused Assembly of First Nations. He quickly made headlines with harsh criticisms of the Indian Act and what he called the unfair division of resources between aboriginal people living on- and off-reserve. Brazeau wanted to get rid of reserves—"little empires created by chiefs and councils"—and redistribute their $10 billion in annual federal funding, a view quite similar to that of the Conservative Party under Stephen Harper.

Even then, in the shaky early years of the Harper government, Brazeau was thinking ahead. "I may take a stab at federal politics," he told the *Ottawa Citizen* in 2007. "I've thought about that. It may be something I'm interested in down the road." That might not have been such a great idea, given what was going on in his personal life. Word leaked that he had been missing child support payments for a boy he had fathered in the early 1990s with a woman from Quebec. He was also accused of sexual harassment through text messages and phone calls by two former staffers at the Congress. Brazeau called the allegations "100 percent false," but mediation consultants were called in.

It also emerged that, while living in Gatineau, Brazeau had been filing tax returns from an address in the Kitigan Zibi reserve that belonged to his father-in-law, Daryl Tenasco. The on-reserve address allowed him to collect an aboriginal tax exemption, compounding the benefits of the six-figure salary he was collecting at the Congress—in effect, collecting a benefit from the reserve status he so harshly condemned. Tenasco later said he wasn't aware Brazeau had been using his address for tax purposes. But tax information and sexual harassment complaints are mostly kept private, so few Canadians were aware of these potentially serious questions about Brazeau's ethics and judgment. Had they known, Brazeau would have had a very hard time getting elected, but it didn't matter—Harper put him in Parliament without the messy ritual of an election.

Harper's decision to name Brazeau to the Senate surprised many, but perhaps not Brazeau himself. As head of the Congress of Aboriginal Peoples, he had sung the praises of the Conservative prime minister. That was no coincidence. The Harper government had been increasing funding for the Congress even as it trimmed support for the more mainstream Assembly of First Nations. In 2007, Brazeau controversially supported a Conservative proposal to extend the Canadian human rights code to reserves, which had always been exempt. So Brazeau and Harper shared interests and each could help the other.

There was one problem: Brazeau wanted to stay on in his $105,000-a-year-plus-expenses job as national chief at the Congress after going into the Senate—in effect, collecting two six-figure salaries funded by the taxpayer. That wouldn't fly, however, and he ended up resigning from the Congress, probably on the frank advice of the PMO's political fixers. The day after he assumed his Senate seat, Brazeau issued a statement that would later ring hollow in the minds of many Canadians: "My goal is and has always been to serve Canada's Aboriginal peoples and my country to the best of my skills and abilities, in a manner that is accountable, responsible and transparent. I am committed to bringing this same discipline to my role as a Senator in the Parliament of Canada. To this end, I have decided to step down from my position as National Chief of the Congress of Aboriginal Peoples."

As a senator, Brazeau immediately attracted notice, most of it negative. A putative champion of downtrodden aboriginals, he was photographed tooling around Ottawa in a Porsche SUV. Word leaked that his expenses from his days at the Congress were being audited, and there was stress in his personal life. He and his wife split up in 2010, and Brazeau moved out of the matrimonial home. At first, he slept on friends' sofas and in hotels, then moved into rented accommodations in Gatineau. He soon informed the Senate administration that he was living at his father's house in Maniwaki, and began filing expense claims for a second residence, his rented townhouse in Gatineau.

Despite calling his appointment a great honour and grave responsibility, Brazeau wasn't all that keen on attending to Senate business, showing up only sporadically. Canadian Press reporter Jennifer Ditchburn revealed in 2012 that Brazeau had the worst attendance record in the Senate over the previous year. She tried to get Brazeau to respond to her story before publication, but he ignored her. After it was published, however, Brazeau went on Twitter, under his handle @TheBrazman: "while u smile Jen, others suffer. Change the D to a B in your last name and we're even! Don't mean it but needs saying." Calling a respected political reporter names in the very public forum of social media would seem, at best, unwise. Ditchburn replied: "Dear Senator: Many a person has made fun of my name and the word 'Bitch.' But never a Canadian senator. That's a first." Brazeau later offered a half-hearted apology.

Then, in early 2012, Brazeau challenged Justin Trudeau to a boxing match to support a cancer charity. After training to get in shape and some trash-talking of Trudeau, Brazeau met the celebrity politician and future prime minister in the ring on March 31 in a hotel convention room in Ottawa. His reputed black belt in karate had made Brazeau a favourite to win, but he was pummelled by the athletic Trudeau, whose wife, Sophie Gregoire, cheered madly from ringside as his mother, Margaret, winced. The referee stopped the fight in the third round after a large welt emerged under Brazeau's eye and with Trudeau pounding him relentlessly. Amid a tremendous din from the well-dressed crowd, Trudeau's red-suited trainer lifted him into the air in victory while Brazeau recovered his wits. "He didn't get me down," Brazeau said after the match. To settle a bet with Trudeau, Brazeau cut his hair and wore a Liberal sweater for a week. Despite the pugilistic humiliation, the event raised $230,000 for the Ottawa Regional Cancer Foundation.

For Brazeau, the fundraiser proved to be his career highlight. On February 6, 2013, CTV's Bob Fife broadcast details of Brazeau's claims to the aboriginal tax exemption and his use of an on-reserve address. Brazeau again took to Twitter, this time to denounce the story and to claim that Fife "has become a racist" against First Nations people. The next day, the Senate decided to send his expenses to Deloitte for review. And that wasn't all that happened on that disastrous day for Patrick Brazeau.

Shortly after 9 A.M., Gatineau city police were called to Brazeau's home after receiving two 911 calls from a woman who told police that the senator had punched her and pushed her down a set of stairs. Brazeau, who was in an upstairs bedroom with the door locked, was arrested and charged with sexual assault and domestic violence. Later, the woman would say an argument over aboriginal politics had gotten out of control. Brazeau was released, vowing to fight the charges through the legal process, but the political damage had been done. The next day, as Brazeau was appearing before a magistrate on the assault charges, Prime Minister Harper announced his expulsion from the Conservative caucus. On February 12, the Senate took the unusual step of suspending Brazeau, which didn't affect his pay but did clip his travel wings and remove his office budget until the end of the parliamentary session. A formal suspension motion said the step had been taken "to protect the dignity and reputation of the Senate and public trust and confidence in Parliament."

On top of that, Brazeau was on the hook for $49,000 in housing claims that the Senate deemed were inappropriate, and the Internal Economy Committee ordered that 20 percent of his wages be garnisheed to collect the money. With trouble on multiple fronts, police and paramedics were called to his address in October 2013 on a report of a man in trouble. It was later reported to be an undisclosed medical incident. Expelled from the Conservative caucus, deprived of his senatorial perquisites, and facing criminal charges, Brazeau seemed like a man spinning out of control. And the Mounties were closing in. On October 8, 2013, they released an application for a production order for Brazeau's bank records, which the RCMP said were needed to investigate potential criminal charges. "Based on the information and evidence gathered to date,"

Corporal Horton wrote, "I believe that Senator Brazeau has committed Fraud and Breach of Trust by filing inappropriate living and travel claims since April 2011." Sounding a plaintive note on Twitter, @TheBrazman quoted from a poem: "I'm wounded now, but I'm not slain. I'm bruised and faint they say. Just let me lie and bleed awhile; I'll not be long this way."

MAC HARB: COUNTRY SQUIRE

Mahmoud (Mac) Harb was born in Chaat, a dusty hill town of about two thousand souls located in Lebanon's turbulent Bekaa Valley, not far from the Syrian border. Seeking a better life, Harb emigrated to Canàda at age twenty to study science and electrical engineering at the University of Ottawa. After graduation, he worked for a while for Northern Telecom, and taught at Algonquin College.

He first ran for public office for a seat on the Ottawa City Council and won, serving from 1985 until resigning to run for the Liberal Party in the federal riding of Ottawa Centre in the 1988 general election. He represented Ottawa Centre for fifteen years, but wasn't known for weighty legislative achievements. Mostly, he performed the usual backbench MP duties of committee, critic, and constituency work. If his political achievements were sparse, his astuteness couldn't be disputed. He was an early caucus supporter of Jean Chrétien as Liberal leader, in defiance of the man under whose banner he was first elected, John Turner. Like some other Chrétien loyalists, his reward would come in the form of a Senate appointment when his useful time in the Commons was coming to an end.

Over his twenty-five years in the Commons and Senate, Harb seemed attracted to causes closer to the fringes of Canadian politics than the centre. He supported legislation to crack down on smoking, which was already in decline across the country. So was the East Coast seal hunt, but Harb seemed determined to stick a harpoon in that, too. His opposition to sealing was ardent, almost singular, but his achievements were slight. In March 2009, Harb tried to introduce a bill in the Senate that would have limited sealing to those with aboriginal treaty rights. It was a spectacular flop. No other senator would second the proposed legislation, a rare occurrence indeed. He tried again with another bill in 2011, which also failed. His quixotic attempts to oppose sealing, ignored in Canada, were enough to gain him fans in the radical animal rights movement. People for the Ethical Treatment of Animals honoured Harb as its "Canadian Person of the Year," a distinction he shared with film and television star Pamela Anderson.

Like Brazeau and Duffy, Harb's problem with the Senate was in not knowing where he lived. Like them, he claimed to reside outside the National Capital Region—in his case, in a farmhouse in the Ottawa Valley hamlet of Cobden, about halfway between Renfrew and Pembroke. He had purchased the building right after going to the Senate, and claiming it as his primary residence made him eligible to collect expenses for a second home in the capital. The problem was that he didn't live there. In fact, no one did. Occasional renovations had been carried out, but never enough to make the place liveable. Indeed, in November 2007, after Harb had been claiming the Cobden farmhouse as his primary residence for four years, an insurance inspector described the property as uninhabited, with "a lot of bird shit in the basement." The report on the house concluded: "house is not fully complete. Not lived in full time. Don't raise coverage anymore." The report, with a list of needed repairs, was forwarded to Harb at his address in Ottawa. In real estate sales and Senate expense claims, location is everything. And the farmhouse had a great location, a little more than one hundred kilometres from Parliament Hill, enabling Harb to collect $22,000 a year from the Senate.

Harb's case would unravel in much the same way as those of Brazeau, Wallin, and Duffy. The Liberal Harb didn't even have the fig leaf of protection provided by the Conservative dominance of the Senate, and he became the all-purpose Conservative whipping boy every time questions were raised about the other three senators. When their names came up, the Tories and their supporters invariably pointed to Harb. And so did the Internal Economy Committee. The Cobden house also became a focus of RCMP inquiries into the way Harb disposed of it. The Mounties found out that, in 2007, the property's ownership had changed in an unusual transaction involving Magdeline Teo, a little-known diplomat from the obscure but oil-rich Asian nation of Brunei. On October 12 that year, according to land registry records, Harb transferred 99.99 percent of the ownership in the house to Teo and retained 0.01 percent for himself. The transfer of ownership was odd enough, but the police also determined that, on the same day, Harb had taken out a mortgage on the property worth $177,000, apparently without disclosing the change of ownership to the lender. Harb paid rent on the Cobden property and in 2011 paid off the mortgage, but the RCMP was suspicious.

"Obtaining a mortgage on the property and then transferring 99.99 percent ownership of the property to Teo on the same day potentially put the bank at risk," according to the RCMP affidavit.

It didn't help the RCMP's perception of the transaction that Teo wouldn't cooperate with its inquiries but gave only a few perfunctory responses to emailed queries from the investigators. She said she and Harb had "a personal relationship," without giving details other than to say she and the senator "do not and never have had a business relationship or any relationship based on our professional lives." That answer seemed to mystify the Mounties, who declared in their affidavit that "the relationship between Teo and Harb has not been determined by investigators...nor is it clear why Harb maintained a 0.01 percent interest in the residence after selling it to Teo, or why she refuses to speak to investigators." It won't be easy getting her to talk, either. The Nation of Brunei, Abode of Peace, reassigned Teo to China. It's still not known why a diplomat from a wealthy sultanate would pay a Canadian senator far more than the market value for a home that was of no residential use to either of them. In May 2011, Teo and Harb sold the Cobden house to a third party.

By then Harb was on the move again, from his house on Clearview Avenue to a new high-rise condo on Prince of Wales Drive, near the Rideau River, south of Carleton University. Later that year, Harb paid $300,000 to purchase another home in the Ottawa Valley, this one at 52 Crosby Trail, in the village of Westmeath, also just outside the magic one-hundred-kilometre circle from Parliament Hill and which he then claimed as his primary residence, although the registry documents for the Westmeath house list Harb's address as his condo on Prince of Wales Drive.

Even Harb's staff didn't know where he lived. The Mounties interviewed Paula Ghaffar, the assistant who processed his expense forms, but Ghaffar wasn't able to offer much help. She said she filled out the expense claim forms based on his schedule and the receipts he provided. She then got Harb to sign the forms, and sent them along to be processed by Senate administration. She told the RCMP she didn't know where he lived. Another assistant, Alison Deakin, told the Mounties that Harb lived in Ottawa at the time of his appointment and later bought the place in Cobden. She thought he once held a family Christmas gathering there around 2003.

After Deloitte told the Internal Economy Committee that his claims were not appropriate, Harb, like the other senators whose claims had aroused suspicion, maintained that the rules were vague and subject to interpretation. The committee disagreed, saying in its Twenty-fourth Report that "it is...our conclusion that the Primary and Secondary Residence Declaration form in force during the scope of these investigations and signed by Senator Harb is amply clear, as is the purpose and intent of the guidelines to reimburse living expenses." Harb showed up at one of the committee meetings accompanied by his lawyer, former Supreme Court justice Michel Bastarache. He said he expected to be cleared by the audit into his claims. He also went to court to try to stop the Senate's efforts to collect money from him.

The secretive Harb continued to say little other than to affirm that he had done nothing wrong and to express confidence that he would be exonerated. Then, suddenly, he had a change of heart. On August 26, 2013, Harb announced he was retiring, handed over a cheque for $231,649.07, and dropped his lawsuit against the Senate. He told CBC reporter Hannah Thibedeau that he was "relieved after 28 years in public service to become a private citizen. The last couple of months have been very hard."

There was at least a little bit of consolation for the now-disgraced former MP and senator. By retiring after fifteen years as an MP and ten years as a senator, Harb was able to retain his pension and benefits for life. He could start drawing his parliamentary pension of $123,000 a year—only $12,000 less than his salary as a senator—immediately. The Canadian Taxpayers Federation estimated that Harb stood to collect $5 million if he lived to be ninety years old.

PAMELA WALLIN: CELEBRITY AND CONTROVERSY

It's fair to say that Pamela Wallin put Wadena, Saskatchewan, on the map. It's also true that Wadena put Pam Wallin on the map—the actual map of the town. Wadena's main drag, Pamela Wallin Drive, takes you to the centre of the town of 1,306. On the way in, you pass a billboard: "Welcome to Wadena, Home of Pamela Wallin." Wallin would call Wadena "the centre of the universe," but it's been a long road away and back.

Wallin got into radio as a radical young student, arguing for feminism and the newfangled concept of "women's studies," but unlike Mike Duffy, it wasn't love at first sight of a microphone. She saw radio as just another forum to discuss her political ideas. But one break led to another, and by 1975 she was on her way to Ottawa and a job on the CBC's morning radio show in the national capital. She was soon on the move again, to Toronto in 1977 and a job on CBC Radio's hottest show, *As It Happens,* with iconic host Barbara Frum. She produced a weekly segment of Ottawa political news, landed an interview with Indira Gandhi, and helped produce coverage of Elvis Presley's death. During the 1979 federal election, she travelled on a campaign plane, and she started plotting her return to Ottawa, only this time to Parliament Hill.

First, though, came gigs at the *Toronto Star* and then over to television, where she became the Ottawa reporter for CTV's *Canada AM.* Even calling West German chancellor Helmut Schmidt "Helmut Shit" didn't slow her down. Wallin would become one of the most recognizable faces on CTV and establish herself as a popular after-dinner speaker. In the 1990s, she was lured over to the CBC, where she co-hosted the ill-fated *Prime Time News* with Peter Mansbridge. When that show got revamped, Wallin was sidelined to current affairs and then eventually out the door. She bounced back with her own company, Pamela Wallin Productions, which, oddly enough, produced programs starring Pamela Wallin. She had moved on from an earlier marriage with few regrets and had become self-sufficient; something like a real life Murphy Brown, only Canadian. The girl from Wadena epitomized success for a female journalist and television personality. Over time, she was awarded a dozen honorary degrees and the Order of Canada, a distinction that eluded her old colleague, Mike Duffy. She even tried her hand at the game show biz. In 2000, she produced and hosted a pilot for a Canadian edition of *Who Wants to be a Millionaire?*

In June 2002, Wallin accepted a posting from Jean Chrétien to become the Canadian consul-general in New York, where, after the September 11, 2001, terrorist attacks, she had co-hosted a "Canada Loves New York" rally with foreign minister and Chrétien crony John Manley. Over the next four years, Wallin became the public face of Canadian diplomacy in one of the world's great cities. In addition to a generous salary and the use of a swanky midtown

Manhattan apartment, records show that Consul-General Wallin did a lot of expensive entertaining, although, in fairness, her expenses were not out of line with her predecessor's, and no one suggested there was anything inappropriate about them.

Her new connections would also lead to opportunities in the corporate world. In 2006, she joined the board of Bell Globemedia, which owned the *Globe and Mail* and CTV. In 2008, she began serving on the board of Porter Airlines. She also served as a director of Toronto wealth management firm Gluskin Sheff + Associates and on the advisory board of BMO Harris Bank. And, controversially, she was a director of Oilsands Quest Inc., which planned to develop a bitumen project in Saskatchewan. The boards all paid daily fees for attending meetings plus expenses and some provided an annual stipend. Others offered stock options or deferred share units, leading the *Toronto Star* to estimate in June 2013 that then-Senator Wallin had collected or potentially could collect about a million dollars from her directorships between 2009 and 2012.

Meanwhile, Stephen Harper was reaching out. He asked Wallin to join with John Manley and three other "eminent persons": former Mulroney chief of staff and diplomat Derek Burney, former Tory cabinet minister Jake Epp, and Paul Tellier, former privy council clerk and chief executive of Canadian National Railways. They were to report on what Canada's future role should be in Afghanistan. In January 2008, the panel recommended strengthened diplomatic, military, and economic measures, and said Canada should emphasize training local police and the Afghan National Army to take over combat duties in that broken country.

From broadcaster to diplomat to businesswoman, Wallin's life was to take another turn in December 2008, when Harper called again, this time to ask her to join the Senate and the Conservative caucus. Wallin thought it over for a few days and said yes; it would be an opportunity to serve her country, she claimed later. Plus, being a senator wouldn't get in the way of her other activities, corporate or otherwise. She planned to be what she called "an activist senator."

She showed up to be sworn to office in the Red Chamber in January 2009 with Duffy, Brazeau, and fifteen others Harper had summoned.

Wallin was just as famous coming from Wadena as Duffy was coming from Charlottetown. But, in common with Duffy, she hadn't spent much time in the old hometown. That would become relevant when people started questioning her expense claims and where the senator from Saskatchewan actually lived. She owned a place in Ottawa until 2011, and stayed in hotels after that. She still owned a condo in Toronto and co-owned a house in Wadena with her sister. She had a co-op studio apartment in midtown Manhattan and a cabin at Fishing Lake, near Wadena. With corporate boards, volunteering, her role as chancellor of the University of Guelph, speaking engagements, and the Senate, she was constantly on the go. "I live in airplanes," she was fond of saying. That would make it harder to determine where she actually resided; it also made her travel expenses seem high, even by the permissive standards of the Senate.

As with Duffy, she initially brushed off the doubters. She told the *Midtown Post*, a local newspaper in her Toronto neighbourhood, that only one person, a Saskatchewan academic, had ever raised the issue of whether or not her peripatetic lifestyle undermined her claim to represent the province in the Senate. "Nobody that I've spoken to, save the one gentleman, has raised any concerns about whether or not I'm an appropriate representative of the province," Wallin said in the 2012 interview. "I've spent most of my life as the unofficial ambassador of Saskatchewan regardless of where I've been and what I've been doing."

Wallin took the Senate transition in stride. In her maiden speech, on February 10, 2009, she signalled the issues she would pursue: trade and foreign relations, promotion of Saskatchewan, and like Duffy, her fervent support for the leadership of Harper and the Conservative Party. Like Duffy, Wallin became a reliable Conservative campaigner. Audit documents suggest she travelled frequently to party functions and campaigned for provincial Tories in Ontario and for federal Conservatives in Saskatchewan. Like Duffy, she gave speeches and posed for pictures with admiring crowds who wanted to meet the famous broadcaster-diplomat-senator. And like Duffy, she got some of her expenses for party businesses mixed up with those of her official senatorial affairs.

In early spring 2013, Wallin's name started to crop up in news stories about Senate expenses. Hers seemed high, topping $300,000 over the two years straddling the period that included the 2011 general election. She spent $13,000 on travel in a month when the Senate wasn't even sitting. Then it emerged that some of the trips home to Wadena had gone via Toronto, sometimes with layovers of several days at the condo. Was that a legitimate part of the trip to Saskatchewan? And if she was spending so much time in Ottawa and Toronto, did she really live in the province she was supposed to represent?

Wallin said she would defend the expenses and if any were found to be offside, she'd do the right thing. On February 7, the same day Brazeau was arrested for domestic assault in Gatineau and a day before Deloitte was hired to go over the Senate books, Wallin told the CBC that she was fully entitled to sit in the Senate. "I am in compliance with the constitutional requirements to serve as a senator," she said. "I own property in Saskatchewan and my home is in Saskatchewan." But she would not say if she had the required proofs of residency: a driver's licence, a provincial health card, proof of voting in a Saskatchewan riding, or her residence of record for tax purposes.

Her statement failed to stop the questions. As the story spread in the media, Wallin decided on a dramatic next move. On February 13, in a *Globe and Mail* op-ed, she defended her travel, her living arrangements, and her right to sit in the Senate. "Wadena is where I reside in my home province," she wrote. She had spent 194 days in Saskatchewan in 2012, and 94 days in Ottawa. Yes, she had a condo in Toronto, but she was really from Saskatchewan—a sign in Wadena said so. She also defended her travel expenses, saying she had never exceeded the total allotted to each senator. As to her attendance, which had also been questioned, she said she had never been docked pay for missing time.

The piece was meant to put aside the questions, and it had a positive impact at least on the prime minister. The next day, Harper told the Commons that, from what he could see, she had no problem. The prime minister's support galvanized Conservatives to Wallin's cause, albeit briefly. Government House leader Peter Van Loan, who would later praise Duffy's "leadership" for paying back his expenses, said "we expect parliamentarians to maintain a residence in their home region and in Ottawa. That is exactly what Senator Wallin has done." He added there was "nothing out of the ordinary" about her claims.

What wasn't publicly known was that Wallin had already been talking to Deloitte's auditors, even though the Senate had not linked her name publicly to the review. We know now that Wallin's expenses were among the first to raise a red flag in the auditor general's review, released in June 2012, which suggests that top Senate Conservatives knew about her problems as far back as that summer. Wallin said later that, somewhere in the process, Senator Tkachuk had advised her to "clean up" her digital calendar by including only entries related to her expense claims. Eventually, almost four hundred entries were changed, a fact some people found suspicious.

Wallin indicated she was cooperating with the review. "I certainly did willingly meet with a representative of Deloitte," she said on February 13, the same day Harper defended her in the Commons. "I have answered all questions and have provided all the necessary information regarding claims," but she had not paid back any money, nor had she been asked to do so. The next day, Tkachuk admitted that Wallin's expenses had been examined in the first of several "random" audits by the Internal Economy Committee following the auditor general's report. "That's why Senator Wallin was referred...and she was referred well before this issue [of other senators' expenses] came up. She was Number One," said Tkachuk. The Senate knew there were issues with Wallin's expenses but, true to form, didn't say a thing to the public.

As Parliament and the media seethed with new revelations about Duffy, Harb, and Brazeau, Wallin's case flew mostly under the radar. Robert Fife's story on May 14 linking Duffy's repayment to Nigel Wright forced Duffy out of the Conservative caucus the next day. On May 17, Wallin issued a statement saying she had cooperated with the audits, but since the matter was still unresolved, she would step aside for the time being. "I have been involved in the external audit process since December 2012 and I have been co-operating fully and willingly with the auditors," the statement read. "I have met with the auditors, answered all the questions and provided all requested documentation. I had anticipated that the audit process would be complete by now but given that it continues, I have decided to recuse myself from the Conservative Caucus and I will have no further comment until the audit process is complete."

It was an odd choice of words, with "recuse myself" suggesting a conflict of interest. Senator LeBreton issued a brief statement that Wallin would later endow with great meaning. Instead of saying Wallin had "recused" herself, LeBreton used a more pejorative term: "Senator Wallin has informed me that she has resigned from Caucus to sit as an independent." There was no defence of the senator and no explanation. LeBreton's brief comment suggested that the Conservatives no longer wanted to talk about their star senator; they just wanted her gone. A month later, Wallin told the CBC's Peter Mansbridge that she had been given an hour to resign from the caucus or face expulsion. "It was clear to me that they wanted me out," she said. "That was, a phone call comes and you're given an hour to resign or you'll be fired, for lack of a better word." She said the calls came from both the Prime Minister's Office and the "leadership in the Senate," which is at odds with LeBreton's statement that Wallin informed her of the decision, not the other way around. Six months later, Wallin would reveal that the calls came from Harper's principal secretary, Ray Novak, and from LeBreton, the same two who had ordered Duffy to resign.

In the interview with Mansbridge, Wallin managed to sound both contrite and defiant. "I'm very sorry, obviously, that I've caused all of this grief for my family, and my friends and my fellow parliamentarians," she told her former colleague. "And I think taxpayers have a right to know." But it was frustrating that the matter was taking so long to resolve. "It isn't over and that's exactly the problem. We were first told we'd have the result in January, then in February, and then in April and then, you know, now maybe the middle of the summer," which is pretty much how it turned out. She denied she had mixed Senate and Conservative Party business, and blamed the problems, yet again, on poor bookkeeping and unclear rules.

As to her residence, Wallin was unequivocal. "We have gone through this. The Senate has signed off on it. Even the Prime Minister sort of said, you meet the requirements. It's a very simple test. You know, do you own $4,000 worth of property in the province that you represent? You declare your primary residence in the province you represent. It's a pretty straightforward thing." She also denied double-billing for party events, and maintained she "did very little direct party work" other than campaigning for Saskatchewan Conservative candidates. Wallin also complained about the media coverage. "I've had camera crews outside the old folks' home in Wadena where my mother who has dementia lives," she complained. "This is nuts."

Wallin also got off a shot at Duffy and the help he got from Wright to repay his expenses. Mansbridge asked whether there had been any discussion with Wright about getting help to make the repayment. "No. No, no, no," she said. "It would have never been discussed....These are my mistakes and I will pay my bills. I have worked every single day of my life and I will continue to do that in one way or another and I have always paid my own bills. Period. Full stop. He did not offer. I did not ask. It was not accepted. My money."

By the time the Deloitte auditors got through with their investigation, the $38,000 she had repaid in the spring would multiply to $138,969. In September, the Senate imposed a deadline to repay the money or have it deducted from her wages. A few days later, it was revealed that she had sold her Manhattan co-op apartment. The selling price was $349,000, $30,000 less than she had paid for it in 2005. For Pamela Wallin, the audit process had been "flawed and unfair." It was also expensive.

Perhaps worse, her political friends were no longer standing by her. Prime Minister Harper brandished the verbal equivalent of a barge pole when he was asked about it in the Commons on May 28. "Senator Wallin has chosen to step outside the Conservative caucus until such time as that audit report and the matters that may or may not be raised in it are resolved." He was asked a week later whether he had seen the Wallin audit, and blandly responded: "I am aware that the audit has taken considerable time, and considerable issues remain unresolved. Beyond that, I am not aware of any particulars."

A few weeks later, Wallin said she had paid back $138,969, including the $38,000 she had repaid earlier in the year. She issued a statement saying she disagreed with Deloitte and the Senate, but didn't want to get into "a protracted legal debate about the matter." She insisted she had been railroaded: "I was not treated fairly by the Deloitte review, which was not conducted in accordance with generally accepted accounting principles, nor have I been treated fairly by the Senate Committee. Evidence that casts doubt on the correctness of the amounts owing was either ignored or disregarded during the review." Accusing the Senate of falling prey to "a lynch mob mentality," she made it clear she was staying put. "I am disappointed and angry about the way in which this matter was handled, and any implication that I behaved dishonestly," she said. "I have not done anything wrong. I am not guilty of any misconduct. Accordingly I will not resign as a senator. I will continue to act for the people of Saskatchewan and Canada, fulfilling the duties of a senator that have been entrusted to me."

But repayment didn't end the affair for Senator Wallin. The RCMP was still investigating, and there was no way to predict where that would go.

PROJECT AMBLE

Senator Mike Duffy,...I believe[,] has committed offenses of Breach of Trust and Frauds on the Government.

— CORPORAL GREG HORTON, RCMP NATIONAL DIVISION

AS REVELATIONS EMERGED ABOUT THE FOUR EMBATTLED SENATORS, police started opening files, saving media reports, and compiling Internet links to the Senate's rules and regulations. The spring of 2013 turned into summer as the team of special investigators in one of the most sensitive units of the RCMP kept building the collection. The Senate issue had burned white-hot into the spring sitting of Parliament, and the RCMP's federal fraud unit had good reasons to be suspicious about what was going on in the Red Chamber. But the Mounties wanted evidence, and for that, they would need warrants, formally known as production orders.

On July 4, the first batch of court documents the RCMP filed seeking production orders in the Senate scandal came to light, and they revealed a lot about what had been going on away from the predictable fury of the Commons and the hubbub in the media. For the first time, the public became aware, from named, credible sources, just how serious the allegations were against Senator Mike Duffy. The potential consequences went beyond getting his knuckles rapped by the Senate for sloppy accounting or even being forced out of the Conservative caucus. Duffy had cast the repayment as his own decision, saying it was made to remove a distraction from the good work he and the Harper government were otherwise doing. We now know that Duffy had been subjected to intense pressure to leave the caucus, and was even given a deadline by Senator Marjory LeBreton and Ray Novak, Harper's longest-serving aide and Nigel Wright's replacement as chief of staff in the PMO.

Beyond the inevitable political fallout for the PMO and for Duffy, the RCMP affidavits laid out a serious criminal case against the senator, based on three distinct allegations of fraud and breach of trust. Any of the three could result in jail time, were Duffy or perhaps Wright to be charged, tried, and convicted. The documents specified the RCMP's grounds for alleging wrongdoing, raised serious questions about the deal with Wright and his cheque, and laid out the connections among Duffy, Conservative Fund Canada, the PMO, and the senior Conservatives on the Senate's Internal Economy Committee. Clearly, the warrant applications showed that the RCMP was not taking the Senate case lightly.

Investigators reviewed Duffy's expense claims and Deloitte's interpretation of what they meant, which led to the allegation of a breach of trust. They looked at the apparently unwritten agreements made to secure Wright's cheque, which they considered a potential fraud on the government. Because of that probable cause, they had embarked on a thorough investigation, code-named Project Amble, of possible criminal wrongdoing. The investigation wasn't based on calls from the Opposition parties, the Senate, or the media, but on straight-ahead police work initiated by the Mounties themselves. The documents also revealed they had been on the case longer than anyone suspected—beavering away since March, when reports surfaced that the Senate was referring expense claims by Duffy, Harb, and Brazeau to Deloitte for external review, and well before the Senate got around on May 28 to voting on whether to refer the Duffy matter to the police. In the two months before the Deloitte results were made public, RCMP investigators gathered information from the auditor general's conclusions, media reports, and available

Senate documents. For two months, they considered whether a Canadian senator and the prime minister's chief of staff had made an agreement that constituted a fraud on the federal government.

Investigators from Project Amble had studied the Senate's rules and reports, obtained Duffy's driver's licence and car registration information through the Canadian Police Information Centre database, and begun preliminary interviews with potential witnesses. They were taking notes when Duffy said publicly in March that he had repaid more than $90,000 in expense claims. They began to construct a case based on a pattern of questionable expense claims, and had patiently awaited the Deloitte reports. In turn, the Deloitte reports caused the Mounties to expand their enquiries and begin sketching out the affidavits that would get them their search warrants. They needed reliable information, but they had to find ways to obtain it without offending Parliamentary privilege. The affidavits filed in support of their production order request also suggested they planned to come back for more evidence later. Perhaps most significantly, the affidavits raised questions about the roles of some of those closest to the prime minister and, ultimately, about the extent of Harper's knowledge of what had gone on in the Duffy-Wright deal.

The main affidavit was filed under the name of twenty-one-year veteran RCMP corporal Greg Horton, of the Sensitive and International Investigations unit at the recently created National Division. Commanded by Superintendent Biagio Carrese, one of the RCMP's most senior investigators and a specialist in fraud and money laundering, the unit's job is "safeguarding Canada's political, economic and social integrity through investigations that focus on corruption and criminality here and abroad." The National Division was created as part of a wide-ranging reorganization of the RCMP, which had been dealing with its own problems in the past few years. Internal complaints by female officers of harassment and sexual intimidation, mismanagement of the RCMP pension scheme, and the Taser killing of Robert Dziekanski in the Vancouver airport and its subsequent cover-up were symptoms of rot within the storied force. Commissioners came and went, without changing hidebound attitudes among the senior leadership.

In November 2011, a new commissioner, Bob Paulson, had been appointed from the ranks, and he set about restructuring the RCMP to better reflect its current environment and the expectations of the Canadian public. He had a lot to prove if he was to win back traditional public esteem for the Mounties, and the National Division was a central element of that reform. It included experts on everything from commercial crime and government corruption to bodyguards and special intelligence officers. The prime minister's personal protection team is operated by National Division. Given their obvious need to demonstrate political impartiality, National Division investigators were motivated to be as thorough as they could be—indeed, they were specially trained to deal with investigations that might have a political dimension. To add expertise on the accounting side, the unit seconded Mark Grenon, a Department of Public Works expert on investigative and forensic accounting and a certified fraud examiner. Project Amble was set up to go deep, and Duffy would get no breaks from them.

Corporal Horton's first set of documents, dated June 24, 2013, and technically an "information to obtain a production order," alleged two types of wrongdoing. First, that Duffy "did commit a breach of trust in connection with the duties of his office by filing inappropriate expense claims." If true, this would contravene section 122 of the Criminal Code, which deals with breach of trust by public officials. The section is not mere window dressing: "Every official who, in connection with the duties of his office, commits fraud or a breach of trust is guilty of an indictable offence and liable to imprisonment for a term not exceeding five years." The second allegation, which falls under the category of "frauds on the government," was that Duffy "for his own benefit did...accept an advantage or benefit of money ($90,124.27) from Nigel Wright, a person having dealings with the Government of Canada." That section of the Criminal Code specifies that it is an offence if "an official or employee of the government, directly or indirectly demands, accepts or offers or agrees to accept from a person who has dealings with the government a commission, reward, advantage or benefit of any kind for themselves or another person, unless they have the consent in writing of the head of the branch of government that employs them or of which they are an official." The head of that branch is Stephen Harper. He was to say, repeatedly and without equivocation, that he never gave any such consent.

Put simply, police go to court to obtain production orders and search warrants when they believe a crime has been committed and when they feel they know where evidence can be found. Project Amble was looking for documents and first-person testimony, but legally, it's no different than a warrant to look for illegal drugs or stolen goods—they need a judge's approval. In this case, the evidence included a lot of documentation detailing Duffy's declarations about his primary and secondary residences going back to his appointment just before Christmas 2008 up to June 1, 2013. The investigators also wanted all his travel expense claim forms, supporting receipts, and other travel records for that four-and-a-half-year period. They wanted a true copy of the Twenty-second Report of the Standing Committee on Internal Economy, Budgets and Administration, the report on Duffy's expenses. And they wanted the billing statements for Duffy's Senate-issued American Express card along with his cell-phone billings, all going back to his first days as a senator. They asked for his Senate attendance records, copies of the documents Duffy submitted to back up his residence claims, a copy of the Senate's electronic calendar showing Duffy's travel and expense claims, an electronic report summarizing all the payments made to Duffy, and all draft reports of the Internal Economy Committee relating to Duffy. And they wanted a copy of the cheque issued to the Receiver General for Canada from the senator in the amount of $90,172.24.

Corporal Horton's affidavit summarized the police case against Duffy and potentially against Wright. It didn't prove any wrongdoing; it was part of the evidence collection process that is the bedrock of police work. But in laying out the case, the affidavits shed light on how seriously the RCMP was taking the allegations that had been roiling Parliament and the national media for months. They made it clear that the RCMP had committed people and resources to the investigation; along with Horton, the application mentioned at least three other RCMP investigators, one holding the rank of superintendent, who were working on the case. Even more significant, the anti-corruption unit's involvement suggested that the case had gone beyond Parliament and its backroom deals to an unpredictable situation governed by police priorities, not political ones.

Horton certified that the RCMP needed documents and information "in relation to an RCMP investigation into the activities of Senator Mike Duffy, whom I believe has committed offenses of Breach of Trust and Frauds on the Government. These offenses are in relation to travel and housing expense claims, submitted in relation to his duties as a Canadian Senator, and in relation to accepting a $90,000 gift to pay back those expenses." Horton laid out the particulars, which portrayed Duffy as a persistent and determined manipulator of the Senate's expense account system and of the rules governing public officials, and suggested that the RCMP had gathered enough evidence to conclude that a crime might have been committed and a full-scale investigation was merited. A key element in the case would be the alleged pattern of behaviour Duffy demonstrated almost from the day he was sworn in as a senator in early 2009. The affidavits painted a picture of a public office holder working the system every way he could.

I believe that Senator Duffy has demonstrated a pattern of filing fraudulent expense claims. He maintains that his primary residence is in PEI so that he can collect housing and travel allowances from the Senate, however uses his Ottawa residence as his primary residence when convenient, such as when dealing with OHIP so that he can obtain medical coverage in Ontario. He has submitted expense claims for Senate business to cover travel costs during the Federal election campaign and filed per diem claims for being in Ottawa for Senate business on days when he was actually campaigning in other parts of the country. He has also submitted expense claims for being in Ottawa on Senate business, on days when he was actually in Florida or elsewhere. Once this matter became the focus of an independent audit, Duffy publicly announced that he paid back $90,000, before the results of the audit were even known. Only later was it revealed that Nigel Wright gave $90,000 to Duffy to cover the cost of the repayment.

In the background of all of this was the Conservatives' fear of the inevitable political fallout from a Harper Senate appointee and some of the prime minister's closest aides becoming mired in an unseemly affair over expense claims. Worry about the Deloitte audit seemed to be at the root of how both Duffy and the Conservative Party reacted to the increasing pressure. The timing suggested strongly that news of a third-party review had set off negotiations between senators Duffy and Gerstein about potential support from Conservative Fund Canada. The affidavit alleged that the $90,000 payment from Wright was arranged only as the Senate's own internal review had played itself out and when it became known that Duffy's, Harb's, and Brazeau's expenses were all being audited by an independent third party, Deloitte. This was a crucial factor for the RCMP. Although the affidavit didn't put it that way, the implication was clear: the Mounties suspected that money changed hands between public officials who were involved in or had knowledge of wrongdoing by a parliamentarian, and that it was exchanged to ensure silence. For the Conservative Party, it was all about the price of that silence. Wright's lawyers, Patrick McCann and Peter Mantas, told the RCMP that Senator Gerstein had been approached and seemed ready to approve about $32,000 for the Duffy bailout from Conservative Fund Canada, but had backed off when the $90,000 figure emerged.

Superintendent Carrese and at least one other Mountie met with McCann and Mantas on June 19 "to discuss the circumstances under which any future interview with Mr. Wright might take place"— in other words, a meeting to set up a meeting. The police wanted to hear what Wright had to say, and no doubt Wright's lawyers wanted to find out as much as they could about what the Mounties knew and where the case was going. Wright's representatives were heavy guns. Peter Mantas is a top litigation expert at Fasken Martineau who had already taken on the Harper government in a suit launched by former cabinet minister Helena Guergis. She had been drummed out of the Harper cabinet and the Conservative Party in 2010 over vague but tawdry-sounding allegations, mainly connected to her husband's business connections. Patrick F. D. McCann, a partner in McCann & Lyttle, is one of the top criminal defence lawyers in Canada, having fought many high-profile cases and public inquiries. He has acted for the defence in some sixty homicide cases.

The RCMP officers told McCann and Mantas that they were investigating both the $90,000 payment by Duffy and Wright's cheque to the senator, "that both Wright and Duffy were subject of that investigation, and that a decision on whether to interview Wright as a suspect or witness had not been made." The Mounties clearly saw Wright as a potential suspect, with the implication that it was in his best interests to cooperate.

Mantas and McCann then related the Nigel Wright version of the story, which contained crucial information not previously made public. Wright's job as chief of staff to the prime minister, as interpreted by the lawyers, "was to manage the Conservative party, part of which was to deal with matters that could cause embarrassment." According to the lawyers, Wright believed Duffy should pay back the money he had claimed for the secondary residence in Ottawa and told him so. But Duffy said he didn't have the money to pay it, and was worried that if he didn't claim the cottage on Friendly Lane as his primary home he'd be declared ineligible to sit in the Senate. The affidavits tied the Conservative Party to Duffy's predicament and the attempt to find a solution. Wright offered to put up the cash himself, "believing it was the proper ethical decision that taxpayers should not be out that amount of money."

As to documentary evidence, the lawyers insisted there was no written contract between Wright and Duffy. They did, however, make a deeply significant admission to the Mounties. "Wright asked for two conditions from Duffy," the affidavit said: "pay back the money right away" and "stop talking to the media about it." The apparent quid pro quo got the Mounties' full attention, because it implied a secret deal between two government officials: money in exchange for prompt repayment and silence. Duffy evidently had agreed to the conditions, because Wright obtained the details about how much he owed, and on March 25 sent a bank draft for $90,172.24 to Duffy's lawyer, Janice Payne, of the Ottawa firm of Nelligan O'Brien Payne. Mantas and McCann insisted that Wright made the payment on his own initiative and "received no direction from anyone to make the offer," adding that "Wright and Duffy knew each other, but were not friends." They confirmed that Duffy was the only senator under investigation to whom Wright offered financial help. Finally, the lawyers said Wright didn't expect to get any of the money back.

Much of what Mantas and McCann told the Mounties proved to be damaging to Duffy's carefully nurtured image, to his legal status, and to the political fortunes of the Harper government. The $90,000 payment alone was bad enough, but there was also the question of who knew what was going on between the senator and Wright. According to his lawyers, Wright said, "some people within the PMO were aware of the arrangement, but Prime Minister Harper was not," and they identified those people as David van Hemmen, Wright's assistant, PMO lawyer Benjamin Perrin, and Chris Woodcock, the director of issues management, along with Senator Irving Gerstein. This, too, would become a much-repeated Conservative talking point when attention eventually turned to Harper: that other people might have known, but the prime minister was kept entirely in the dark. Harper himself would say that many times, gradually escalating the point until, by the fall, he was accusing Wright of lying to him. Wright's lawyers told the RCMP that they "were not aware" of any link between Wright's payment to Duffy and the changes senators David Tkachuk and Carolyn Stewart Olsen had made to the Twenty-second Report, the changes that Duffy had demanded so that the Senate would "go easy" on him.

The Twenty-second Report of the Internal Economy Committee, or Senate Report 22 as it was described in the affidavits, is central to the RCMP case involving Duffy and Wright. It gave rise to the investigators' strong suspicion that ranking Conservatives had altered the report at the last minute to remove critical references to Duffy—in other words, to go easy on him. How that came about is a tangled story all its own and one that didn't happen quickly. The auditor general's report was released on June 13, 2012, but it wasn't until November 21 that the committee started looking into Patrick Brazeau's expense claims for a secondary residence in the Ottawa area. A couple of weeks later, Duffy's name got dragged into the mix. On December 6, the committee decided to consider Senator Mac Harb's expenses as well and to undertake a much broader review of similar expense claims by senators.

Bob Fife's May 14 CTV story linking Duffy, the repayment, and Wright started investigators focusing on whether there had been an earlier version of Senate Report 22, one that might have been much harder on Duffy had it not been for the intervention of Tkachuk and Stewart Olsen. The CTV story led to Wright's resignation from the PMO and, according to the RCMP, "further revelation that there was in fact an initial or draft Senate Report 22 which was more critical of Duffy. The final Senate report however was less critical of Duffy, which lends credence to the media reports, that there was a deal in place." The affidavits also made it clear that Tkachuk and Stewart Olsen weren't keen to explain their roles in the preparation of Senate Report 22. Tkachuk pleaded illness, but the Mounties interviewed Stewart Olsen on June 21. She said several versions of the report had been considered during meetings held on May 7, 8, and 9, when it was tabled, but claimed she didn't remember what changes had been made on what days. She admitted that "she and Senator Tkachuk discussed the report outside of the sub-committee meetings," but didn't say what they discussed. The Mounties weren't entirely convinced.

Senator George Furey, the only non-Conservative on the Internal Economy Committee's three-person steering committee, had a better memory of the events. He told the investigators that the first draft of the report "contained three main criticisms of Duffy." The steering committee made some changes to the report on that day. When they met the next day, according to the RCMP, "Tkachuk proposed that they remove two of the three criticisms. Furey objected, but was the minority on the committee and Stewart Olsen agreed with Tkachuk. The report was amended." A day later, May 9, the full committee was given the report, "at which time the Conservative majority removed the third and final criticism of Duffy from the report." Again Furey protested, but it was a done deal. Tkachuk moved to present the report to the full Senate, noting even then that "the process that we have gone through has raised serious questions in the media and among Canadians about our institution and our ability to govern our own activities. This was a crisis, pure and simple." He then presented the report on Duffy; the Twenty-third Report, on Brazeau; the Twenty-fourth, on Harb; and the reviews from Deloitte. Furey rose in the Senate to say that Tkachuk had presented the reports as if they were unanimous, but that he had dissented on some of the changes. He didn't go into detail, at least not that day and not in front of the full Senate.

The Mounties used public reports and information they had gathered from interviews to conclude that Wright and Tkachuk had been in contact during the audit of Duffy's expenses. As Horton's affidavit noted, "Tkachuk has also been in contact with Duffy during the audit process and in fact informed him of some of the audit findings such as identification of the NCR [National Capital Region] per diem claims for days spent in Florida, prior to Deloitte filing a written report," although "Tkachuk has publicly denied any influence was put on him about what would be written in the Senate Report 22." The next line in the affidavit is a ripper: "Based on all of the information set out above, I believe that there was an agreement between Duffy and Wright involving repayment of the $90,000 and a Senate Report that would not be critical of him, constituting an offence of Frauds on the Government. Wright's own lawyers partially confirm this by saying that Wright had two conditions of Duffy in return for the money, to pay it immediately and stop talking to the media about it."

Duffy had already stopped talking to the auditors. His lawyer, Janice Payne, wrote to Deloitte on May 26 noting that her client had made the repayment and, "in the circumstances, the review that Deloitte has been asked to undertake is now unnecessary. The considerable time required for Senator Duffy to compile the extensive information and documentation required of him by Deloitte as well as his participation in the review of that material, to say nothing of the public expense involved in the same, is no longer needed."

The original report also shot down Duffy's public claims that the Senate's expense rules and forms were unclear. Secondary residence expenses can be claimed only if a senator lives "more than 100 kilometres from Parliament Hill" and that "your Subcommittee considers this language to be unambiguous, and plainly, if a Senator resides primarily in the NCR, he or she should not be claiming living expenses for the NCR." To that point, the original Twenty-second Report found that "Senator Duffy's travel patterns were consistently Ottawa-PEI-Ottawa, demonstrating that Ottawa was his primary or default location." It noted that "Senator Duffy owns a residence in PEI and spends considerable time there, in particular during the summer months," but the fact he continued to live in Ottawa ran counter to his claims that the place in Cavendish was his primary residence.

With pressure from the media and the public building almost every day, the secretive Internal Economy Committee finally was flushed into the open with a public meeting on May 29. It reviewed Deloitte's findings about Duffy's claims and recommended that the committee "be authorized to refer such documents, as it considers appropriate, to the proper authorities for the purposes of the investigation." As we've seen from the affidavits, the proper authorities—namely, the RCMP—were already on the trail.

Investigators went well beyond the location of senators' residences and their travel and expense claims. They also went after election spending reports by at least twelve Conservative candidates for whom Duffy had campaigned in the run-up to the 2011 general election: MPs Gerald Keddy, Greg Kerr, John Carmichael, Robert Goguen, Tilly O'Neill Gordon, Rodney Weston, Scott Armstrong, Wladyslaw Lizon, and Natural Resources Minister Joe Oliver, and unsuccessful candidates David Morse, Gin Siow, and Sandy Lee. The Mounties also obtained a DVD from the Senate containing electronic copies of Duffy's expense claims, as well as his declarations of primary and secondary residences and other documents. It was provided to Project Amble without a warrant by the Senate's deputy law clerk, and included a letter dated June 7 from Senate clerk Gary O'Brien to Superintendent Carrese. From that information, it became clear that the RCMP was also investigating Senator Mac Harb. The hunt was widening, with unpredictable results for all concerned. However, it's one thing to launch an investigation and quite another to obtain a conviction on a criminal charge. In fact, some experts were already saying that it was unlikely any charges would stick, given the Senate's unique rules and the strict letter of the law on criminal matters.

Rob Walsh is a former law clerk of Parliament and quite possibly Canada's leading expert on the laws affecting parliamentarians. For thirteen years he advised Parliament on legislation and served as its chief legal counsel. He told the author that prosecutors would have a hard time making charges stick against Wright because as the PMO chief of staff, he didn't receive a direct benefit from bailing out Duffy. Walsh's opinion was that the sections of the Criminal Code cited in the RCMP affidavits didn't necessarily apply, because Wright derived no personal gain from bailing out Duffy. Although the transaction certainly looked bad for having "all the trappings of a bribe," it was quite a different matter to prove that in court. The public might have made up its mind, but Walsh suggested that the RCMP would need expert legal advice of its own on how to proceed with the case. Police and prosecutors would have to prove the transaction was carried out for "corrupt purposes," a definition which is open to interpretation by the courts. He disputed, as Wright and Duffy would, whether Wright obtained any benefit from paying Duffy's expenses. There might have been a potential benefit to the Conservative Party had the exchange remained secret, but that would be a difficult matter for a court to sort out. "It blurs the line between a criminal transaction and a political transaction," Walsh said.

The expenses and residency claims were a different matter. Walsh suggested the Raymond Lavigne case was similar to the allegations against Duffy. Lavigne had blamed unclear Senate rules and procedures for his expense account problems, but the courts rejected that argument for the simple reason that he should have known that what he was doing was wrong. Lavigne was convicted of fraud for abusing his Senate expenses, and "the courts might well decide that the Lavigne case does set an important precedent." The courts "might say 'you could have sought clarity on the rules, you should have asked questions'."

Yet, any case would be shaky, Walsh said, if it is built on the findings of the Senate's auditors or on reports commissioned for Parliament, such as those of Deloitte into senatorial spending. Law and tradition dating back to the 1689 Bill of Rights prevent the Crown or its courts from using parliamentary speech as evidence in court proceedings. That's why they call it "parliamentary privilege." It is the same constitutional measure that guarantees Parliament and all its individual members the right to unrestricted free speech in debates, committees, and reports. They can't be sued for what they say in either chamber of Parliament, and it's why parliamentarians often won't repeat outside the Commons allegations they made a few minutes earlier inside it. In the criminal investigation of the senators, the RCMP would be able to use what it learned from the Senate and Deloitte process only as starting points. Still, common sense has to enter the picture somewhere. In the Senate, "you have unclear rules but sophisticated players," Walsh says, which makes some of the excuses seem lame at best. "The concept of primary and secondary residences is pretty clear."

Expense and residency claims weren't the only tracks the hunters at Project Amble were following. In August 2013, the RCMP filed requests for production orders for Duffy's personal banking and credit card records, claiming Duffy had used at least three credit cards in addition to his Senate American Express card. The Mounties needed the bank records to show whether or not the expenses Duffy had claimed actually had been paid into his accounts.

In October, Corporal Horton was back with more requests for documentation, this time on two accounts at the Bank of Nova Scotia. The warrants sought information about a mysterious series of payments Duffy's office made to his former CTV colleague, Gerald Donohue, who admitted to the RCMP that he had "produced no tangible work product for Duffy," according to an affidavit filed on October 8. That suggested to Horton that the senator had "used his office for a dishonest purpose, other than the public good. In doing so, he committed Breach of Trust and Fraud." Donohue told the investigators that he "never funnelled any of the money back to Duffy," but the transactions were suspicious enough that the Mounties alleged that Duffy "did by deceit, falsehood or other fraudulent means defraud the Senate of Canada of $64,916.50 by awarding consulting contracts for little or no value for service, contrary to section 380 (1) of the Criminal Code."

In his affidavit, Horton said the lack of tangible results suggested Donohue "was awarded contracts and paid an inflated rate for the type of service purportedly provided." There had been talk of advice to Duffy on website design, although Donohue told the Mounties he had never seen Duffy's site. Further, Horton alleged, Gerald Donohue didn't own a consulting business, he lacked any experience as a government consultant, his contracts and invoices were vague, he received large lump-sum payments with little explanation or measurable service, and his inflated hourly rate of $200 had been selected by Duffy.

Maple Ridge Media was the biggest recipient of funds from Duffy's office budget, but not the only one. The senator also purchased consulting work from three prominent Prince Edward Island Conservatives. Teresa Wright reported in the *Guardian* that the RCMP had spoken to Wayne Hooper, Jason Lee, and Peter McQuaid about their services to the senator. All ran legitimate consulting firms and had provided services at fees much lower than those paid to Maple Ridge Media. All were reliable Conservatives. Hooper and McQuaid had both worked for former Tory premier Pat Binns, now a Conservative senator. Hooper was appointed to a federal job by the Harper Conservatives and got tangled up in accusations of political hiring at the Atlantic Canada Opportunities Agency. Lee is the son of former Tory premier Jim Lee and, according to Wright's story in the *Guardian*, a fundraiser for the provincial party.

It was clear that the most recent crop of RCMP affidavits suggested new legal troubles for Senator Duffy. It was also clear that the release of the affidavits was going to produce political fallout for the Harper government. In the Commons, the Opposition parties used them to attack the government's handling of the scandal, further damaging the Conservatives' claim to be the party that would clean up Ottawa. Questions were raised about the ethical standards of more senators, including Harper's trio, Tkachuk, Stewart Olsen, and LeBreton. Just what was their role in the whitewashing of Senate Report 22? Had they pressured Duffy or others to walk the plank to protect the prime minister? Bob Fife's May 14 story linking Duffy's repayment to Wright had serious potential consequences for the prime minister's office. The Conservatives repeatedly denied that Harper knew anything about Wright's decision to cut the cheque, but many people found that explanation a bit too tidy. Stephen Harper was known as a micro-manager. Had he really stayed out of the worst ethical scandal to face his government?

ALL THE PRIME MINISTER'S MEN

The prime minister was not aware of the payment.

— OFFICIAL STATEMENT FROM THE PRIME MINISTER'S OFFICE

IN POLITICAL TERMS, THE BIGGEST PROBLEM WITH THE SENATE EXPENSES fiasco was that everyone could understand it. It wasn't a complicated government program or policy "initiative" that challenged the interpretive skills of professional analysts. It wasn't as important as an international trade agreement or the war in Afghanistan, but Canadians, no matter which party they support, don't tolerate politicians fudging expenses. That is what made the issue so difficult for Prime Minister Harper, who generally excelled at keeping clutter out of his messaging. Every voter can understand the simple fact that Harper's people—his senators and members of his senior staff—have been up to their necks in something distasteful at best and possibly even illegal.

In June 2013, Gerald Comeau, a Mulroney-era Tory and no-nonsense Acadian from Nova Scotia, replaced David Tkachuk as chair of the Senate's Internal Economy Committee. Comeau had no time for senators who made inappropriate claims and said later that the rules were unclear. "It's kind of hard to have sympathy with that...I mean most people know where they live. Knowing where you live should be pretty straightforward," he told the author in an interview. James Cowan, at that time the Liberal leader in the Senate, didn't buy the excuse that the rules weren't clear, either: "The guidelines were clear, but they were broken," he said. When the public perceives that privileged people are abusing the public trust, there's trouble coming for the reigning government. That has happened many times—the Liberals' sponsorship scandal brought the Conservatives to power in Ottawa, and expense scandals have roiled governments in Newfoundland and Labrador, Nova Scotia, and Saskatchewan, with voters kicking out the government in the latter two cases. Once voters connect the government to such abuses, that government is walking wounded.

As the undisputed top political figure in Canada, the prime minister has to accept some measure of accountability when things go wrong among his appointees. Mac Harb is a Liberal appointed by Jean Chrétien, and Tkachuk and Marjory LeBreton are Conservatives appointed by Brian Mulroney. But it was Harper who named LeBreton as government leader in the Senate and who appointed or approved almost everybody else in this story: Mike Duffy, Pamela Wallin, and Patrick Brazeau as senators, Irving Gerstein to head Conservative Fund Canada, Nigel Wright, Benjamin Perrin, Chris Woodcock, and David van Hemming in the Langevin Block. His majority had installed Tkachuk and Carolyn Stewart Olsen on the Internal Economy Board's powerful steering committee.

When the revelations started to spin out of control and danger washed over the decks, the PMO started to jettison heavy baggage, like Brazeau, Duffy, and Wallin. The overriding objective was to limit the damage, because by then it was way too late to prevent it. At every step along the way, Conservatives from Harper on down would do what they could to deflect criticism, dissuade investigation, and, possibly, deceive the Canadian people. They would put pressure on the senators themselves and, in Duffy's case, demand their silence. Harper had always said he "didn't come to Ottawa to defend the Senate," but at every turn, right up until Deloitte's reports were made public and the RCMP confirmed that it was investigating, that's exactly what he did. Until CTV's Robert Fife broadcast his scoop on Wright's connection to Duffy on May 14, Harper made it appear he knew what was going on and that everything was above board. On May 9, Harper had tried to put the matter behind him, telling the House of Commons that "an independent external auditor was brought in to examine all of these expenses. He looked obviously at the expenses of three particular senators who have had some difficulty. The auditor has concluded that the rules in place were not clear...Senator Duffy some months ago repaid the money." As the Harper PMO got dragged further into the mire, there would be no more talk about a spot of bother or difficulty. The rules that, in the spring, "were not clear" eventually would become very clear indeed.

The prime minister's role in the Senate expenses affair was opaque to say the least, partly because of the firewalls built to ensure he didn't get burned even if everyone else went up in smoke. It wasn't entirely because Harper himself feared taking the hit. His leadership was vital to the Conservative Party's reputation, and every crack in the reputational wall was a potential threat. He was the leader who brought the Conservatives to power and was the party's strongest asset. He was the man who disciplined the notoriously fractious conservative movement in Canada by insisting on centralized control. In Harper's Team, Tom Flanagan portrays Harper as engaged in everything from policy development to campaign messaging, fundraising, and patronage. Harper took a personal interest in how Conservative Fund Canada was managed and kept topped up. By all accounts, he is a man of tremendous personal capacity, a tireless worker, and a lightning-fast study. As the party's authentic leader, he had a duty, one might say, to protect himself.

From his first days in office, the party's greatest asset protected himself with layers of central control. On orders from the top, every event that involved a Conservative MP and every government announcement had to be vetted by the Privy Council Office, the bureaucratic instrument of the PMO. Nothing was too small, right down to the ribbon-cutting photo ops and media requests for routine information. The prime minister's people even tracked the number of signs erected with the glad news of "Canada's Economic Action Plan": in March 2010, there were 5,337 of them. Communications staffers in all government departments worked closely with the Privy Council Office, which is housed in the Langevin Block along with the prime minister. Every move had to be approved by central control, even if it resulted in absurdly long delays to release straightforward information.

Fife's story about the Wright-Duffy connection changed the tune coming from the Langevin Block. Because it drew a line from the troubles of one senator straight into the heart of the Harper government, that one news story transformed the affair from the wrongdoing of wayward senators to a potentially far more damaging narrative that has entangled some of the people closest to the prime minister. New Democrat MP Charlie Angus has called it "a brand new phase of the scandal" because it ties the most powerful PMO operative, Wright, to a secret payment to a government official, Duffy. Wright's lawyers told Project Amble that their client had informed other PMO officials as well, although Wright said the prime minister wasn't one of them. Harper has said many times that he knew nothing about the deal cooked up in his offices in the Langevin Block, and that he found out about the transaction only through Fife's story and heartily disapproved.

Yet, on May 16, 2013, the PMO said Wright still had the "full confidence" of the prime minister. The next day, a spokesman said

Wright was "staying on" in the PMO. But he wasn't staying on. Four days after Fife's story ran, Wright "resigned." As he went, he stated that he hadn't informed the prime minister "either before or after the fact" about the Duffy deal: "My actions were intended solely to secure the repayment of funds, which I considered to be in the public interest, and I accept sole responsibility." And "sole responsibility" would be in the script of all of the prime minister's statements about the affair for months to come. Over that time, Harper would heap all the blame on his former right-hand man, eventually changing the story to say that Wright hadn't resigned but been dismissed. Suggesting he had been kept in the dark as much as anyone else, Harper threw his loyal aide straight under the bus.

On May 21, the Conservative caucus allowed journalists to cover Harper's remarks to its weekly meeting, a rare event. The cameras and reporters were herded out right after Harper spoke, but he wanted to make sure the Canadian people heard his message. "I'm not happy," the prime minister said. "I'm very upset about some conduct we have witnessed, the conduct of some parliamentarians and the conduct of my own office." He alluded to a 2005 speech in which he had pledged a new era of public accountability, a promise that now seemed laughable amid the revelations about the Senate. "Let me repeat something else I said in that same speech in 2005, and let me be very blunt about it. Anyone, anyone who wants to use public office for their own benefit should make other plans or, better yet, leave this room." That was the right thing to say, except that the Conservatives who were accused of using public office for their own benefit weren't in the room to hear it.

There's no question that the Opposition parties sensed a rare opportunity to dent Harper's credibility. As the parliamentary session ended, NDP leader Thomas Mulcair conducted repeated interrogations of Harper during Question Period. His simple, direct questions made Harper's talking points seem disingenuous. Liberal leader Justin Trudeau submitted written questions, trying to find a paper trail, the supposed "letter of understanding between the Prime Minister's former Chief of Staff, Nigel Wright, and Senator Mike Duffy regarding the payment of $90,127 to cover Senator Duffy's living expenses." He didn't get the letter.

As Canadians grew angrier by the day, the prime minister portrayed his castoff colleagues as the ones to blame. "It was Mr. Wright who made the decision to take his personal funds and give those to Mr. Duffy so that Mr. Duffy could reimburse the taxpayers," Harper said in Question Period on June 5. "Those were his decisions. They were not communicated to me or to members of my office." By then, he had even stopped adding "senator" to Duffy's name; from now on, he was simply Mr. Duffy. The trouble is, that's not what Wright's lawyers told Project Amble. They said Wright recalled informing at least three other PMO staffers about the cheque. They included people very close to the prime minister: Wright's aide, van Hemmen, Harper's in-house lawyer, Perrin, and the PMO's director of issues management, Woodcock. Wright said Senator Gerstein was also in the loop as head of Conservative Fund Canada. So, the prime minister was either misinformed about the situation or gave an inaccurate account of it to the House.

On July 6, two days after the RCMP affidavits surfaced with Wright's revelation that other PMO staff and Gerstein knew about the transaction, Harper elaborated on the I-knew-nothing theme. "I think if you read the affidavit it makes very clear that the decision to pay money to Mr. Duffy out of Mr. Wright's personal funds was made solely by Mr. Wright and was his responsibility," Harper told a news conference. "Obviously, had I known about this earlier I would never have allowed this to take place. When I answered questions about this in the House of Commons I answered questions to the best of my knowledge." That the boss didn't know seemed out of character for Harper, considering his reputation for hands-on management and his demanding style with his staff. Rob Walsh, the former law clerk of Parliament, told CTV the day after the affidavits became public that it was "implausible or irresponsible to have not known this was going on."

The prime minister's partisan critics didn't buy it either. "It's a real stretch that supposedly nobody knew and nobody asked any questions," remarked Senate Liberal leader Cowan. He said it was obvious that the word had been put out to fix the problem and heap all the blame on Duffy and Wright: "The money was paid and the report [into Duffy's expenses] was changed by lead government senators that we now know were in touch with the PMO"—a reference to Tkachuk and Stewart Olsen and their attempt to whitewash the Senate report on Duffy—"What is the connection here?"

To the Harper government, there was no connection. The prime minister's official spokesman at that time, Andrew MacDougall, was reluctant to get into the substance of the Wright-Duffy arrangement. MacDougall, who soon left the PMO for a private sector job in London, issued a statement saying "this file was handled by Nigel Wright and he has taken sole responsibility.... [T]he affidavit is clear that the prime minister was not aware of the payment." Except, again, the affidavits didn't make that clear at all. They didn't say that the prime minister wasn't aware, just that the faithful Wright said he didn't tell him. In the same way the affidavits weren't proof of the allegations against Duffy and Wright, neither did they prove that the prime minister knew nothing about the deal. Wright issued a statement through his lawyer: "I have offered and given my assistance to the investigation and I intend to continue to do so. I have no further comments at this time." Wright was now speaking only through his lawyers, and they were handing over evidence to the RCMP.

One of the senior staffers who Wright said knew about the payment is former top PMO lawyer Benjamin Perrin. From his new home in British Columbia, Perrin offered a finely crafted statement insisting that he "was not consulted on, and did not participate in, Nigel Wright's decision to write a personal cheque to reimburse Senator Duffy's expenses." He also added cover for his former boss: "I have never communicated with the Prime Minister on this matter." Perrin distanced himself from "Wright's decision" to pay Duffy, but didn't specifically deny that he knew what had happened.

In politics, words matter, and it's important to understand exactly what the prime minister's people were denying or seeming to deny. In statement after statement, Harper and his official spokespeople insisted he had nothing to do with "the decision by Nigel Wright" to pay off Duffy. But there was much more to it than one man's decision, if it was his alone, to write a cheque. It reflected on Harper's judgment call to name the senators in the first place, right up to the concerted efforts by top Senate Conservatives to keep the problem under water. But it didn't stay submerged, and the party was paying the price. As the scandal accumulated facts and infamy, Canadians became angrier and more mistrustful of politicians in general and of the Harper government in particular. The Conservatives were polling over 40 percent support in the summer of 2011, after the majority election and before the Senate scandal erupted. By the fall of 2013, they were at less than 30 percent public support, and the trend line was lower in every region of the country. The Conservative heyday was over.

In the meantime, more baggage was going overboard. Among the first to go was Chris Woodcock, who had been Harper's man responsible for managing political flare-ups like the Duffy case. He went to work for Natural Resources Minister Joe Oliver. Van Hemmen went to the Finance Department, and Perrin, as we've seen, was in British Columbia. There were changes in the Senate, too. On July 4, a day after a visit from two RCMP investigators, Marjory LeBreton announced she intended to resign as government leader. After the summer cabinet shuffle, she was replaced by little-known Senator Claude Carignan, who took up the cudgels against the outcast senators. Tkachuk, citing health reasons, stepped aside as chair of the Internal Economy Committee; his job was taken for the next few months by Gerald Comeau.

The meetings in the Langevin Block during the second week of February had involved a who's who of the Senate expenses affair. Mike Duffy was there one day, Gerstein and Tkachuk the next. Tkachuk confirmed that he updated Wright on the Senate situation, but denied they discussed a bailout plan for Duffy. We know from the RCMP documents that Duffy had approached Gerstein, who had considered writing a cheque, then balked. Over those two days, the players came and went from Room 204 in the Langevin Block, but other than Duffy's assertion that he met with Wright during his visit, we don't know who in the PMO the others met or what was discussed. The RCMP released another eighty-plus pages of emails in November, but there still wasn't a thing on the record to suggest the prime minister was present at any of those meetings. But was he briefed? That's not clear either.

It's possible Harper didn't know. Rob Walsh says he wouldn't be surprised if Harper was purposely kept out of the loop on the Duffy deal even if it was "implausible or irresponsible" for the prime minister to keep his hands off the file. "We know that Wright had an ongoing brief to sort out the Mike Duffy problem," Walsh says. "It could be that the prime minister just left it to him and that he was not to know the specifics, by design." It wouldn't be the first time a prime minister's aides kept the boss in the dark, simply to provide a deniability buffer around the leader should things go wrong. His opponents contend that Harper should have known, and if he didn't, he wasn't doing his job.

Duffy told me in Cavendish in the summer of 2013 that the whole story would come out only in court. At one point, he called for a public inquiry to get to the facts, implying that the prime minister would be put on the spot about his knowledge of the matter. But Walsh said it was unlikely that Duffy could force the prime minister to testify, even in a criminal proceeding. Under the doctrine of parliamentary privilege, the prime minister can't be compelled to testify in a court while Parliament is in session because it potentially would interfere with his rights as a parliamentarian. He could be called as a witness only earlier than forty days before the beginning of a new session of Parliament or forty days after a session has ended. Since the prime minister decides when Parliament is prorogued and when new sessions begin, it's child's play to make sure the window never opens. If Duffy's lawyers were to demand him as a witness and Harper wouldn't or couldn't appear, a judge might rule there was no chance of a fair trial. That would leave the Crown little choice but to drop the charges. Other senators, such as Tkachuk, Stewart Olsen, or LeBreton, might make similar arguments. They might be accused of hiding behind the shield of parliamentary privilege, but a court might decide they have every right to do that. As it turned out, no parliamentarians other than Duffy and George Furey were ever called to testify in court.

When Parliament broke for the summer, Harper announced he intended to prorogue the session and start up fresh in the fall. As the Second Session of the Forty-first Parliament opened in mid-October, Harper's still-unclear role in the scandal and his orders to his Senate operators put his government in the deepest jeopardy it had ever faced. During some of the most extraordinary days anyone could remember in the Red Chamber, the Conservatives would turn their guns on the trouble-causing senators. But the attempt to isolate the Senate Three and bury the story would backfire spectacularly on the Harper government.

OCTOBER CRISIS
IN THE SENATE

This was a setup, planned by the Senate leadership
under the direction of the PMO.

— SENATOR MIKE DUFFY, OCTOBER 28, 2013

STEPHEN HARPER'S DECISION TO PROROGUE PARLIAMENT AND COME back with a new agenda gave him some breathing room while he considered how to navigate around the increasingly hazardous situation in the Senate. It would mean that the government's legislative agenda from the previous session would be suspended. The prime minister could also turn the page politically with a new Speech from the Throne and, perhaps, change the scandal-marred storyline of the last session. He was close to finalizing an ambitious trade deal with the European Union, which the Conservatives hoped would demonstrate Harper's economic leadership and get people talking about something other than the stench coming out of the Red Chamber.

It didn't turn out that way. Parliamentarians and distinguished visitors gathered on October 16 in the Senate to hear Governor General David Johnston read the speech. Senators Duffy, Wallin, and Brazeau were all invited, but weren't in the chamber to hear it. Duffy had submitted a letter saying he needed sick leave to deal with his heart condition, which had been aggravated "by months of unrelenting stress." With the Governor General reading and the prime minister looking on, the speech laid out the government's agenda for the new session, including plans to balance the budget, sign the European trade deal, legislate new consumer regulations, and crack down further on crime. At more than seven thousand words, one of the longest such speeches in Canadian parliamentary history, there were but three sentences about the Senate: "The Government continues to believe the status quo in the Senate of Canada is unacceptable. The Senate must be reformed or, as with its provincial counterparts, vanish. The Government will proceed upon receiving the advice of the Supreme Court." The government was still interested in Senate reform, but that wasn't a central preoccupation. Getting rid of distractions was job number one.

The new session had barely opened when the New Democrats took the offensive. Ontario MP Charlie Angus raised a point of privilege, accusing Harper of lying to the Commons for his repeated insistence that neither he nor anyone in his office had any knowledge of the deal between Duffy and Nigel Wright. In Question Period, Opposition leader Tom Mulcair demanded to know what the prime minister's involvement really was. He accused Harper of fostering a "climate of corruption" in the Senate matter. But Harper couldn't respond—he wasn't there. He was already on a jet to Brussels to sign the European free trade agreement. Instead, his combative new parliamentary secretary, Paul Calandra, held the party line: "Mr. Wright handled this file on his own, [the prime minister] had no knowledge of the payment until May 15," the day after Fife's story connecting Duffy and Wright. Calandra, from Markham, Ontario, had been named to the post after another Ontario MP, Dean del Mastro, was charged with campaign irregularities by Elections Canada and forced out of the Conservative caucus.

The Opposition parties would keep up their attacks for weeks to come, but the Commons almost became a sideshow. The real action was going on down the hall in the Red Chamber. And the threat to the Harper government wasn't coming from anyone in the Official Opposition, but from his own appointees and former colleagues: the three senators accused in the expenses fiasco. On October 17, the first full day of the new session, Senator Claude Carignan, the new government leader in the Senate, introduced motions calling for the suspension without pay of senators Duffy, Wallin, and Brazeau. The accusation was "gross negligence" in the management of Senate funds, and immediate suspension was necessary to protect "the dignity of the Senate." If the motions passed, the Senate Three would be deprived of their employment, health benefits, and access to Parliament. And they would have no way to defend themselves. No hearings were planned and no further attempt was to be made to collect evidence of either innocence or guilt. The Conservatives aimed to ram the motion through, and if the Liberals objected, they would be cast as defenders of the Senate status quo. No doubt this law-and-order approach sounded good to whoever dreamed it up—probably Harper himself. It would turn out to be a damaging misstep because it removed any motivation for the senators to keep quiet or cooperate. They were backed into a corner, with nowhere to turn and nothing left to lose. Each in his or her own way would lash out.

The suspension motions were immediately controversial. Constitutional experts weighed in, saying the Senate had no right to remove the sessional pay of its members absent conviction of a notorious crime or treason. Some Liberals and even some Conservative senators expressed misgivings about taking such a drastic step without giving the accused so much as the right to reply. There was talk of kangaroo courts and a Star Chamber, the secret English Privy Council court of the 1600s that operated without indictments or witnesses—Conservative senator Hugh Segal described the process as precisely that. It only got worse, as all three senators under suspicion already had decided to counterattack. The stage was set for some of the most dramatic scenes in Senate history.

On Monday, October 21, the Press Gallery was notified that Duffy's lawyer, Donald Bayne, would hold a news conference in Room 130-S, a small media theatre downstairs in the Centre Block. Bayne is a veteran criminal law specialist with the Ottawa firm of Bayne Sellar Boxall. With the media crowded into the low-ceilinged room, Bayne spoke for forty-five minutes, laying out his argument that Duffy had broken no law, had not been charged with anything, and the Senate was proposing to throw him out without so much as a hearing, despite the Conservative leadership's having reassured Duffy on several occasions that he was operating within the rules. Calling it "a mob rush to judgment," Bayne made it clear that his client had evidence of his own and was prepared to use it "should, for example, Senator Duffy be charged and we have to defend ourselves." Bayne made public a mountain of evidence showing the complicity of the PMO and senior Conservatives in a cover-up to hide the expense claims and lie to the Canadian people. Bayne said PMO operatives and Senate Conservatives had continuously ratcheted up the pressure on Duffy, finally resorting to threats. "The PMO had decided they wanted to sweep a political embarrassment to their Tory base under the rug, and they threatened Senator Duffy with wholly unconstitutional and illegal procedures of throwing him out of the Senate without a hearing if he failed to go along with it." Duffy had become more than a distraction; he was a liability with the party's vital core voters.

This was strong stuff, and Bayne said he could prove what he was saying. He quoted from the now-famous February 20 email, the one Robert Fife had seen in reporting the story of the Duffy-Wright connection. In it, Duffy tells his lawyer that Wright had called him to say that top officials "have been working on lines and a scenario...that would cover all of [Duffy's] concerns, including cash for repayment." There was an "or else" clause as well: if Duffy didn't go along with the scenario and speak the lines to be written for him, David Tkachuk and Carolyn Stewart Olsen would get him kicked out of the Senate. Bayne had lots more where that came from, saying ominously that "[t]here is a clear and long and substantial evidentiary chain. The email that I just read you from Nigel Wright is but the tip of a big evidentiary iceberg. I have those emails. The RCMP have most of those emails."

Bayne's timing was suggested by Duffy himself, and it was perfect: right before the daily Commons Question Period. Mulcair and the NDP demanded to know what the prime minister knew about the alleged conspiracy. The Liberals took a similar tack, with Justin Trudeau saying the affair betrayed a failure of leadership by Harper. And in the Senate, voices started to be raised to object to Carignan's motions to suspend the senators. They were cautious voices and, at first, only those of Liberals. George Baker of Newfoundland and Labrador called it an abuse of process, and said he would vote against the motion. Jim Munson said something similar: "I believe in fairness, I really believe in fairness. I believe in due diligence and I believe in due process. I will be voting against this Conservative motion." Liberal leader James Cowan at first seemed to back the motion, then quickly modified that. He too wanted due process for the three accused.

Bayne's performance succeeded in raising doubts about the tactics used by Carignan and other senior Conservatives, but it was just the start of the counterattack. The next day, Duffy himself took the stage and made it clear that, if he was going to take the fall, he was not going alone. Standing in his new place in the back row of the Senate chamber, far from his former Conservative caucus mates, Duffy gave the prime minister, his office, and the senators who had done so much to bring him low both barrels. He didn't bother arguing about the rules or the Senate's processes, but went straight for the jugular. In a vintage Duffy performance, and with a sense of outrage and anxiety ringing in his voice, the senator insisted that Wright had approved his expenses as recently as December 2012. He then tied the prime minister directly to the supposed conspiracy. On February 13, he said, after the weekly Conservative caucus meeting and two days after his visit to Room 204 of the Langevin Block, "I met the Prime Minister and Nigel Wright, just the three of us." Duffy said he tried to explain to Harper that he hadn't broken any rules, but the prime minister waved him off. It wasn't about the rules, Harper allegedly replied, calling the affair "inexplicable to our base" and ordering the senator to pay back the money.

Duffy then sketched out what he called "this monstrous political scheme" hatched by the prime minister's staff. In Cavendish, he said he had taken a series of calls from Nigel Wright. In one of them, Duffy told Wright that he didn't want to pay back the money because he didn't believe he owed it. And besides, he didn't have the cash. "'Don't worry,'" Duffy said Wright told him, "'I'll write the cheque. Let the lawyers handle the details; you just follow the plan and we'll keep Carolyn Stewart Olsen and David Tkachuk at bay.'" Duffy claimed the negotiations then expanded to include at least two lawyers from the PMO, one or more from the Conservative Party, and Duffy's lawyer Janice Payne. While this was going on, Duffy said, he started getting "nasty and menacing messages" from Conservative senators telling him to "do what the Prime Minister wants. Do it for the PM and for the good of the party." He said one senator, so far unnamed, told him if he didn't go along with the arrangements, "the Conservative majority on the steering committee of the Board of Internal Economy, Senator Tkachuk and Senator Stewart Olsen, would issue a press release declaring me unqualified to sit in the Senate." That was the stick. There was also a carrot: "If you do what we want, the Prime Minister will publicly confirm that you're entitled to sit as a senator from PEI and you won't lose your seat."

Duffy sketched out the deal he was to agree to. It was the same deal he had revealed to me, supposedly on background, that August day in Cavendish. "There was an undertaking made by the PMO, with the agreement of the Senate leadership, that I would not be audited by Deloitte, that I'd be given a pass," he told the hushed Senate. "Further, that if this phony scheme ever became public, Senator LeBreton, the Leader of the Government of the day, would whip the Conservative caucus to prevent my expulsion from the chamber." Duffy said that a string of emails had flown back and forth between Cavendish and Ottawa, emails he made sure to save. He claimed to have been shocked later to hear that, when the CBC asked for the emails via an access-to-information request, the PMO claimed it didn't have a single relevant document in its voluminous files. Duffy also said he was told not to worry about the Deloitte audit because "they've got all they need. It doesn't matter. Don't bother."

All that had changed on the night of May 14, Duffy said, when Fife's piece on the deal went to air. The PMO blew a fuse.

> I was called at home in Cavendish by Ray Novak, senior assistant to the Prime Minister. He had with him Senator LeBreton, Leader of the Government in the Senate. Senator LeBreton was emphatic: The deal was off. If I didn't resign from the Conservative caucus within 90 minutes, I'd be thrown out of the caucus immediately, without a meeting, without a vote. In addition, she said, if I didn't quit the caucus immediately, I'd be sent to the Senate Ethics Committee, with orders from the leadership to throw me out of the Senate.

If true, this was a plain attempt to intimidate a sitting parliamentarian, a criminal act. Duffy insisted he still had rights, and they should be respected. This wasn't "Iraq or Iran or...Vladimir Putin's Russia." Senators should not be subjected to bullying by the "unaccountable power of the PMO."

It was a bravura performance, suggesting that, although wounded, the senator still had some fight. As the CBC's Terry Milewski put it, Duffy "has gone nuclear and he's aiming not just at the PMO but at the Prime Minister himself." The speech monopolized the daily political shows and exploded in the social media. It even provoked the prime minister into doing something he hates to do: answer questions in the Commons.

Since the spring, Harper had been giving repetitive stock replies according to his carefully crafted talking points or ignoring questions entirely. But now he fought back. Under questioning by Mulcair, the prime minister disputed Duffy's story about meeting "just the three of us." Harper said he was doing what was right for the country and the party: "The issue is not a matter of perception. You can not claim an expense you did not incur. That is not right, that is not proper, and that will not be tolerated in this party." In all, Harper answered twenty questions that day and didn't waver. He denied, again and again, any knowledge of the deal. And he paid back Duffy in kind, mocking his claims of being railroaded. "Mr. Duffy now says he is a victim because I told him he should repay his expenses," Harper growled, as Conservatives MPs yelled and pounded their desks. "You're darn right I told him to repay his expenses." That was strong stuff from the understated prime minister, and the clip was played endlessly on that night's TV news.

Marjory LeBreton also mounted a counterattack, rising later in the Senate to dismiss Duffy's version of events as that of a master storyteller, a yarn spun with little regard for the truth. She denied his claim that the post-caucus meeting with the prime minister and Wright had been anything more than a quick chat. Duffy's assertion that he was offered "a pass" on the Deloitte audit was "utterly preposterous...a blatant falsehood." She fully supported sending Duffy's expenses to the auditors, and Duffy was lying to suggest otherwise: "I will use the slang word for falsehood. That statement is a whopper," LeBreton said. But, curiously, she confirmed that she and Novak had given Duffy an ultimatum: "Mike, this is the only option that can ensure your future livelihood," is how she put it. To many listening, that sounded a lot like a threat. To the Mounties, who were reading emails exchanged among senior Conservatives, her claims rang a bit false.

Then, just an hour or two later, the prime minister's Senate problem took another unexpected twist. This time, it was Pamela Wallin who alleged bullying and manipulation by the PMO and senior Senate Conservatives. Like Duffy, Wallin chose the privilege-protected Senate chamber to unleash her broadside. Speaking to one of the suspension motions, Wallin's three-thousand-word speech, a defence of her record and a stinging condemnation of the Conservative leadership, would compete for lead-story status with the prime minister's "darn right I told him" quote from the Commons. She called the investigation into her expenses "a charade" arising from "a purely politically motivated set of charges in a chamber that has not demonstrated it is prepared to rise above party politics." Like Duffy, Wallin aimed her rhetorical guns at the prime minister's people and by implication, Harper himself.

> This issue is no longer about expenses or audits or transparency or accountability or even about the reputation of this chamber—it about the abuse of power....If, as I suspect, Senator Carignan is taking direction from the PMO, then this process is not in the interests of an independent, functioning and effective Senate....[I]t is intended to intimidate, not only me but others in this chamber. It is about political expediency, to get rid of someone it considers to be a political liability.

And Wallin had venomous criticism for two of her former colleagues, senators LeBreton and Stewart Olsen. Wallin said she believed as many as fourteen serious leaks had been made to the media, all of them spun to attack her character. "We believe those leaks were orchestrated in large measure by Senators LeBreton and

Stewart Olsen," she said. Wallin was on the attack, and it was getting personal.

> [Stewart Olsen and LeBreton] could not abide the fact that
> I was outspoken in caucus, or critical of their leadership, or
> that my level of activity brought me into the public eye and
> once garnered the praise of the prime minister. They re-
> sented that—they resented me being an activist senator....
> In this chamber, Senator Marjory LeBreton derided me,
> accusing me of having an inflated view of my role. "This
> narcissism," [LeBreton] said, "is the crux of the situation
> before us." In fact, the crux of the situation is not about
> narcissism—not hers or mine or anyone else's—the crux of
> this matter is the lack of due process and a flawed system
> that allows personal vendettas to be indulged.

Wallin also said that she had been kicked out of the Conservative caucus in almost the same way Duffy had, via a phone call from LeBreton and Novak, a day after Duffy got the call from the same two fixers.

> I received a panicked phone call ordering me to resign
> immediately from the Conservative caucus. It was after 5
> [PM] Eastern time and Senator LeBreton and...Ray Novak
> said they were speaking on behalf of the prime minister,
> and that my being a part of the Conservative caucus was
> now an embarrassment to the prime minister....I was told
> again they were speaking for the prime minister, he want-
> ed me gone....[W]e negotiated with the two a statement
> that said I would recuse myself from caucus, not resign. I
> had not done anything wrong. Less than 10 minutes later,
> Senator LeBreton broke the deal and publicly declared
> that I had resigned.

In Wallin's view, she had been subjected first to "a show trial," then a betrayal.

Wallin hit hard at the core of the Conservative Senate leadership, for whom she had worked so diligently. She had done everything she was asked: speaking out for the Senate, chairing an important committee, supporting her government and leader, and raising lots of cash for the Conservative Party. Along with Duffy, she had co-hosted the party's national convention in 2011. And this was how she was being repaid. It was a stinging attack, backed up with many pages of letters and emails which Wallin said proved she had been a victim of manipulators in the party's senior circles. The petty jealousy of two other senators had made it so much worse by poisoning her image in the media. If Duffy had gone nuclear, Wallin went chemical.

Ottawa reeled—there seemed to be no other topic on the agenda. The antique Senate does not allow cameras, so the networks broadcast a raw audio feed of the speeches over an archive image of the Senate floor. That, too, was technically forbidden, but the Senate didn't dare stop it. Canadians seemed transfixed. It was all over talk radio, the lead story in newspapers, and sprawled over the ubiquitous social media. It had the elements of a classic tragedy: famous and powerful characters first seduced by power, then betrayed by its dangers. And it was all happening in public. Duffy and now Wallin were denying the ethical claims of a party that had come to power promising accountable change after the scandals of the Liberal years. Now, two former Conservatives were alleging that the party's senior leadership was abusing its power, covering up malfeasance, and making backroom deals to thwart inquiries into what was really going on inside the Harper government.

The next day, it was Patrick Brazeau's turn. Brazeau rose to say he had been approached that morning by Carignan in a room off the Senate floor and offered "a backroom deal." "The deal was that if I stood in this chamber, apologized to Canadians and took responsibility for my actions, that my punishment would be lesser than what is being proposed," said Brazeau. He refused it, maintaining his innocence. But the story fit perfectly with the scenarios laid out by Duffy and Wallin. Carignan seemed to confirm the substance of Brazeau's story: "I spoke to him...saying how can we help you? Propose something. Let us know how we can bring corrections...apologize, perhaps a lighter sanction, we can come up with something." So, despite all the high-minded talk from the Conservatives about transparency and accountability, here was the government leader in the Senate offering a quiet deal to make a problem go away. If anything has been consistent about the Harper government's behaviour during the Senate scandal, the desire to make problems go away quietly is it.

Inconsistencies were now popping up everywhere, even from the prime minister himself. On October 28, having previously said Wright had resigned when the Duffy deal came to light, Harper told a radio talk show in Halifax that Wright had been dismissed. Harper also admitted in the Commons that "very few" people in his office had known about the arrangements, in contrast to his previous statement that no one knew. The details, he had said on June 5, "were not communicated to me or to members of my office," a statement he later said had been "based on the information I had at that time."

And the Conservative leadership's insistence that the senators be suspended without pay also seemed to be tempering. The party's Senate caucus appeared to be working on a plan to stop short of suspension without pay, at least for Wallin and Brazeau. For a few brief moments, it seemed as though the Harper government was recovering its balance. But it wouldn't last.

Mike Duffy rose in the Senate in the afternoon of October 28 and delivered another devastating blow to his former party's credibility. Saying he had come to the Senate "directly from the Heart Institute," where he had been receiving treatment, Duffy said he was fighting back against the "avalanche of untruths and character assassination" to which he had been subjected by the Conservative leadership. He said the Internal Economy Committee had tried to ambush him over trivial expense claims, which he said resulted from honest mistakes. "I can only conclude that this was a setup, planned by the Senate leadership under the direction of the PMO and designed to destroy my credibility with Canadians, if and when I ever went public about the real story behind the 90,000 [dollars]." That was just the start. Duffy had the cannon double-shotted, and he was firing for effect.

LeBreton had dismissed his earlier allegations as lies. Well, Duffy said, he had emails that proved his story, and he was ready to name names. The email chain included Benjamin Perrin, the former PMO lawyer who had issued the careful "non-denial denial" about his role in the Wright-Duffy deal. It included Arthur Hamilton, a Bay Street lawyer who had acted for the Conservative party in the robocalls case, the Helena Guergis affair, and the Gomery Commission into the Liberals' sponsorship scandal. Duffy accused the prime minister of being behind "this nefarious scheme," using Wright as his point man and Hamilton as fixer. Within a few days, the RCMP would come looking for those emails from the senator.

Duffy had another startling revelation: the $90,000 payment wasn't the only one that came his way during the negotiations; the Conservative Party had also paid his legal bill. "One cheque from Nigel Wright? No, ladies and gentlemen: there were two cheques, at least two cheques," Duffy thundered. "The PMO, listen to this, had the Conservative Party's lawyer, Arthur Hamilton, pay my legal fees. He paid for my lawyer, Arthur Hamilton, a cheque, $13,560. That is right, senators: not one payment...but two." The prime minister had arranged to pay Duffy's legal bills "because...this was all part of his strategy, negotiated by his lawyers and the Conservative Party's lawyers, to make a political situation, embarrassing to his base, go away."

The whole affair, in the Duffy version, was a "monstrous fraud [that] was the PMO's creation from start to finish," although the RCMP would suggest later that Duffy had started it with his demands of Wright and the party. Still, Duffy had other emails which suggested that LeBreton and Tkachuk were operating from scripts written by the prime minister's men. They had even worked out the deceptions that were to be fed to the news media, lines that were "rehearsed with me right up until minutes before I went on television," Duffy said, referring to his televised announcement that he would repay the money.

There was also the matter of the bank loan Duffy had referred to in May when Robert Fife asked him about the Wright connection. Duffy said he and Heather had taken out a loan, when the cash really came from Wright. The prime minister's men had made much of this supposed lie, but Duffy said the cover story came straight from the PMO. "When the media asked, 'Where did you get the money to pay the ninety thousand,' the PMO told me to say, 'My wife and I took out a loan at the Royal Bank.' That line was written by the PMO to deceive Canadians as to the real source of the $90,000."

There was more to come from the scorched-earth senator. He suggested that Conservative Party funds had gone into the deception campaign, money raised from faithful grassroots supporters whose names populate the Conservative databases. Their money had been used to back up a sham manipulated by the puppet masters in the PMO for political gain for a party that had lost its way. "They have no moral compass," he said of the prime minister's men. "Oh, they talk a great game about integrity, but, in my experience, they demonstrate every day that they do not understand the meaning of the phrase 'the truth, the whole truth and nothing but the truth.'"

Later, as the smoke cleared over Parliament Hill, the party issued a statement confirming that Duffy's legal bill had been paid out of party funds. "At the time these legal expenses were incurred and paid, Mike Duffy was a member of the Conservative caucus," said a statement issued by Conservative spokesman Cory Hann. "The Conservative Party sometimes assists members of caucus with legal expenses." That was the line the prime minister used in Question Period the next day during an extraordinary exchange with the

NDP's Thomas Mulcair. The Opposition leader rose twenty-six times, and every question he asked was about the Senate scandal. If Duffy had taken money he wasn't entitled to, then why did the Conservatives pay his legal bill? What did the Conservative Party actually pay for? Why did the prime minister keep changing his story? In response, Harper insisted that neither Duffy nor Wright had told him the truth about their arrangements. If anyone had been deceptive, it was Duffy and Wright, and he had been "very clear" about that from the start. Duffy and Wright had concocted a regrettable scheme behind his back. That was why Wright was out of a job and why Duffy should get the same treatment: "It's time for the Senate to act and remove him from the public payroll."

But the Conservative government had not been consistent or clear. When Duffy paid the $90,000, Harper's people had praised him for his "leadership" in refunding taxpayers. At that time, they said Wright was protecting the public by supplying the cash that paid Duffy's disputed expenses. "Nigel Wright did an exceptionally honourable thing," in making the payment, Conservative MP Pierre Poilievre had said in May. By late October, according to the prime minister's new opinion about his former top aide, Wright was a deceiver who deserved to be fired. That was Harper's line for many days afterward, an encore performance after the "darn right" answer the week before. His words weren't wasted.

Down the hall, Senator Carignan was moving as fast as he could to put the three distractions out on their ears. The motions to suspend the senators had been elevated to the status of government business, which made it possible under parliamentary rules to limit debate severely. It was a frequent tactic of the Conservatives in the Commons, and the new Senate leader had no hesitation using it, for political reasons that had nothing to do with finding out what really went on in the expenses affair. Carignan wanted the votes taken and the senators suspended before the start of the party's policy convention in Calgary, due to open three days later. Thousands of grassroots Conservatives would be there. They were hearing from their friends and neighbours what Canadians thought about the Senate and Harper's handling of it. New polls suggested that fully 60 percent of Canadians were following the scandal in the media. In the 2011 election that had brought Harper to power, 61.4 percent of eligible Canadians voted. If the six out of ten Canadians who were following the crisis were all voters, the Conservatives were in deep trouble.

Moreover, the upcoming convention threatened to be eclipsed by yet another dark development in the scandal: the release of more RCMP affidavits, this time into Wallin's expenses. As RCMP Constable Michael Johnson wrote, "there are reasonable grounds to believe that two offences have been committed...breach of trust in connection with the duties of office" and "by deceit, falsehood or other fraudulent means defrauded the Senate of Canada of money by filing inappropriate expense claims." The news also emerged that it had cost the Senate $390,000 to conduct those audits, close to three times the amount under dispute.

Once the convention got under way, its big moment came with Harper's speech to almost three thousand delegates. It had been keenly anticipated for what he would say about the Senate and how he planned to extract his government from the mire. It turned out he didn't have a lot to say, preferring to repeat his earlier assurances that anyone caught offside on their expenses would face the sternest consequences. Certain unnamed senators had violated the rules, he said, "knowingly or without regard to the rules, over a long period. These senators have shown little or no remorse for these actions.... [W]hile we do not know whether these actions were criminal, that is not relevant. In private life you would be fired for doing anything resembling this... and Liberal Senators continue to block action. The Senate should do the right thing now and suspend those senators without pay." He blamed his lack of progress on Senate reform on the other parties "and the courts," even though no court had blocked any reform initiative he had introduced. How could it? There were no proposals to block.

The Conservative rank-and-file also got an update on the party's rather plush finances from Senator Gerstein in his role as head of Conservative Fund Canada. The party was rolling in cash, Gerstein reported. It had $14 million in the war chest and was debt-free, even after spending $220 million on partisan activities over the previous ten years. Gerstein also seemed to dispute some facts in the RCMP documents, while confirming others. The senator said he told Wright the party wouldn't pay for Duffy's disputed expenses, even though it did lay out more than $13,000 to cover the senator's legal fees related to the audit. But he did confirm what Duffy and Wright had been saying through their lawyers—that Gerstein had been involved in the discussions all along.

The convention over, Parliament resumed, and high up on the agenda was the delayed suspension of the three troublesome senators. It all came down on November 5, a history-making day in the Senate, when its members voted to suspend the three for alleged "gross negligence" in handling their expenses. After almost a year of building scandal and months of revelations, accusations, investigations, and denials, the actual vote took barely more than half an hour, starting just after 5:30 P.M local time. Duffy stayed home, but Wallin and Brazeau looked on from their seats as Speaker Noel Kinsella gave a ruling which separated the votes on the three suspensions, so that each senator would be censured individually. He then called the votes on Motion Number Five, the actual Senate order that would take away the pay, offices, and all but the basic benefits of senators Duffy, Wallin, and Brazeau. Each motion—a charge, indictment, and sentence in one handy package—made the same accusation of "gross negligence in the management of...parliamentary resources." The motions laid out exactly what penalties would be imposed. It was all very tidy, and the Conservative majority carried each motion easily. Hearing the fifty to twenty-nine vote in favour of his suspension, Brazeau got up from his seat and walked down toward the Liberal benches. He stopped and shook Jim Munson's hand, saying "thanks for your support."

Munson replied: "good luck. Take care of your kids." Brazeau trudged out of the chamber, down the steps, and out of the Centre Block without saying another word.

The Conservative senators who had been so deeply involved in the affair, Marjory LeBreton, David Tkachuk, Carolyn Stewart Olsen, Irving Gerstein, and Claude Carignan, were no doubt relieved to see the votes wrapped up. Duffy and the others would now be deprived of their platform to make accusations against them or the Harper government. The three would no longer enjoy the protection of parliamentary privilege, limiting what they could say. They would have no Senate income, a serious matter for someone facing potential criminal charges. The Internal Economy Committee took custody of their offices, and the three were gone. This was what the prime minister wanted, and despite the delays, it was mission accomplished for the Senate Conservatives. Harper now had a ready line to use with the media and in the Commons: the matter was settled, the senators were gone, problem solved.

Outside the chamber, Senate Liberal leader James Cowan called the suspension votes "a highly questionable and perhaps even illegitimate process." The Senate had failed to safeguard the principle of fair play in the case of the wayward three. Munson commented, "I voted for fairness. No matter how anyone feels about Senators Brazeau, Wallin, Duffy...it is important to remember rights in Canada." He told the author later that week that the Conservatives "were just making it up as they went along. I've never seen anything like it in my life."

Carignan emerged from the chamber and read from his PMO-prepared talking points, blaming the Liberals for slowing down the suspension votes and never once accepting any responsibility for the former colleagues he had just voted out. The only one of the three accused senators to speak was Wallin. She left the chamber and walked to the Gallery microphone in the Senate foyer for a twelve-second comment: "It's a sad day for democracy....[I]f we can't expect the rule of law in Canada, then where on earth can we expect it?" Within hours, the Senate cancelled the three senators' credit cards, BlackBerry accounts, email, and security access cards. Their staff were fired; they couldn't even get into their offices unless accompanied by a security guard.

The Conservative majority in the Senate had carried the unprecedented suspension vote obviously in the hope that it would cause the scandal to die down and let the Harper government move ahead. The problem was that, by the time the three senators were kicked out, the political damage had already been done. Doubts had arisen about Harper himself, with polls suggesting many Canadians believed he knew much more about the Duffy-Wright deal than he was admitting. By the end of the year, the Conservatives would be at their lowest level of public support in almost ten years.

POLICE, POLITICS, AND THE ROAD AHEAD

All his life [Mike Duffy] was driven by two things:
status and money. Those were his fatal flaws.

— CTV'S CRAIG OLIVER, SEPTEMBER 2013

AFTER ALL THAT HAS HAPPENED, IT IS TYPICAL OF THE TENOR AND TONE of our politics that Senate abolition is now a favourite topic. It seems to be the simplest and easiest way to put an annoying spectacle to rest, for everybody. Simple solutions, however, rarely succeed in politics. No matter how cavalier the behaviour of individual senators, the Senate is still a constitutionally enshrined institution of Parliament. It's not optional: provinces have the right to representation in the

Senate, and those rights have been diminished, on the orders of one party, to cover up the misdeeds of that party's own adherents and possibly those of its leader. That fact could make meaningful reform of the institution much harder to achieve. Stephen Harper had once had the goal of a "Triple-E" Senate: equal, elected, and effective. It had been a central plank of the platform of the Canadian Alliance, which he had led, and before that of the Reform Party, of which he was a founder, policy director, and MP. Today, the goal seems farther out of reach than ever.

Like so many prime ministers before him and the one who would succeed him, Harper was bedevilled by the contradictions of an unelected chamber in a democratic Parliament. The paradox has been debated since Confederation, when the Senate was enshrined as a regional balance to the powers of the elected Commons. New Brunswick, Nova Scotia, and Quebec (then called Lower Canada) had demanded it during the talks that led to Confederation in 1867. But the solution wasn't perfect, and Parliament had considered reform measures as early as 1874. The Senate itself took it on in 1909, with no result. In 1965, some progress was made when the mandatory retirement age for senators was set at seventy-five. There were languid discussions on reform during the 1960s and 1970s before Pierre Trudeau proposed a House of the Federation with 118 senators, half chosen by the federal government following an election and half chosen from the provinces after their elections. That didn't happen. And, of course, there have been calls for a Triple-E Senate since the 1980s. But nothing else of any significance happened until the patriation of the Constitution in 1982, when the Senate was given a limited veto over certain kinds of constitutional changes. Senate reform was included in the sweeping amendments proposed in the Meech Lake and Charlottetown accords, both of which failed the tests of the amending formula and turned into political nightmares for the Mulroney Tories. The Charlottetown proposal in 1992 called for elections and an equal number of senators from each province, and the Senate's relevance would have been bolstered by more power to delay or veto bills coming from the Commons. But none of that happened, mostly because Senate reform was tied to a package of other changes that Canadians did not accept.

When he came to power in 2006, Harper proposed that the provinces start electing senators to fill new vacancies, and his government introduced a bill in the Senate to impose an eight-year term limit. The Conservatives proposed a second bill at the end of 2006 that would have provided for "consultation of the electors... in relation to the appointment of senators." In fact, the rookie prime minister seemed so intent on reform that he promised never to appoint an unelected senator. In the 2006 election, the official party platform promised that "a Conservative government will not appoint to the Senate anyone who does not have a mandate from the people." But during five years of minority governments, dissolutions, prorogations, and two general elections, none of Harper's reform bills was ever passed. Instead, he has appointed many unelected senators, every one of them a Conservative. By the time he had been in office for seven years, Harper had appointed senators at the fastest rate of any prime minister since Sir John A. Macdonald. It is simply a paradox for the party's core supporters that Harper kept on appointing senators even after campaigning against that in every election.

He even named senators who were rejected by voters in elections. Newfoundlander Fabian Manning was elected to the House of Commons in 2006, but was taken down when the Conservatives were shut out in that province in 2008. Nonetheless, Harper appointed Manning to the Senate in January 2009, where he served until the 2011 general election was called. Manning resigned from the Senate to run, only to be defeated again. Harper then reappointed him to the Senate right after the election. Former Canadian Football League commissioner Larry Smith was summoned to the Senate in 2010, but quickly said he would run for a seat in the Commons. He ran in the Quebec riding of Lac-Saint-Louis in 2011 and came third. Harper restored him to the Senate.

On February 1, 2013, the Harper government said it would refer a series of questions about the Senate to the Supreme Court of Canada. At the same time, it launched a parallel reference in the Quebec Court of Appeal. It asked both courts for expedited treatment of the reference because Senate reform "is a matter of great public importance that should be settled as soon as possible." In essence, the high court references ask for guidance on whether the federal government has the constitutional power to establish fixed terms, conduct provincial or national elections for senators, change the property qualifications, or even abolish the Senate. If abolition is sought, would unanimous provincial consent be required? Or might the Senate be changed with the agreement from seven provinces with 50 percent of the population, the threshold for the constitutional amending formula? If the Senate is to carry on, can reform be achieved "by Parliament acting alone?" Can term limits be imposed, say, for eight to ten years or perhaps for the life of two or three Parliaments?

The Harper plan hit a jagged pothole in October when the Quebec Court of Appeal ruled that creating Senate elections in the provinces or imposing term limits was unconstitutional. It said Ottawa could not proceed unilaterally and that significant changes to one of Canada's founding institutions had to be approved according to the constitutional amending formula: seven out of ten provinces representing at least half of the population. That is a high standard to meet, especially with the political whirlwind being reaped in the Senate.

In the meantime, Harper ordered "further steps in the area of Senate expenditure and accountability"—in other words, more specific rules on managing expenses. Such changes wouldn't require consultations with anybody outside the Senate itself, let alone pesky provinces or constitutional lawyers. And although, constitutionally, the prime minister can't order the Senate to do anything, senators would have no choice but to make change happen. In his caucus speech on May 21, Harper assigned Senator Marjory LeBreton to "accelerate changes to the Senate's rules on expenses and close any loopholes in those existing rules....I expect Conservative senators, regardless of what opposition you may face, to get that done in the Senate." The boss concluded with an implied threat: "There is much work to be done. When distractions arise, as they inevitably will, we will deal with them firmly." Two months later, LeBreton was dropped as government leader in the Senate and shuffled out of the Harper cabinet. Carolyn Stewart Olsen resigned from the Internal Economy Committee in October. Both had become distractions.

They had also become magnets for public scorn when the RCMP released another batch of court documents in late November. Eighty pages of emails, correspondence, and interrogation records were included in the latest Project Amble search warrant application, which added a new allegation of bribery against Duffy and Wright. The documents provide a rare insight into the inner workings of the Senate and the PMO as the Conservative brains trust grappled with the Duffy problem. The emails show particularly how Nigel Wright tried and failed to have LeBreton, Stewart Olsen, and David Tkachuk manage Duffy and keep the repayment from becoming a political problem for the Conservatives. That they failed became a source of frustration for Wright and set off back-biting among the senators, who tried to outdo each other in currying favour from central command. The emails show that the PMO tried to keep a lid on the audit process and to exempt Duffy as part of the over-all deal to pay off his expenses. Senior PMO staff even dispatched Irving Gerstein to call a senior contact at Deloitte to find out how the audit was going.

The emails collected by Project Amble also point to many statements by the players, including Duffy, LeBreton, and Stewart Olsen, that vary substantially from the facts and cast new doubt on some statements by the prime minister. Greg Horton, who was fast becoming the most famous corporal in the RCMP, concluded that LeBreton and Stewart Olsen, in particular, repeatedly had given at best vague and perhaps misleading statements about the matter, and he was asking for RCMP technicians to be given permission to retrieve all the emails and attachments of the Senate accounts assigned to LeBreton, Stewart Olsen, Tkachuk, and Duffy for the period around the time of the deal.

The documents also suggest strongly that Wright held a personal conviction that Duffy should repay the money, or at least that the public shouldn't have to pay. That was what had led him to pay off Duffy's bills from his own bank account. Wright's personal initiative, if that's what it was, created problems for his boss that might never had occurred if the payment hadn't been made. The payment might have been morally right, but politically it was very wrong. The RCMP documents might not make a direct connection to the prime minister, but they have drawn many of his close associates into the bog. In May 2016, the RCMP's fraud and breach of trust charges were dropped when the Crown said it was unlikely to get a conviction.

Pamela Wallin's lawyer suggested he would go to court to fight her suspension, but he never did. Like Duffy and Brazeau, Wallin remained suspended without pay until Parliament was dissolved in August 2015 for the election. Also, like Duffy, she wasn't talking about the scandal any more.

What of the actors in this less-than-Shakespearian tragicomedy? History will assess Stephen Harper at least partly on his track record with the Senate and call into question his judgment and supposed powers of political insight. Some of his senators certainly let him down, perhaps because they had been elevated for the wrong reasons in the first place. Call it bad karma, or a series of unforced errors. The Harper government's ethics had certainly become a central issue in national politics, with dire results in 2015. Canadians recognized that it was Harper's Senate at the heart of the scandal and while never linked by hard evidence, he couldn't escape responsibility. He had appointed fifty-nine of its members, and the Conservatives maintained strict majority control over almost all Senate committees, including Internal Economy. When things went so wrong in the Red Chamber, many Canadians blamed Harper.

In the meantime, the Senate began to take steps of its own to address its lack of accountability. Senator Gerald Comeau, who took over from Tkachuk as head of the Internal Economy Committee before announcing his own retirement, accurately predicted one important step: that senatorial expenses would be posted online. The Nova Scotia senator suggested that "the Senate has taken a hit" in the scandal, and it's in the institution's own interest to repair the damage. "In this day and age, [accountability and transparency] do matter. We are in the public eye and must use their money wisely." Inevitably, he said, "there's going to be more scrutiny because of the mistakes that have been made."

It also turned out that Rob Walsh was right about the Senate's rules and the Criminal Code. Nigel Wright was never charged with bribing Duffy, even though Duffy was charged with accepting a bribe from Wright. Walsh, as the former law clerk of Parliament, is an undisputed expert on the rights and responsibilities of the institution's members and he felt Wright couldn't be prosecuted successfully for bailing out Duffy. But that's just the legal side of it. It was very clear that Wright committed, at minimum, a colossal error in political judgment. It cost him a brilliant career in government and the trust of his former mentor and boss, Harper. Wright ended up going back to Onex, in its London offices, and testifying at Duffy's trial. He wasn't talking to the media.

Other PMO officials who knew about the Wright-Duffy arrangement would be called to testify about it in court, but faced no sanction at all, other than the public scrutiny brought on by questions about what they knew about the deal and why nobody, apparently, told the prime minister.

Three suspended senators paid the direct price for the scandal, but their friends-turned-enemies on the Conservative side in Senate were also badly discredited. Marjory LeBreton, who had toiled in Conservative backrooms since 1962 and in the Senate since 1993, moved to the back benches then retired with a full pension at age seventy-five, right before the 2015 federal election. Irving Gerstein would carry on at the Conservative Fund Canada and would serve in the Senate until his scheduled retirement in 2016. David Tkachuk will be in the Senate until 2020, but was off the Internal Economy Committee; like a growing list of other Conservatives, he was interviewed by the RCMP about his role in the Duffy matter. Carolyn Stewart Olsen rejected any criticism of her own expenses, but was tarred by her role in helping to whitewash the Deloitte report on Duffy and suppress the truth about what happened.

Mac Harb retired from the Senate and paid back more than $220,000 he was said to owe in inappropriate claims. But his combined Commons and Senate pensions add up to more than $123,000 a year, for life. If he lives to be eighty, the people of Canada will have paid him more than $2.4 million. In 2016, he was still facing fraud and breach charges but it's doubtful his pension would be affected even by a criminal conviction.

Pamela Wallin's lawyer suggested he would go to court to fight her suspension, but he never did. Like Duffy and Brazeau, Wallin remained suspended without pay until Parliament was dissolved in August 2015 for the election. Also like Duffy, she wasn't talking about the scandal any more.

Even more than Duffy's did, Brazeau's Senate troubles set off a spiral of personal and legal troubles. He was given a conditional discharge on the sexual assault charge against him, but he appeared to be deeply troubled. He worked for a while as a strip club manager and tried his hand at journalism but neither worked out. In January 2016, Brazeau was admitted to hospital in critical condition after an apparent suicide attempt. He was still facing charges, although his trial date was put back to 2017.

Duffy was spending his time in Ottawa, where he was getting treatment for his chronic heart problems. He, too, was keeping an uncharacteristically low profile, but for some it wasn't low enough. Corporate Research Associates of Halifax released a poll in October 2013 suggesting even fellow Islanders had made up their minds about their senator: 85 percent of respondents thought Duffy should resign from the Senate, while only 6 percent thought he should stay. Predictably, the poll became a topic on the political talk shows. On CTV's *Power Play*, which had replaced *Mike Duffy Live*, host Don Martin hashed it over with *Globe and Mail* reporter Bill Curry and Duffy's old CTV colleague, Craig Oliver. Martin said the numbers suggested "a pretty strong indication that Mr. Duffy is the least-wanted senator in Canada." Oliver said he had been travelling across Canada, and "I think you could get a similar poll to the PEI poll, pretty close on, in pretty much any province in the country...I was amazed at the furor in the land. And a lot of it was about Duffy. For some reason he has become the star in terms of aggrieved Canadians feeling like senators are stealing money."

Oliver was also approached for an interview for this book. He had worked with and against Duffy for decades on Parliament Hill and was among his critics at CTV. He's reluctant to speak publicly about their relationship now, but did observe that "this was a guy who grew up awkward and fat and didn't fit in. All his life he was driven by two things: status and money. Those were his fatal flaws."

Another long-time friend turned cold is Island Liberal MP Wayne Easter. He says Duffy's transformation from neutral journalist to Conservative attack dog to beleaguered senator under suspension is a tragic tale of ambition and downfall. "It's a remarkably sad story. A lot of Prince Edward Islanders were proud to see a fellow Islander on TV. He was a national celebrity. And now, it's almost a visceral hatred that people feel." Easter says Duffy "became Harper's little man" and lost himself in the process.

The scandal, controversy, and suspension finally achieved the seemingly impossible, the silencing of Mike Duffy. The senator retreated to his circle of close friends, rarely communicating with anyone not trusted absolutely. He heeded Don Bayne's advice and settled in for the coming trial, except this time it wouldn't be in the court of politics or public opinion. This time, it would be for real.

EPILOGUE: TRIAL, VINDICATION, AND REVENGE

*Senator Duffy, in the last two to three years, has been subjected to
more public humiliation than any other Canadian in history.*

–DONALD BAYNE AT THE CONCLUSION OF
SENATOR MIKE DUFFY'S TRIAL, APRIL 21, 2016

THE LINEUP STARTED EARLY ON THE CHILLY MORNING OF APRIL 7, 2015,
outside the Ontario provincial courthouse in Ottawa on Elgin
Street, a few blocks from Parliament Hill. Spring was tardy that
year across eastern Canada and snow still lingered on the ground.
Everyone in the growing crowd of reporters and curious citizens was

bundled up against the wind. Across the sidewalk from the main doors, the television networks had erected a platform for cameras and reporters, watched over by bemused court security guards. The queue was for anyone who wanted to witness the case scheduled for Courtroom 33. It started at the main door and snaked south along Elgin Street, buzzing with anticipation. The fraud, breach of trust, and bribery trial of Senator Mike Duffy was finally starting and there was no way to predict how it would turn out.

Anticipation had been building since the previous July, when Duffy found out that he would face thirty-one criminal charges arising from the Senate scandal and the detailed investigation by the RCMP's task force, Project Amble. His lawyer, Donald Bayne, had actually scooped the Mounties by telling the media in advance that his client would be charged. The charges were formally announced by the commanding officer of the National Division, Assistant Commissioner Gilles Michaud, leaving the strong impression that the case against Duffy was a very serious matter indeed. Bayne immediately announced that he would argue that his client was not guilty of any of the charges and would fight every one of them.

Even that early, it was apparent that the trial would not be quick and it certainly would not be cheap. Duffy, still suspended without pay from the Senate, prepared for it by taking out a $550,000 second mortgage on the house in Kanata. With so many charges, a long and complicated trial was all but guaranteed, but even the experts couldn't have foreseen how long it would take or the impact it would have on national politics. The court initially set aside forty-one days for the proceeding, expecting it to conclude in June. Bayne's pit-bull defence would drag the trial on much longer than that—right into the middle of the 2015 election campaign and beyond.

The charges broke down into four main categories: fraud over $5,000 and breach of trust related to his Senate expense claims, amounting to $90,000; frauds unrelated to Senate business; fraudulently issuing contracts to a third party using Senate funds; and bribery in the Nigel Wright matter. The third-party contracts went to Gerald Donahue, the old friend from CJOH and CTV. Duffy was charged with bribery for accepting the $90,000 payment from Nigel Wright, but Wright was not charged for offering it.

Hearing and deciding the trial would be Ontario Justice Charles Vaillancourt, selected after Duffy elected to be tried before a judge alone, with no jury. Justice Vaillancourt was a thirty-one-year veteran of the bench, a former criminal defence attorney who normally presided over courts in Toronto. The legal community respected Vaillancourt as a no-nonsense jurist. He had adjudicated at least one case with political overtones, ruling that an Ontario cabinet minister should have butted out of a potential court case.

The trial would play out before an audience of reporters and members of the politically curious public, including a sprinkling of students as well as an observer from the Conservative Party. Duffy would spend his long days in court staring straight ahead or taking notes on the testimony. During breaks, he chatted quietly with his support group; it usually consisted of Heather, longtime Ottawa journalist pals John Warren and Bill Rodgers, or his old buddy, Hugh Riopelle and his wife, Marie. Spectators needed passes to come and go from the courtroom, but that was mostly a crowd-control issue. The wristbands were issued first thing in the morning, so arriving early was the best way to get a seat inside the court-room. Latecomers were shepherded into an overflow room, where they could monitor the testimony. Outside, a platoon of reporters and cameras lingered to capture the arrivals of the star performers and supporting cast: Crown prosecutors Mark Holmes and Jason Neubauer, Duffy's RCMP nemesis, Corporal Greg Horton, and, of course, Bayne.

Even before the trial made him a household name across Canada, Donald Bayne was a wealthy, well-respected criminal law-yer and a partner in the Ottawa firm of Bayne Sellar Boxall. He had been a star scholar-athlete at Queen's University, where he played quarterback for the Golden Gaels before going on to earn a master's degree in law at the London School of Economics. Bayne settled on criminal law as his specialty, although he also acted as an advocate at high-profile public inquiries such as those into the Canadian Army's problems in Somalia and the treatment of wrongly accused terror suspect Maher Arar, who was later awarded $10 million because he had been negligently identified by Canadian officials as a terrorist, arrested, detained in Syria, and tortured. By the time the Duffy trial started, Bayne had already won some of the most prestigious honours in Canadian law. But it was this case, and the media circus around it, that would make him truly famous.

Bayne was up against two experienced and respected prosecutors, Assistant Crown Attorney Mark Neubauer and Deputy Crown Attorney Mark Holmes, both from the Ontario prosecution service. Holmes was mainly known for his many successful murder prosecutions. Neubauer had done his share of gory trials, but had also prosecuted some complicated fraud cases.

The Crown case relied on the assertion that Duffy had corruptly and intentionally defrauded the Senate, contrary to its rules and regulations, via his expense and residence claims. So the first part of the trial would be consumed with Senate administrators and officials, explaining how the system worked and how Duffy used it. Bayne interrogated the former law clerk of the Senate, Mark Audcent, over the rules, finding many holes in them along the way. There was testimony from some of the people who got money from the covert fund Duffy had set up through Gerry Donohue at Maple Ridge Media. Evidence was introduced about how Duffy came to start claiming expenses for the house in Kanata after declaring the Cavendish cottage as his primary residence. Documents from Duffy's personal bank accounts were entered as evidence.

The court heard that Duffy and other senators would pre-sign expense forms to speed up processing and that, like others, Duffy relied on his office staff to keep track of his expenses and his claims for reimbursement. In almost every case, Bayne put the witnesses through a thorough cross-examination. No stone went unturned and sometimes, just as he appeared to have finished his exhaustive cross-examination on a point, Bayne would turn the stones over again. Partly because of Bayne's persistent attention to detail, the trial plodded along through May and into June, when it finally went beyond just evidence about Duffy and his expense accounts. Finally, everyone would hear the story behind Nigel Wright's famous cheque and its circuitous route from a U.S. account to a Canadian account, then to Janice Payne's firm, then via Duffy to the Receiver General of Canada.

Along with the testimony came exhibits, thousands of pages of financial and bank records, expense claims, and even Duffy's diaries from his years in the Senate. They were called diaries, but they were actually more like calendar entries with brief notations of significant events, including Senate paydays and many lunches and dinners with sundry pals and political types. The diaries recorded that in March 2009, for instance, Duffy visited Northern Ireland and Scotland with a parliamentary delegation. After a few days in Belfast, the delegation travelled to Edinburgh, where it toured the famous castle and enjoyed a pub meal. Duffy spoke at a gathering about "political jokes," and afterward noted, as always with himself in the third person that "MD agrees to send jokes to Tavish Scott," a Scottish MP and leader of the Liberal Democrats.

The diaries contain hundreds of entries for Duffy's medical appointments, and his Senate days missed due to illness. They follow him to Senate and party events, public functions in P.E.I. and across Canada, as well as documenting personal matters. They record his busy schedule travelling the country to raise funds for the Conservative Party, although Duffy saw himself more as "friend-raiser," who would "expand the pool of accessible voters," rather than the more traditional term, "bagman." In any case, the Crown invested these political calendar notations with great significance, alleging that Duffy had inappropriately mixed Senate and partisan business. It turned out to be a tough claim to prove.

While the trial dragged on, calculations were going on in the top reaches of the Conservative Party, leading to a series of fateful decisions. The Harper majority government had been in power since May of 2011 and its time was just about up. It was switching to full-on re-election mode and dipping into the bag of electoral tricks the Tories had created for their parliamentary majority. The Conservatives had options going into the 2015 election, which had been fixed in law for October 19. The fixed date was a Conservative reform, as was some fine print in the so-called Fair Elections Act, which, among other provisions, changed the way campaigns could be financed. It also removed limits on the campaign's duration, meaning election periods potentially could go on much longer and cost a lot more than they ever had in the past. That bit of electoral minutiae went unnoticed in the media. Even the opposition parties had somehow missed it, but it was noticed by Alice Funke, the Ottawa-based publisher of the online Pundits' Guide to Canadian Elections. In January 2015, Funke published an analysis suggesting that the changes could allow a well-funded party to stretch the official campaign period beyond the ability of opposition parties to match its spending. That would present a potential advantage to the governing Conservatives, who were sitting on a war chest larger than those of the NDP and the Liberals combined. And it wasn't just the national campaigns. Funke warned that the new rules meant well-financed local campaigns would have huge advantages over less well off rivals. The Harper Conservatives had also changed the law to make it more difficult for campaigns to borrow start-up money, further entrenching their financial advantage. Funke was a voice in the wilderness and few observers paid heed to her analysis. That all changed in August.

On the morning of August 2, a Sunday, an emailed notice went out to the Parliamentary Press Gallery. The Prime Minister would be at Rideau Hall to meet with Governor General David Johnston. The Gallery didn't take long to figure out what that meant: Parliament was being dissolved, the official election campaign was on, and it would be a marathon of seventy-eight days, the longest in Canadian history. Funke had been prescient; the Tories were taking advantage of their fundraising edge. A Nanos poll published that day put the Conservatives slightly in the lead at 32 per cent support, with the New Democrats at 30 per cent and the Liberals trailing at 29. Other polls disagreed, but none put Harper dangerously behind. So the prime minister was able to force a smile when he showed up at Rideau Hall with his wife, Laureen. Harper disappeared into the building for the meeting with Governor General David Johnston, which was brief, and emerged to take five questions from the media. He said the election would be all about the economy and national security. Even though the campaign would set records for spending and cost to the public, Harper insisted that parties would pay the freight and not taxpayers.

With the campaign finances stacked in their favour, the Conservatives must have thought they had better than a fighting chance to repeat as a majority government. Still, they had been in power a long time and people were getting tired of them. Seven cabinet ministers and some senior MPs had already retired. But the Conservatives had a consistent pitch: lower taxes for some Canadians, and a hawkish stance on national security, including on the global refugee crisis. And the Tories had Harper, the undisputed champion in the heavyweight division of national politics.

The Conservative campaign team must have considered the potential effects of the Duffy trial on their plans. Nigel Wright was due to testify a few days after the election call, opening a potential can of worms just as the campaign was lifting off. The Conservatives had released the hounds on Duffy two years before and nodded agreeably as the Mounties got involved. Now with the court's agenda outside the control of the Harper apparatus, the Conservatives decided that any damage from Wright's testimony would be limited. They could still blame Duffy individually while deploying Senator Gerstein's bankroll to full advantage. The Conservatives would highlight Harper's experience and leadership while attacking Tom Mulcair and Justin Trudeau. Saturation attacks, the Tories felt, would overcome the hits likely to be taken from Wright's revelations.

After all, Wright had been one of them, so the Conservatives knew what he could reveal. It probably wouldn't be that bad.

The dissolution of Parliament had an important impact on Duffy's life, too. It meant his suspension and those of Wallin and Brazeau would expire. They'd go back on the Senate payroll, although another quiet Conservative change kept the suspension on their pension plans.

From Rideau Hall, Harper headed straight to Montreal for a tour event. As he would throughout the campaign, he repeated over and over that the Tories were the only party offering security in an uncertain world and that to choose the NDP or the Liberals would mean economic chaos and a field day for terrorism. He knew his core party support of around 30 per cent was solid and probably wouldn't be distracted by anything at the Duffy trial. The goal of the campaign was to add another 7 to 8 percentage points to the core vote to keep him in office for another four years.

It didn't turn out that way.

Harper's first days on the campaign would be as good as they would get. On August 12, ten days after the launch, Wright was called as a witness in the Duffy trial. He would spend six days testifying, laying out in astonishing detail the efforts the Harper PMO had made to stifle the Senate scandal, to herd Duffy toward acknowledging misuse of Senate funds and paying them back, and to manipulate public opinion about the whole affair. Wright, who had co-operated with the RCMP and turned over massive amounts of information, also provided eyewitness testimony about Duffy's alleged "monstrous scheme." It was an unprecedented insider account of how the Harper PMO really worked.

While it wasn't the decisive factor in the campaign, the Duffy case and the wider Senate scandal did much to undermine Harper's credibility as a prime minister who would not tolerate ethical lapses in his government. With hard evidence of the PMO's manipulations emerging at the trial, Harper could no longer deny that he was running an office that placed more stock on results than ethics. And everywhere Harper went, he was dogged by questions about Duffy and the Senate. The Conservative campaign stuck with its plan to only answer a few questions a day, but on many days the only questions were about Duffy. Harper's irritation became apparent and Tory audiences took the cue, often shouting down questions from the media, blocking cameras or trying to intimidate reporters. One of those Harper supporters became an internet sensation for yelling at reporters and calling them "lying pieces of shit." When they asked his name, the man, later identified as Earl Cowan, yelled at them to "go stuff yourselves."

In his testimony, Wright cast his role in the affair as that of an honest broker, trying to put the wayward senator back on track while never doubting Duffy's eligibility to represent P.E.I. in the Senate. He believed he had done nothing wrong, other than make a political mistake. In fact, Wright insisted he had kept taxpayers whole by covering the money in dispute between Duffy and the Senate. Still, many Canadians wondered how the bribery charge could stand against Duffy for corruptly accepting the $90,000 from Wright, but with no charge made against Wright for giving him the money. By the time it was dealt with in the trial, the Crown seemed disinterested. The RCMP Commissioner had already said publicly there was no evidence of a criminal act by Wright in making the payment. When Duffy testified at the end of the trial, the Crown didn't even ask him about the famous $90,000 cheque.

Still, much would be made about who knew what and when as other former Conservative staffers took the stand. Benjamin Perrin, the PMO lawyer through most of the period, testified that he got drawn into the web of unsavoury dealings between Harper's office and Duffy's then-lawyer, Janice Payne. He vetted offers and was bidden to appeal to Duffy, through Payne, to go along with the PMO's arrangements. Perrin left the PMO soon after all this happened and went back to teaching law at the University of British Columbia. He testified that he wasn't always comfortable with the PMO's tactics, which were orchestrated by Wright. Wright told Perrin what kind of tone to take with Payne in the Duffy matter and suggested pressure tactics. Wright's emails reflect Wright's escalating irritation with Duffy and his problems. Finally, he decided to pay the $90,000 himself and told Chris Woodcock that in an email. Justice Vaillancourt's noted in his decision that: "Mr. Wright had decided that he will personally provide the "repayment" money the scenario requires, although it must appear to have come from Senator Duffy as an act of honourable Tory contrition, and on March 8th, he clearly and succinctly advised his subordinate (Mr. Woodcock) in a brief email sent directly and only to Mr. Woodcock that 'For you only: I am personally covering Duffy's $90K'. Mr. Woodcock claimed that he read the rest of this brief email from his boss, but not this line."

It was manipulations like this and the overbearing treatment of the senior Senate Conservatives, the whitewashing of a potential review of Duffy's finances by Deloitte, and the PMO's bully boy tactics that annoyed and disgusted Justice Vaillancourt. He would have much to say about that in his written decision.

While the trial stopped and started through the fall, the world kept revolving. The election campaign turned into a dogged test of stamina for all the parties. Instead of an election about the economy and national security, it morphed into one that was all about change. People were tired of Harper and his dark ways, which had been revealed pretty starkly at the Duffy trial. Desperately, the Conservatives tried to play on voters' fears about hordes of Syrian refugees heading to Canada. That backfired spectacularly, with both Mulcair and Trudeau promising to take in thousands more refugees than the government promised. Trudeau held his own in debates and kept up a positive, reassuring tone with voters. The Conservative campaign seemed deaf to the desire for change in the electorate. By early October, it was clear that the change vote was dominating and that it was going en masse to the Liberals.

On election night, Justin Trudeau and the Liberals were swept into power, ending almost ten years of Conservative rule. Harper spoke to the party faithful to thank them for their support but issued a news release announcing he was resigning as Conservative leader. Duffy's case hadn't sunk the Conservatives, but it sure hadn't helped.

After hearing from Wright, Perrin, Woodcock, and Senator George Furey, among others, the Crown wrapped up its case. Now it was Bayne's turn to set out the facts as he and Duffy saw them, a narrative that would have great influence on Justice Vaillancourt. And Bayne's star witness would be none other than Duffy himself. After weeks of speculation about whether he would ever testify and risk a harsh cross-examination, the senator entered the witness box on December 8. Over the next several days, he would tell his story: how he wanted to represent Ontario to avoid problems around eligibility, how Harper insisted that he represent P.E.I. until the scandal blew up and how the PMO started to threaten the senator with the loss of his seat. Duffy testified that he had always followed the Senate's expense rules to the best of his understanding. He said he tried to get clarification on the residency issues from Tkachuk and even Harper and was told that he qualified because he owned land in P.E.I. worth more than $4,000. He testified that he claimed per diems for his Kanata home because that's what he was told to do by Tkachuk, although Tkachuk would continue to insist that wasn't true. Duffy claimed he made every claim for expenses "openly, forthrightly, completely in the open and completely transparently and honestly."

As to Wright and the "monstrous scheme" behind the $90,000 cheque, "I'd fought and I'd fought and I'd fought, and I'd tried every kind of resistance. When they pulled that knife out [removal from the Senate] and held it over my head, I felt I had no other choice."

Testifying was risky for Duffy, or would have been if the Crown had the goods on him. It didn't, and in cross-examination Holmes was able to trip Duffy up on some small details but not on anything vital to the issues in the trial. There were times when Duffy's bluster occasionally boiled through, but never enough to make Vaillancourt think he lacked credibility. If he really was an innocent man, there was no wonder why he would be angry at a process that got him suspended from his job, cost him $270,000 in Senate salary, a small fortune in legal fees, and, almost as important, his reputation. "I am so fed up with this," he complained one day from the witness box.

With Duffy testifying under Bayne's relentless guidance, the trial seemed to morph into an inquisition against the Harper PMO. There were no charges against anyone in that office, but the evidence presented left a powerful impression on the judge. In his decision, Justice Vaillancourt observed that Neubauer described Duffy's actions as "driven by deceit, manipulations and carried out in a clandestine manner representing a serious and marked standard expected of a person in Senator Duffy's position of trust." He didn't see it that way at all. "I find that if one were to substitute the PMO, Nigel Wright, and others for Senator Duffy in the aforementioned sentence, that you would have a more accurate statement."

Fittingly, Duffy was the last witness and the evidence portion of the trial came to a close. In the Crown's final summation of the case weeks later, Holmes and Neubauer stuck to their allegations that Duffy had acted corruptly by misusing Senate funds and by taking a bribe from Wright. Holmes also questioned Duffy's credibility as a witness, with the obvious implication that if he could fall short of the truth in court, he could not be trusted. "He's not reliable and he's not at all concerned, it would seem, about just conjuring up facts," Holmes said. "It may work in broadcasting, but it is outrageous for a witness to do that at a criminal trial."

Bayne wrapped up by insisting that the worst Duffy had done was commit a few administrative errors, never anything criminal. And if the senator had agreed to the deal with Wright, it was due solely to the pressure and manipulation of the truly corrupt party: the Harper PMO. Harper spoke to the party faithful to thank them for their support but issued a news release announcing he was resigning as Conservative leader, effective immediately. He planned to retire from politics in September 2016.

"There isn't a single charge worthy of a guilty verdict," Bayne told the court as Duffy looked on stolidly. "The only right verdict is not guilty. The man has been through a horrendous ordeal. He's been humiliated and ridiculed. Few have been through his ordeal."

With final arguments made, Justice Vaillancourt said he would render his findings on April 21. The 308-page decision, given three years after the scandal first became a hot political issue, was a slam dunk for the defence, a triumph for Duffy and Bayne, and a blistering indictment of the Harper government. Justice Vaillancourt was particularly harsh on the Crown case, which he said was poorly conceived and badly argued. He considered Duffy's claim of 10 Friendly Lane as his primary residence to be "inaccurate" but not fraudulent. And he rejected the Crown's theory that Duffy was trying to avoid questions about whether or not he was eligible to sit as a senator from P.E.I.

"The Crown submits that Senator Duffy wanted to shield himself from scrutiny of his very eligibility to sit as a Senator from Prince Edward Island. I do not agree," the judge wrote. "Quite frankly, this whole area is not before the court and for good reason. The Prime Minister of Canada appoints Senators. If there are issues regarding eligibility, those concerns are addressed by the Senate and not the courts."

Justice Vaillancourt gave a lot of weight to the fact that Duffy testified on his own behalf, with all the potential risks that entailed. He noted that key aspects of Duffy's story went unchallenged by the Crown, leaving only the defence argument on the record. That was a key factor for the judge, who placed great emphasis on the presumption of innocence and the heavy burden of proof carried by the Crown. Unlike the court of public opinion, guilt in a criminal matter has to be proven beyond a reasonable doubt. He mostly believed Duffy over the Crown witnesses, who didn't much impress him with their sincerity. "At the end of the day, I find that Senator Duffy is an overall credible witness," he wrote.

Justice Vaillancourt dismissed twenty-seven charges and found the senator not guilty of four. Duffy was therefore acquitted on all counts. By the end of the day on April 21, 2016, he was a free man. He walked out of the courthouse wearing a thin smile but not uttering a word to the throng of media. Bayne had no such hesitation, declaring his client vindicated with a "resounding acquittal," after enduring a living hell. "I would say Senator Duffy has been subjected in the last two and a half to three years to more public humiliation than probably any other Canadian in history," he said.

Within hours, Senate Law Clerk Michel Patrice issued a statement that the acquittal "gives rise to the reinstatement of Senator Duffy as a member of the Senate in full standing with full salary and office resources." Duffy could go back as he saw fit, his status restored. Parliament resumed sitting on May 3 and Duffy was back in his office the day before, getting ready to retake his seat as an independent member of the Red Chamber.

He would find that things had changed. Duffy returned to a Senate that, while still unelected, had experienced some long-overdue changes since he was last there in October 2013. It was less partisan, with an independent senator representing the Trudeau government but who was not a member of the Liberal parliamentary caucus. Not only were most senatorial expenses now posted online, but the expense rules were also tightened and made clearer. Travelling senators now had to provide a specific purpose for each trip and receipts for expenses such as meals and taxis. They were warned unambiguously that "Senate resources shall not be used to fund travel that is incurred to pursue the private business of personal interests" of senators. If private business took place during official travel, senators had to pay for any expenses incurred. Per-diem rules were tightened up for senators claiming second homes or hotels in Ottawa. Now, they could claim expenses only for days when the Senate or its committees were in session or when party caucuses met. The traditional but now disgraced "honour system" was being replaced by modern rules and regulations.

Beyond the new rules, the Senate also called in the Auditor General for a more thorough look at the books. The auditors found problems with expenses and other claims of dozens of senators. Nine cases were forwarded to the RCMP, but it was unlikely they would move forward given what happened in the Duffy case. Some senators took their cases to an independent dispute resolution process supervised by retired Supreme Court Justice Ian Binnie. He eventually found that fourteen current senators and former senators were found to owe about $177,000, which all got paid back. And for the first time in Canadian history, the Senate got an Ethics Officer to referee the Senate's first-ever Ethics and Conflict of Interest Code. The Senate claimed the new code to be "among the toughest in the Commonwealth," although that's a hard claim to verify. In any case, the improvements suggested the Senate finally had awoken to the fact that Canadians were demanding change.

But there was still some way to go. Chris Montgomery, the former director of parliamentary affairs for Senator LeBreton and one of the few Tory insiders to resist the Duffy deal, urged the Senate to keep up the pace of reform. "With increased independence comes increased responsibility," Montgomery wrote in Policy Options. "Senators must take every step to put in place tough, transparent, rules-based policies to govern their conduct. There are risks to not taking action. The next time there is a significant scandal involving the Senate, the sour taste in Canadians' mouths as a result of the Duffy trial will turn bitter, and the entire political apparatus will be free to cut ties with the institution."

Finally, one big question remained: had Harper known about the $90,000 cheque? Famously manipulative and controlling, Harper was a fiend for detail, although it emerged at the trial that he didn't write many memos or leave much of a paper trail. He would read emails on a laptop but not write them, preferring to scribble on Post-It notes when he wanted to comment. "There were no fingerprints," was how Duffy described it.

Harper was never called to testify but the court heard that Ray Novak knew all about Wright's cheque. He had been notified by email and according to Conservative campaign spokesman Kory

Teneycke, it would be "inconceivable" that Novak would keep important such information from his boss.

Three days after Duffy was acquitted, Bayne made it clear what he thought about the question. Bayne sat for an interview with Robert Fife, now with the Globe and Mail but still hosting the CTV program Question Period. Fife asked Bayne whether he believed that Harper really didn't know what his office was doing. "Do I personally believe that? Having seen that? For what it's worth, and I'm a biased observer now, no. It strains credulity."

A few days later, a curious op-ed piece showed up in the Ottawa Citizen. In it, lawyer Robert Staley revealed he had been representing Harper since mid-2013 in respect to the Duffy matter and that at all times, the former PM had behaved in exemplary fashion. His argument went like this: Harper directed that all information be given to the investigators and to the courts, a decision that "had a profound impact on Mr. Duffy's criminal case." Further, "the record also showed that the prime minister was not privy to Mr. Wright's decision." As Harper himself does, Staley refers in every instance to "Mr. Duffy," never to "Senator Duffy," as if the mere mention of his appointee was too painful to bear.

Although Conservatives would repeat many times during the election campaign that the record proved that Harper was kept out of the loop, it doesn't actually prove that at all. The trial failed to prove that Harper did know, but it left the question unanswered. Few Canadians believed Harper had played an impartial role in the Duffy matter and that his actions were always above reproach. That view was reflected in the 2015 election results. But Harper hadn't changed his mind on Duffy's behaviour. According to Staley, Harper still believed that what Duffy did was unacceptable. "It was and is my client's view that public office demands a higher standard than conduct that falls short of criminality," wrote Staley, reflecting the view still held by many Tories that the problem was always 100 per cent Mike Duffy.

After a fair trial, the court decided that Duffy's handling of Senate funds, his expense and residency claims, and the payment from Nigel Wright were not crimes and that the senator was not a criminal. Yet only Duffy and his lawyer seemed convinced that everything Duffy did was appropriate. He was going back to a Senate that had changed, mostly unwillingly, because of his actions. He was out of the Conservative caucus, which would oppose any attempt to get back his lost wages.

Mike Duffy turned seventy in late May 2016. He had five years to go in the Senate before mandatory retirement, if his health held up. It had been a turbulent time for Duffy, for the Senate, and for the Conservative party that had adopted him, profited from his work, and eventually condemned him to public ridicule, a costly trial, and an uncertain place in Canadian political history.